TRANSMEDIA ADAPTATION IN THE
NINETEENTH CENTURY

TRANSMEDIA ADAPTATION IN THE NINETEENTH CENTURY

~

Lissette Lopez Szwydky

THE OHIO STATE UNIVERSITY PRESS
COLUMBUS

Copyright © 2020 by The Ohio State University.
All rights reserved.

Library of Congress Cataloging-in-Publication Data
Names: Szwydky, Lissette Lopez, author.
Title: Transmedia adaptation in the nineteenth century / Lissette Lopez Szwydky.
Description: Columbus : The Ohio State University Press, [2020] | Includes bibliographical references and index. | Summary: "Illustrates how novels gained cultural traction as they underwent reinvention and renewal through adaptation. Discusses Mary Shelley's *Frankenstein*, Boydell's *Shakespeare Gallery*, Dickens's most iconic works, and many more nineteenth-century works"—Provided by publisher.
Identifiers: LCCN 2019053063 | ISBN 9780814214237 (cloth) | ISBN 0814214231 (cloth) | ISBN 9780814277959 (ebook) | ISBN 0814277950 (ebook)
Subjects: LCSH: English fiction—19th century—Adaptations—History and criticism. | English literature—19th century—Adaptations—History and criticism.
Classification: LCC PR771 .S99 2020 | DDC 823/.809—dc23
LC record available at https://lccn.loc.gov/2019053063
Other identifiers: ISBN 978-0-8142-5587-2 (paper) | ISBN 0-814-25587-6 (paper)

Cover design by Jordan Wannemacher
Text design by Juliet Williams
Type set in Adobe Minion Pro

CONTENTS

List of Illustrations	vii
Acknowledgments	xiii
INTRODUCTION A Historical Model of Adaptation, Transmedia Storytelling, and Convergence Culture	1
CHAPTER 1 Adaptation in the Nineteenth Century; or, the Convergence of Censorship, Spectacle, Commercialism, and Aesthetics	27
CHAPTER 2 Professional and Celebrity Networks: Authors, Actors, Adapters	63
CHAPTER 3 Visual and Textual Adaptations in Literature and Fine Art Forms	97
CHAPTER 4 Culture-Texts and Storyworlds across Nineteenth-Century Media	139
CHAPTER 5 Nineteenth-Century Tie-Ins, Commercial Extensions, and Participatory Culture	175
CONCLUSION A New (Popular) Literary History: Adaptation and Canon Formation	209
Bibliography	223
Index	247

ILLUSTRATIONS

FIGURE 1.1　Performance program for Andrew Halliday, *Notre-Dame de Paris,* Adelphi Theatre, Monday, April 24, 1871. Image courtesy of Matthew Lloyd (http://www.arthurlloyd.co.uk).　44

FIGURE 1.2　Playbill announcing revival of Richard Brinsley Peake, *Presumption; or, The Fate of Frankenstein,* Theatre Royal Covent Garden, December 7, 1830; detail. A collection of playbills from Covent Garden Theatre, 1829–30. British Playbills, 1754–1882. © The British Library Board. Nineteenth Century Collections Online.　44

FIGURE 1.3　T. P. Cooke as Frankenstein's Creature in Jean-Toussaint Merle and Antony Béraud, *Le Monstre et le Magicien* (1826) in Paris. Cooke was the "original Frankenstein," first appearing as the Creature in Peake's *Presumption* (1823) in London. © National Library of France, Paris.　55

FIGURE 1.4　Set of miniature theatrical prints of characters from Jean-Toussaint Merle and Antony Béraud, *Le Monstre et le Magicien* (1826). © National Library of France, Paris.　56

FIGURE 1.5	Green monster print from Jean-Toussaint Merle and Antony Béraud, *Le Monstre et le Magicien* (1826). © National Library of France, Paris.	57
FIGURE 1.6	Green monster print from Jean-Toussaint Merle and Antony Béraud, *Le Monstre et le Magicien* (1826). © National Library of France, Paris.	58
FIGURE 1.7	Creation scene from *Frankenstein; or, The Model Man* (1849) from the *Illustrated London News*, January 12, 1850. Image © The British Library Board. All Rights Reserved. Image reproduced with permission of the British Newspaper Archive (https://www.britishnewspaperarchive.co.uk).	59
FIGURE 1.8	Ferdinand Dugué, *Le Monstre et le Magicien* (1861), an adaptation of Merle and Béraud's 1826 play. © National Library of France, Paris.	59
FIGURE 2.1	Alexandre-Marie Colin, *Byron as Don Juan, with Haidee* (1831). Image © The Matthiesen Gallery, London.	71
FIGURE 2.2	O. Smith as Robert Baptiste in *Raymond & Agnes*, adapted from Matthew Lewis's novel *The Monk* (1827). Image Courtesy of The Billy Rose Theatre Division, The New York Public Library Digital Collections.	77
FIGURE 2.3	Richard Mansfield as Dr. Jekyll and Mr. Hyde (1888). Image courtesy of The Newberry Library, Chicago.	78
FIGURE 2.4	"December: Jekyll and Hyde," The Richard Mansfield Calendar for 1900 (1899). Public Domain. Digital image courtesy of The British Library.	78
FIGURE 2.5	Ellen Terry as Ophelia (1878). Image © National Portrait Gallery, London.	81
FIGURE 2.6	Sarah Bernhardt as Hamlet (1899). Public Domain. Image courtesy of The Library of Congress Prints and Photographs Division Washington, DC.	82
FIGURE 3.1	John William Waterhouse, *La Belle Dame sans Merci* (1893). Public Domain. Wikimedia Commons.	100
FIGURE 3.2	Frank Dicksee, *La Belle Dame sans Merci* (1901). Public Domain. Original held at Bristol Museum and Art Gallery.	101

Illustrations

FIGURE 3.3 William Holman Hunt, *Isabella & the Pot of Basil* (1868). Public Domain. Original held at Laing Art Gallery, Newcastle upon Tyne, England.   102

FIGURE 3.4 John White Alexander, *Isabella and the Pot of Basil* (1897). Image © Museum of Fine Arts, Boston.   103

FIGURE 3.5 Francis Wheatley, View of the Interior of the Shakespeare Gallery (1790). Image © Victoria and Albert Museum, London.   107

FIGURE 3.6 Engraving of Henry Fuseli's painting, *The Enchanted Island before the Cell of Prospero*. Illustration of a scene from Shakespeare's *The Tempest*. Engraved by Peter Simon for the Boydell Folio of images housed in the Shakespeare Gallery (published 1803). Gertrude and Thomas Jefferson Mumford Collection, Gift of Dorothy Quick Mayer, 1942. Public Domain. Image courtesy of The Metropolitan Museum of Art, New York.   112

FIGURE 3.7 William Blake, *Satan Arousing the Rebel Angels*. Illustration to Milton, *Paradise Lost* (1808). Image © Victoria and Albert Museum, London.   120

FIGURE 3.8 William Blake, *The Circle of the Lustful: Francesca da Rimini*. Illustration to Dante, *The Divine Comedy* (c. 1825–27). Public Domain. Image courtesy of The Metropolitan Museum of Art, New York.   122

FIGURE 3.9 Gustave Doré, *Paolo and Francesca* (1861), engraved by Ausman. Illustration to Dante, *The Divine Comedy: The Inferno*. Public Domain. Courtesy of The Victorian Web.   122

FIGURE 3.10 Eugène Delacroix, *La Morte de Sardanapale* (1827), after Byron's tragic closet drama *Sardanapalus* (1821). Public Domain. Wikimedia Commons.   125

FIGURE 3.11 Eugène Delacroix, from Byron's *The Corsair* (1831). Watercolor. Public Domain. Digital image courtesy of the J. Paul Getty Museum Open Content Program.   127

FIGURE 3.12 Eugène Delacroix, Faust in the Prison with Marguerite (1828). Lithograph illustration to Johann von Goethe, *Faust* (1825). Image courtesy of The National Gallery of Victoria, Melbourne.   128

FIGURE 3.13	Gustave Doré. Illustration to Miguel de Cervantes, *Don Quixote* (1863). Public Domain. Image courtesy of Wikimedia Commons.	130
FIGURE 3.14	Gustave Doré. Illustration to Samuel Taylor Coleridge, *The Rime of the Ancient Mariner*, German edition (1877). Public Domain. Digital image courtesy of The British Library.	131
FIGURE 4.1	Robert William Buss, *Dickens' Dream* (1875). Unfinished watercolor. Image courtesy of The Dickens Museum, London.	143
FIGURE 4.2	Title page for stage adaptation of *A Christmas Carol* by C. Z. Barnett, published by Dicks' Standard Plays, no. 722 (1883). Image © The Museum of London.	145
FIGURE 4.3	Gustave Doré, *Vivien and Merlin Repose* (1868). Digital image courtesy of Alamy Stock Photo.	164
FIGURE 4.4	Julia Margaret Cameron, *Vivien and Merlin* (1874). Albumen photograph. Public Domain. Digital image courtesy of the J. Paul Getty Museum Open Content Program, Los Angeles.	166
FIGURE 4.5	Julia Margaret Cameron, *Vivien and Merlin* (1874). Albumen photograph. Public Domain. Image courtesy of The Metropolitan Museum of Art, New York.	167
FIGURE 4.6	Julia Margaret Cameron, *The Parting of Launcelot and Guinevere* (1874). Albumen photograph. Public Domain. Digital image courtesy of the J. Paul Getty Museum Open Content Program, Los Angeles.	167
FIGURE 4.7	Jessie M. King. Illustration to William Morris, *The Defense of Queen Guinevere* (1904). Image courtesy of Alamy Stock Photo.	171
FIGURE 5.1	Illustrated front page of "The Dwarf; or, The Deformed Transformed" from *Endless Entertainment* (1825). Public Domain, Google Digital Collections.	185
FIGURE 5.2	Illustrated front page of "The Monster Made by Man; or, The Punishment of Presumption" from *Endless Entertainment* (1825). Public Domain, Google Digital Collections.	186

FIGURE 5.3	Sample wooden toy theater featuring pasted paper scenery and characters from Redington's *The Corsican Brothers* (1857). Image © The Museum of London.	195
FIGURE 5.4	Title sheet for Redington's *Characters and Scenes in Oliver Twist* (c. 1870). Image © The Museum of London.	197
FIGURE 5.5	Pollock's scenes in *Baron Münchausen,* featuring the façade of John Redington, Printer, Bookbinder & Stationer storefront in London (c. 1857). © Look and Learn / Peter Jackson Collection.	199

ACKNOWLEDGMENTS

THIS BOOK almost never happened, for numerous reasons—many times over.

Most recently, I am grateful for the professional staff at The Ohio State University Press, and for the encouraging feedback and helpful suggestions from my external reviewers.

I am thankful to supportive friends and colleagues at the University of Arkansas. Yajaira Padilla, Robin Roberts, and Susan Marren read drafts and provided invaluable suggestions for revisions, as well as support, enthusiasm, and friendship. I couldn't ask for better friends and colleagues in Toni Jensen and Jo Hsu. Dorothy Stephens wrote countless recommendations supporting my application for grants and fellowships. Sean Connors provided unbounded energy, intellectual enthusiasm, and kind support at a crucial point in this project, and I look forward to continued collaborations with him. I'm fortunate to live among and work closely with so many great people including Lisa Margulis, Martin Miller, John Walch, Shana Gold, Mary Beth Long, Davis McCombs, Padma Viswanathan, Geoff Brock, Raina Lyons, David Jolliffe, Gwynne Gertz, Steven Rosales, Kathy Sloan, Leigh Pryor Sparks, Lisa Corrigan, Stephanie Schulte, Bret Schulte, Stephanie Adams, and Scott Sutton, as well as the staff at the University of Arkansas Mullins Library. The National Endowment for the Humanities has supported my work on adaptation, arts integration, and public humanities.

Many mentors supported earlier stages of this project. Paul Youngquist taught me how to be a more dynamic thinker and writer, and fostered a sense of much-needed irreverence for institutions and disciplinary conventions. Nicholas Joukovsky spent countless hours storying the Romantic period, animating abstract names into real people. Janet Lyon provided a brilliant and inspiring model of intellectual rigor and generosity in theory and practice. Robert Lougy and Robert Caserio ignited my interest in Dickens. Vincent Lankewish showed me how to be a more empathetic scholar and teacher. Kit Hume poured herself into preparing so many of us for academic careers, and her commitment to professional mentoring is unmatched.

I developed dozens of friendships and colleagues at Penn State University, especially those who shared my love of late-night conversations over wine, poker—and sometimes dancing. The regular "Buffy" crew always helped me work through ideas about adaptation and the possibilities of popular culture—Stacey Sheriff, Jessica Raley, Nico Yunes, Pia Deas, Doc Rissel, and Tim Arner, as well as Antonio Ceraso, Dustin Stegner, and Lindsey Simon-Jones. There are too many people to name, but Eric Bowman, Steven Thomas, Jeff Gonzalez, Lynne Feeley, and Kyla Edwards Maldonado deserve special shout-outs. Adam Haley is an amazing editor, writing coach, and friend, supporting me especially in some of the most frantic moments of this book's birth. John Secreto has become a brother to me over the years.

I remain forever grateful to friendships developed during a four-year hiatus from academia—they have forever shaped me as a scholar and educator, especially Sandi Richter.

As a first-generation college student, I would have never made it to graduate school without the mentorship of dedicated professors while at the University of Miami: Anthony Barthelemy, Kathryn Freeman, Jeffrey Shoulson, Russ Castronovo, and (the late) Zack Bowen. And I would have never set foot on that campus as an undergraduate were it not for the guidance and energy of amazing high school English teachers, especially Michael Garcia.

I've presented portions of this book at several conferences over the years, and the feedback received during many conversations has been instrumental. Colleagues in the field (some up close, some from afar) who have invaluably shaped my thinking and provided feedback, encouragement, support, and professional models include Glenn Jellenik, Thomas Leitch, Julie Grossman, Michael Gamer, Jeff Cox, Dennis Perry, Dennis Cutchins, Devoney Looser, Pamela Gilbert, Jay Clayton, Fred Burwick, David Sigler, Kyle Miekle, Nora Crook, Kate Newell, P. C. Fleming, and Jonathan Rey Lee. A special nod goes to the SECU-19c consortium for their advice and encouragement as I prepared to submit the book manuscript for publication. I know I am forgetting people—I apologize, and I thank you too.

Portions of this book have appeared in other publications, particularly my contribution, "Adaptations, Culture-Texts, and Literary Canonization," in *The Routledge Companion to Adaptation,* edited by Katja Krebs, Dennis Cutchins, and Eckart Voight, first published in 2018, and reproduced with permission of Informa UK Limited through PLSclear.

The late Diane Long Hoeveler published my first scholarly article and enthusiastically supported my research. Since then, I've been fortunate to work with students who have provided enthusiastic sounding boards and examples of how adaptation can shed new light on literature and storytelling, especially Garrett Jeter, Kristin Figgins, Sharon Fox, Zach Meyer, Michelle Pribbernow, Jeff Wright, Austin Dean Ashford, Elizabeth DeMeo, Zach Harrod, Shiloh Peters, Laurel Loh, Shavawn Smith, Jessi Schnebelen, Erin Daugherty, Katie Voss, Molly Bess Rector, Brooke Bennett, Samantha Morgan, Julianna Tidwell, Zach Turner, Mikey Reynolds, Angela Blake, Brianna Grimmett, Skye Ferrell, Jackson McNeal, and many more.

My parents Basilio and Gloria Szwydky, as well as my sister Anna Iglesias, instilled in me the work ethic and stubbornness that academia requires. Their models form the engine of the immigrant experience. A shout-out to *mis primos*—Jorge Maldonado, Beatriz and Richard Perez, and Omar Lopez—thanks for always letting me be the type of weird that I am. My mother-in-law Ramona Kizziar is an eternal source of compassion and encouragement, as are my sisters-in-law Natalia Martinez and Nikki Davis.

I couldn't ask for a better partner, colleague, editor, coach, and cheerleader than my husband Geffrey Davis, who makes—all of it—possible. His belief in the work we do sustains us. Many of this book's contours owe their shape to his careful ear and our endless conversations. Our son Carlos is the most patient, loving, caring, kind, creative, and compassionate human I've ever met. I bask daily in the radiance that these two amazing sources of light cast into the world, and I am nourished from my proximity to their warmth. This book is especially for Carlos and Geffrey. Thank you for being my sunshine, as well as my roots.

It will come as no surprise that my own interest in adaptations began long ago with *Frankenstein,* and so this book and my work beyond it owe much to the continued historical and cultural force of Mary Wollstonecraft Shelley and her many hideous progenies.

INTRODUCTION

A Historical Model of Adaptation, Transmedia Storytelling, and Convergence Culture

ADAPTATION IS typically understood as a secondary feature of storytelling—a "derivative" practice, the antithesis of artistic "originality." Despite the fact that adaptation drives much of the history of fine art, it's more closely associated with popular culture. Adaptation's ubiquity in contemporary storytelling is regularly explained through consumerism and technology unique to our time. Today, we expect to see transmedia storytelling in blockbusters from Harry Potter to the Marvel and DC Universes, where audiences can follow the characters into films, spin-offs, and video games. We might even acknowledge that the pervasiveness of these adaptations bolsters their overall commercial success. This is the contemporary culture industry—a for-profit, media-driven, storytelling machine that combines several arts and entertainment industries.

Unfortunately, this presentism obscures how much of today's transmedia trends are inheritances of the past, intensified through industrialization, capitalism, and an ever-expanding audience. Terms used to describe contemporary adaptation and transmedia storytelling apply to similar cultural phenomenon from the eighteenth and nineteenth centuries. For example, Henry Fielding's first forays into prose fiction were parodies in the form of character extensions. The satirist's two-time target was Samuel Richardson's *Pamela; or, Virtue Rewarded* (1740), and Fielding began with *An Apology for the Life of Mrs. Shamela Andrews* (1741). The following year he extended this storyworld with *The History of the Adventures of Joseph Andrews* (1742), a mock-heroic novel "written in Imitation of the Manner of Cervantes, Author of Don Quixote," whose protagonist is Pamela's sibling. Through intertextual allusion, *Joseph Andrews* not only extends the related, fictive worlds created by Richardson and later developed by Fielding, but also links them loosely to the storyworld of Miguel de Cervantes's seventeenth-century Spanish novel *Don Quijote de la Mancha* (1615), itself a popular culture-text in the eighteenth century that included a stage adaptation *Don Quijote in England* (1734), also written by Fielding.[1] As Fielding worked on his *Pamela* parodies, Richardson wrote his own sequel, *Pamela in Her Exalted State* (1741).

This back-and-forth between Richardson and Fielding and other writers who joined in with additional adaptations, parodies, and extensions was central (not tangential) to *Pamela*'s early reception, with Robert Stam calling *Pamela* "perhaps the first English novel to achieve the status of what would later be called a 'media event.'"[2] The following decades saw scores of *Pamela* parodies, sequels, and souvenirs, including handheld fans, as well as an exhibit featuring one hundred miniature wax-works figurines recreating tableaus from the novel. Dramatizations appeared in multiple genres, including comedy and opera, all with varying degrees of critical and commercial success.[3] Richardson's later novel *Clarissa; or, The History of a Young Lady* (1747) was also regularly adapted, including an array of theatrical versions, abridgements, and extensions.[4] In this whirlwind of transmedia adaptations, Richardson found his works alongside those of Aphra Behn, Daniel Defoe, and Jonathan Swift, all turned into plays, paintings, engravings, and various textual expansions.[5] The eighteenth and nineteenth centuries are full of similar examples in Europe and the United States, and this book covers some of the most iconic exemplars primarily (but not exclusively) in the field of British cultural production.

My overarching argument in this book is that a longer, historical view of adaptation challenges common assumptions about transmedia storytelling, the convergence of media industries, and the ubiquity of adaptation in

---

1. Paulson, *Don Quixote in England* (1997); Fielding, *Don Quixote in England* (1734), *Complete Works* (1967).
2. Stam, *Literature through Film* (2005).
3. Keymer and Sabor, *The Pamela Controversy* (2001); Kreissman, *Pamela-Shamela* (1960).
4. Bueler, *Clarissa: The Eighteenth-Century Response* (2010). Bueler notes that the dramatic career of George Colman (the Elder) was launched by the success of *Polly Holcombe* (1760), a play that relied heavily on audience knowledge of *Clarissa* (xiii).
5. Welcher and Bush, *Gulliveriana* (1970); O'Malley, *Children's Literature, Popular Culture, and* Robinson Crusoe (2012); Blaim, *Robinson Crusoe and His Doubles* (2016); Bolton, *Women Writers Dramatized* (2000); Cook and Seager, *The Afterlives of Eighteenth-Century Fiction* (2015).

contemporary culture. My goal is to flip the interpretive script that designates adaptation as an afterthought or as a derivative object that primarily exists through its relationship to an "original" source. Even when approached productively and embraced by scholars as evidence of homage or cultural staying power, too many times adaptation is metaphorically used to describe the "afterlife" of texts.[6] I situate my research alongside such works—not to dismiss them, but to extend their understanding of the centrality of adaptation to literary production and history. My position is that adaptation is actually the mechanism that breathes life into story itself. Adaptation doesn't resuscitate literature; it's a galvanizing force that drives storytelling. Adaptation is the *only* way that a story can become truly culturally relevant. Positioning adaptation as a primary entry point into the study of literature, culture, and history reveals that, although forms and media continuously change and evolve, the process that undergirds the historical trajectory of storytelling—adaptation—remains stable and perpetual.

The following book links the past and the present through the prevalent cultural practice of adaptation in order to rethink the future of literary history and adaptation studies. My transhistorical approach—situated at the intersections of literary studies, theater and art histories, and media studies—helps us make new connections across forms and media, and over time. Adaptation drives storytelling in all of these formats through a series of ongoing, interdependent processes that have been central to cultural production for centuries. A historical and arrayed view of adaptation and transmedia storytelling, the convergence of art and media industries, and the history of participatory forms of audience engagement reveals that today's transmedia, adaptation industry is actually an intensification of earlier commercial models inherited from the nineteenth century.

As a nineteenth-century scholar who also strives to be a critically aware consumer of contemporary popular culture, I see adaptation in all facets of my daily life—education, research, entertainment. We find adaptations across film, television, stage, graphic novels, illustrated editions for children, young adult fiction, erotic retellings, traditional board and card games, as well as digital forms that include video games and web series made exclusively for distribution on YouTube and social media. You'd be hard pressed to find any "classic" novel *without* one or more adaptations. A spectacular or iconic movie image might provide the cover art for a modern trade edition. In most cases, adaptations range wildly, especially as one adds prequels, mash-ups, and loose

---

6. For this "afterlife" trend, note the following titles: Kucich and Sadoff, *Victorian Afterlife* (2000); Clayton, *Charles Dickens in Cyberspace* (2003); Rigney, *The Afterlives of Walter Scott* (2012); Cook and Seager, *The Afterlives of Eighteenth-Century Fiction* (2015).

appropriations into the matrix. For mega-famous texts like *Pride and Prejudice, A Christmas Carol, Jane Eyre, Wuthering Heights,* and *Dracula,* innumerable adaptations and extensions exist. While the valuable approach of in-depth adaptation histories for singular culture-texts informs this book, I focus on the broader implications of such studies (rather than their conclusions) for the fields of adaptation studies, literary history, and media studies.

A transhistorical view of adaptation shows us how contemporary popular culture has inherited the artistic and the business practices of commercial entertainment industries that converged around the turn of the nineteenth century. Literature and art created during this time reflect the ubiquity of adapting, appropriating, and remixing literary and artistic production. From European Romanticism to Victorian medievalism, figures involved in the period's major aesthetic movements remade older stories to incorporate evolving cultural climates and technological advances. As the following book shows, adaptation was central to storytelling across all sites of production in both high art and mass culture, providing a way for literature and art to respond to social and political revolutions. Adaptation also played a major role in the rise of the novel as the nineteenth century's dominant literary form, just as it helped to make film the most pervasive narrative form in the twentieth century and continues to drive the progression of twenty-first-century storytelling.

Multiple forces coalesced politically, aesthetically, and commercially in the period's art and culture; industrialization, rapid urbanization, the birth of consumer culture, and early capitalism converged. Literacy rates rose rapidly during this time, catalyzed in part by new print technologies that steadily decreased the price of books and other printed texts, which in turn created greater consumer demand for storytelling across forms and media. The rise of urban centers allowed for a competitive, commercial theater culture, as well as the explosion of print culture. The literary periods we now term "Romantic" and "Victorian" developed alongside transformative revolutions that included the abolition of slavery across several nations, the gradual enfranchisement of the working class, and the increasing role of women in public and professional spheres, and these social transformations were reflected in and supported by commercial, mass culture.

The sheer number of adaptations on London stages in the eighteenth and nineteenth centuries deserves more consideration as a cultural phenomenon as opposed to a singular practice tied to the respective cultural histories of individual literary works. The early reception histories of the first novels show us how central adaptation was to the history of the novel itself and its rise as the dominant literary form. For instance, Aphra Behn's *Oroonoko: or, The*

Royal Slave (1688) was adapted into a successful stage play by Thomas Southerne as *Oroonoko: A Tragedy* (1695). Southerne's play went through dozens of revivals and remakes over the next 150 years, making his adaptation the most widely circulated version of *Oroonoko* in the eighteenth and nineteenth centuries. Likewise, Daniel Defoe's *Robinson Crusoe* (1719) and Jonathan Swift's *Gulliver's Travels* (1726) were regularly adapted as plays, pantomimes, sequels, parodies, political satires, illustrated books, and toys for children.[7] Thinking about these practices in the rise of the gothic mode across forms and media in the eighteenth and nineteenth centuries, David Jones admits struggling with the idea of projecting "the marketing concepts and jargon of our own age" onto the past, yet he agrees that "it is clear that by the 1760s, patterns of appropriation, both commercial adaptation and artistic 'cross-pollination,' were very well established," as all of the following commercial practices—dramatizing novels into plays; painting literary subjects; selling portraits of stage actors in costume; and parodying politicians in street ballads, staged pantomimes, or printed caricatures—were "successively coded aesthetically, indeed fashionably, into the communities of production as well as sites of outlet and dissemination, and a ready market in broadsides, squibs and parodic sideshows."[8]

Many of these adaptations were produced soon after the publication of the books on which they were based, circulating alongside (not after) their respective "originals." In the 1790s, Ann Radcliffe, Matthew Lewis, and other major gothic novelists saw their works staged in an array of theatrical genres and printed as abridgements and imitations.[9] Sir Walter Scott's novels were a staple of London's theatrical world throughout his career.[10] Mary Shelley's *Frankenstein; or, The Modern Prometheus* (1818) went through at least fifteen stage adaptations during the 1820s.[11] Between 1848 and 1898, at least eight versions of Charlotte Brontë's *Jane Eyre* (1847) were staged.[12] Sensation fictions such as Mary Elizabeth Braddon's *Lady Audley's Secret* (1862) and Wilkie Collins's *The Woman in White* (1859) and *The Moonstone* (1868) were turned into spectacular domestic melodramas shortly after their publications as well. Well-known authors often added their own versions to the mix, as with Victor Hugo's *La Esmeralda* (1836) for Paris theaters, an adaptation of his earlier

---

7. Mack, *The Genius of Parody* (2007).
8. Jones, *Gothic Machine* (2011), 8–9.
9. Saggini, *The Gothic Novel and the Stage* (2015).
10. Bolton, *Scott Dramatized* (1992); Rigney, *The Afterlives of Walter Scott* (2012).
11. Forry, *Hideous Progenies* (1990).
12. Stoneman, *Jane Eyre on Stage* (2007).

novel *Notre-Dame de Paris* (1831).¹³ Collins also adapted his two most famous novels, *The Woman in White* (staged in London in 1871) and *The Moonstone* (staged in 1877), once other dramatists' adaptations of both stories had faded from view.¹⁴ Charles Dickens, perpetually at odds with the dramatists adapting his novels faster than he could finish them, staged public readings and critiqued loose copyright laws in hopes of having more direct influence on public performances of his works.

The eighteenth- and nineteenth-century theater and print industries thrived on adaptation, appropriation, and other forms of narrative recycling. Theatrical careers were built around the adaptation of literature, history, and current events, and actors became celebrities by bringing literary and historical characters to life on stage. Professional playwrights churned out adaptations of novels, poems, myths, and historical events as fast as they could, with the repertoires of the period's most prolific dramatists full of adaptations. Theater managers saw adaptations as relatively safe investments and ran their businesses by capitalizing on bestselling titles. The lack of copyright for page-to-stage adaptations made this practice particularly lucrative, but popular stories were also adapted into textual forms such as abridged or illustrated editions and marketed for a range of ages and prices. Publishers invested heavily in illustrators and engravers that could satisfy consumers' growing demand for visually appealing books. Painting, sculpture, and illustration transformed texts, injecting them into the period's vibrant visual culture. Fine art and mass culture converged around adaptation as stories were turned into an array of commercial products including chapbooks, literary-inspired memorabilia, and children's toys. Adaptations were everywhere in the nineteenth century, just as they are today.

In a world increasingly understood as global through the workings of empire, colonization, and capitalism, adaptations had international reach in the nineteenth century, and they functioned as a major site of transnational, cultural, and political exchange. Like the geographically dispersed setting of Mary Shelley's *Frankenstein,* the gothic story traveled back and forth between England and France from the 1820s through the 1860s. The French melodrama *Le Monstre et le Magicien* (1826) by Jean-Toussaint Merle and Antony Béraud was itself adapted into a new English play by John Kerr as *The Monster and the Magician; or, The Fate of Frankenstein* (1826). Victor Hugo's

---

13. Szwydky, "Victor Hugo's *Notre-Dame* on the Nineteenth-Century London Stage" (2010).

14. Pedlar, "'The Woman in White' on the Victorian Stage" (2012). http://wilkiecollinssociety.org/opening-up-the-secret-theatre-of-home-wilkie-collinss-the-woman-in-white-on-the-victorian-stage/.

historical romances were regularly staged in England throughout the century as melodramas, ballets, burlesques, and operas, where the characters of *Notre-Dame de Paris* appeared in at least five known versions. A search of the period's newspapers in digital databases returns countless hits describing plays "adapted from" France, Italy, Germany, and other countries. A similar dynamic characterized the exchange between English and American narratives. James Fenimore Cooper's nautical novels *The Pilot* (1823) and *The Red Rover* (1827) were turned into hit melodramas for London stages in the 1820s.[15] Harriet Beecher Stowe's *Uncle Tom's Cabin* (1852) was adapted into at least a dozen distinct stage versions during London's 1852–53 theatrical season alone. Charles Dickens's novels were regularly staged in the United States, with H. Philip Bolton cataloging performances from the theatrical centers of Boston, New York City, Philadelphia, Chicago, St. Louis, and San Francisco.[16] Robert Louis Stevenson's *The Strange Case of Dr. Jekyll and Mr. Hyde* (1886) premiered in New York City within six months of its publication and immediately became a transatlantic stage hit that turned the lead actor, Richard Mansfield, into an international celebrity.

While nineteenth-century characters especially continue to inhabit modern and contemporary society, examples abound from antiquity, and this was also true during the nineteenth century. Adaptation was central to European Romanticism and Victorian medievalism across forms and media in both fine art and mass culture. Alongside battle scenes and political leaders, historical painting drew its subjects from mythological, biblical, and literary sources. Ancient myths and medieval legends served as regular sites of artistic adaptation and cultural remediation. Adaptation and transmedia storytelling, including the combined use of text and images in multiple mediums, has always been central to the circulation of narratives.[17] Classicists acknowledge the collaborative role of drama, painting, sculpture, and pottery in the art of storytelling and cultural mythmaking through a "cultural system of iconography" developed in the inscriptions on ancient Greek vases depicting the stories of mythological heroes and historical events.[18] Medieval manuscripts combined text and image to retell stories from the Bible and to establish national

---

15. Burwick and Powell, *British Pirates in Print and Performance* (2015).
16. Bolton, *Dickens Dramatized* (1987). Although Bolton's catalog is self-described as "incomplete," it lists more than three thousand dramatizations of Dickens's works. For details about a performance of *Bleak House* staged in San Francisco in 1875, see Smith, "J. P. Burnett's *Bleak House*" (2016).
17. For a historical survey, see Hunt, Lomas, and Corris, *Art, Word and Image* (2010). For a media studies perspective that includes art, music, film, and digital forms, see Ryan, *Narrative across Media* (2004).
18. Oakley, *The Greek Vase* (2013); Shapiro, *Poet and Painter in Classical Greece* (2005).

myths, such as the legends of Camelot. Nineteenth-century illustrated books brought multiform storytelling into the middle-class home through the fusion of mechanically reproduced text and image. Twentieth-century film transformed this visual medium into the century's dominant form of storytelling. Twenty-first-century new media allows gamers to immerse themselves in storyworlds dominated by virtual simulations. Although they come from widely different historical moments, all of these cultural objects and practices are linked through their patterns of recycling, repetition, and adaptation, differing from one historical context to the next through the available technologies and media revamped by new fashions, trends, and societal change.

The varied examples discussed throughout this book may raise a series of questions about definitions and types of adaptations: What do we mean when we say "adaptation"? What shapes can adaptations take? How much engagement with a precursor text is necessary for an adaptation to be considered an adaptation? Are adaptations always readily identifiable *as* adaptations? Does form or medium affect whether we categorize works of art as "originals" or as "adaptations"? Answers to these questions map familiar terrain in the existing scholarship and are regularly discussed in the introductory chapters of book-length adaptation studies.[19] Such repetition can be partly explained by the diffuse and interdisciplinary nature of adaptation studies, making it difficult to trace a clear and visible history of (and terminology for) adaptations and adaptation studies.[20] From a historical perspective, part of what makes the study of adaptation especially compelling lies in the difficulty of narrowing down a transhistorical cultural phenomenon that can refer to many products and processes at the same time. "Adaptation" is a highly malleable term with flexible meanings. As a noun, it can refer to a specific work of art such as a film or a play; as a verb, it can refer to a creative process (as in the art or act of adapting a work into a new form). "Adaptation" can refer to a single transformation (the same story in two or more forms) or explain how an ur-text and related archetypes evolve over time across various forms and media.[21]

Another obstacle is an overemphasis on "high" versus "low" or "mass culture" in academic discourse. We typically attach adaptation to popular culture, despite the fact that examples abound in high art throughout history.[22] Similar

---

19. Murray, *The Adaptation Industry* (2012); Slethaug, *Adaptation Theory and Criticism* (2014); Newell, *Expanding Adaptation Networks* (2017). See also Leitch, *The Oxford Handbook of Adaptation Studies* (2017).

20. Elliott, "Adaptation Theory and Adaptation Scholarship" (2017).

21. Bortolotti and Hutcheon, "On the Origins of Adaptation" (2007).

22. Scholars have argued that early twentieth-century films regularly adapt novels for the screen to heighten the new medium's "respectability" as an emerging art form. See also Huyssen, *After the Great Divide* (1987).

tensions drove literary and artistic criticism in the eighteenth and nineteenth centuries as literature and art became more accessible to a wider audience, and its aesthetics evolved to reflect changing political and social climates. In adaptation and literary studies alike, high/low binaries are often reinforced by medium, form, or genre, particularly as these categories seem determined by the structure of the modern academy. Several scholars critique the disciplinary silos of modern academia for focusing too narrowly or isolating artistic archives instead of emphasizing comparative approaches.[23] Dramatic forms of storytelling (plays, films, television) dominate adaptation studies while kitsch transmedia examples and adaptation commodities (novelization, fan fiction, video games, toys, tourism) are relegated almost exclusively to the less-studied domain of mass culture. Similarly, literary studies often privilege established literary forms (drama, poetry, prose) over marginalized sites of storytelling (graphic novels, children's media, fan culture).

The following book invites all of these forms into the conversation, following Timothy Corrigan's view that

> between disciplinarity and adaptation, between literature and film, adaptation studies provide . . . especially ambiguous, risky, unstable, and enormously interesting opportunities today. When opened out beyond questions of specificity and fidelity, adaptation studies necessarily and productively trouble and open disciplinary boundaries (both those of literary studies and film studies). It is in that gap that many of the most compelling ideas appear.[24]

To this effect, centering adaptation studies allows us to see how adaptations often functioned as equal or sometimes even primary sites of cultural engagement—especially since many audiences never read the "original" works. In this formulation, the cottage industries that grew around Scott, Hugo, Dickens, and Stowe during the nineteenth century aren't coded primarily as markers of authorial achievement; rather, they helped these writers become famous in their own day and largely determine the extent to which they remain culturally visible in the present. Adaptations become the primary

---

23. In adaptation studies, see Elliott, *Rethinking the Novel/Film Debate* (2003) and Newell, *Expanding Adaptation Networks* (2017). For genre studies perspectives, see Dowden and Quinn, *Tragedy and the Tragic in German Literature, Art, and Thought* (2014); Calè, *Fuseli's Milton Gallery* (2006). For a media studies perspective, see Hausken, "Textual Theory and Blind Spots in Media Studies" (2004).

24. Corrigan, "Literature on Screen" (2007), 42.

way that such writers are transformed into popular, canonical, iconic literary figures in the twentieth century and beyond.[25]

Contemporary disciplinarity often masks the complex network of interactions involved in storytelling. What's more, media-specific, aesthetic-driven, and class-based barriers intensify the invisibility of adaptation by relegating it to a secondary or derivative status situated primarily in the domain of popular culture. These modern disciplinary barriers are also historically inaccurate and perpetuate faulty assumptions about the creation, circulation, and experience of literature in both the past and the present. Adaptation studies provides an interdisciplinary lens to view these dynamics in a new critical light, especially when read alongside aesthetic practices like allusion and ekphrasis.[26] To reframe discussions and resituate adaptations as works of art on their own terms, adaptation scholars frequently turn to Mikhail Bakhtin's notion of intertextuality and Gerard Genette's theories of transtexuality and paratexts in order to establish dialogical relationships between printed texts and other forms.[27] For adaptation scholars such as Thomas Leitch, adaptation exists on a spectrum of critical engagement that includes curation, celebration, and critique, all of which can happen through close engagement, compression, significant expansion, and brief or extended allusion.[28] Understanding adaptations as intertextual engagements across forms and media connects them to broader questions of literary, artistic, and cultural production from a longer historical view.

Many of the formats in which we encounter adaptation and transmedia storytelling today have been around for centuries. As Martin Meisel notes in his foundational study of the interplay of text, image, and performance in the "Sister Art" tradition of the eighteenth and nineteenth centuries, illustration was understood by visual artists as carrying "a sense of enrichment and embellishment beyond mere specification; it implied the extensions of one medium or mode of discourse by another, rather than a materialization with a minimum of imaginative intervention."[29] In the nineteenth century, the "shared structures in the representational arts helped constitute not just a

---

25. The notable exception in literary studies are author- or text-based cultural histories, but even these tend to support traditional canons or ideas of authorial or textual greatness that reinforce the high/low binary in art and literature more than they trouble this divide.

26. Leitch, *Film Adaptation and Its Discontents* (2007); Newell, *Expanding Adaptation Networks* (2017).

27. Cutchins, "Bakhtin, Intertextuality, and Adaptation" (2017); Stam, "Beyond Fidelity" (2000). Genette echoes heavily in the work of both Stam and Hutcheon, two foundational theorists in contemporary adaptation studies.

28. Leitch, *Film Adaptation and Its Discontents* (2007).

29. Meisel, *Realizations* (1983), 30.

common style, but a popular style" that Meisel terms *realization*, both a process and an aesthetic connecting the representational arts of literature, drama, and picture in such a way that "each form and each work becomes the site of a complex interplay of narrative and picture" and storytelling.[30] An array of formats and commercial products provided additional sites for extensions through parodies, continuations, and imitations. (Film, television, and new media adaptations function in much the same way now.) Until the Berne Convention for the Protection of Literary and Artistic Works in 1886, characters and incidents that today would undoubtedly fall under copyright restrictions were considered public property.[31] In this preregulated, commercial environment, authors, artists, publishers, producers, readers, and audiences found a virtual free-for-all through adaptation and transmediation.

Similarly, this book answers a call for transhistorical connection and interaction between nineteenth-century scholars and contemporary media theorists, covered in an exchange between Leitch and Kamilla Elliott. Leitch sees a problematic divide among contemporary adaptation scholars and Victorianists that is noticeable only to those who have been trained and/or participate in both fields. This glaring gap in the scholarship, according to Elliott, is a failure from both groups. On the one hand, adaptation studies have focused too much on film, radio, television, and other period-specific media, thereby excluding those who study historical periods before the twentieth century. On the other hand, literary studies largely values textual works over other storytelling forms. Elliott explains that adaptation studies has not made a broader impact in historical period studies, particularly Victorian studies, because of literary studies' adherence to "*media* hierarchies . . . inherited from formalism and New Criticism," to which I would add critiques of the culture industry as envisioned by Frankfurt School theorists. As a historically trained scholar who studies adaptation, Elliott places much of the blame on literary studies' emphasis on texts and failure to give media its appropriate status as context:

> Victorian scholars have been reluctant to cede that other media are just as much a part of literary context as history, politics, philosophy, psychology, economics, and society. A superannuated adherence to medium specificity and devotion to high culture, even among radical political scholars, keeps other media cordoned off *as context* by media boundaries and categorical divides. Victorian studies can learn from adaptation studies to take more interest in intermedial engagements—in the very transtextuality, inter-

---

30. Meisel, *Realizations* (1983), 4, 3.
31. Brewer, *The Afterlife of Character, 1726–1825* (2005).

mediality (etc.) that populates the table of contents in adaptation studies handbooks, treating them not solely as forms but also as contexts and environments.[32]

Elliot's own research brings together the two areas of study not only in studying the adaptation of Victorian texts into film, but also adaptation practices in "Victorian interart adaptations and intermedial technologies" such as painting, portraiture, and illustrated texts. She suggests that studying adaptation "as a historical continuum across forms" can help bridge the divide between contemporary adaptation theory and scholarly conversations taking place in historical periods that predate film.

My approach opens up the intermediality of nineteenth-century adaptation, laying out what's at stake for all sides in this approach. Thus, this book should be read as both a historical intervention into adaptation studies and as an adaptation-focused, cultural studies intervention into literary studies. Despite four decades of scholarship to draw upon, adaptation studies still doesn't have a well-known history of its own outside of specialized circles.[33] Because adaptation studies are largely spearheaded by film studies (specifically as it developed in relation to literary studies in university English departments), much of the conversation remains situated within film and television. For this reason, historical work that explicitly situates itself within "adaptation studies" rarely looks before the silent film era. There are, of course, a few notable exceptions. Yet by and large, the precinematic age typically shows up in passing references or in highly visible exemplars like William Shakespeare, who has not only been adapted more than one can count, but whose own work was also driven by adapting histories, legends, poems, and other popular plays. However, as this book shows, adaptation as a cultural practice (even in its commercially driven forms) has a long and rich history that should figure more prominently in adaptation studies, even those focused on contemporary examples.

The reverse is also true. Nineteenth-century cultural histories that include literary adaptations would benefit from conversations taking place in contemporary adaptation studies. For example, existing reception histories of major authors or specific texts often provide much needed details about dramatiza-

---

32. Elliott, "What Can Victorian Studies Learn from Adaptation Studies?" (2017).

33. The last decade has seen a boom in theoretical frameworks for understanding the cultural and educational power of adaptations as an interdisciplinary exchange between the narrative and visual arts through scholarship spearheaded by Stam, *Literature through Film* (2005); Stam and Raengo, *Literature and Film* (2005); Hutcheon, *A Theory of Adaptation* (2006); and Leitch, *Film Adaptation and Its Discontents* (2007).

tions, subsequent reprints, new editions, and film adaptations.[34] Yet even these heavily researched, groundbreaking studies provide only partial snapshots of adaptation's contribution to cultural histories. These books do a great job of socially contextualizing adaptations, tracking deviations from their "originals," and situating them in the reception histories of their respective authors. However, without a broader historical view, the takeaway for some readers is largely a version of "fidelity discourse" that has been the bane of adaptation studies, especially in the last decade.[35] Without the theoretical approaches and discursive threads of adaptation studies, historical case studies that focus on a single text or author (unintentionally) promote the idea that specific novels or authors are extraordinary in their ability to draw in new audiences when adapted to new mediums. What's more, many reject the term "adaptation" unless it's used to describe a very specific cultural product, such as a play directly derived from a textual source and used as evidence for the text's or author's excellence. I argue for more inclusive definitions and approaches that open a more productive framework for understanding the convergence of literature, art, and cultural production.

An assumption that specific authors or particular texts drive adaptation (as opposed to the other way around) creates blind spots in existing scholarship. For example, Juliet John's meticulously researched and provocative book *Dickens and Mass Culture* (2010) convincingly situates the Victorian novelist within the nineteenth century's industrialized, cultural milieu. Yet, the two later chapters that focus on adaptations place Dickens at the center of a cultural phenomenon instead of making him a major node in a larger network of cultural production fueled by adaptation and transmedia storytelling. Such conclusions are driven by author- or text-based approaches to adaptation. Without foregrounding adaptation as a primary method of approaching literature and culture, we will never get satisfactory answers to the question that undergirds one of the major assumptions of literary and adaptation studies: "What is it about X that makes them/it a constant presence in popular culture through adaptation?" Reversing this logic, the cultural history of adaptation suggests that specific texts or authors become iconic because of adaptation, not the other way around.

While it's tempting to rationalize the early and continued adaptation of specific authors or particular works as markers of inherent "greatness"—the

---

34. Forry, *Hideous Progenies* (1990); Meer, *Uncle Tom Mania* (2005); Rigney, *The Afterlives of Walter Scott* (2012); and three books by Glavin including *After Dickens* (1999), *Dickens on Screen* (2003), and *Dickens Adapted* (2012).

35. See Murray's introduction to *The Adaptation Industry* (2012) for an overview of this debate's evolution.

sheer frequency and range of adaptation in the nineteenth century proves this "derivative" practice instead had a primary role in cultural production and circulation. Adaptations increased the visibility of stories, introduced them to new audiences, and drove sales of both theater tickets and printed books. Sometimes the text being adapted was by a well-known or great-selling author. Sometimes the text was too obscure to easily identify as an adaptation in the first place. Sometimes it wasn't even a "text" being adapted. Historical and current events were dramatized, illustrated, and appropriated just as frequently as traditional and popular literature. Sometimes adaptations themselves were adapted into new adaptations. Placing less emphasis on individual authors or texts and more on the material conditions, commercial practices, and political effects of adaptation in the period engenders a very different historical picture of adaptation as a cultural practice. For this reason, this book focuses on cultural icons and culture-texts. More than the relationship between a text and a single adaptation, the term culture-text breaks down (or opens up) the ubiquitous text/adaptation binary that adaptation studies regularly defends itself against.[36]

Instead of close readings of adaptations and their sources, I emphasize the material and cultural conditions that allowed adaptation to thrive so pervasively in the nineteenth century—conditions that have continued to intensify over more than two centuries. Where close reading practices ask readers to pay particular attention to the closed form of the "text," the model for transhistorical adaptation that I use here more strongly resembles "distant reading" practices that ask readers to extrapolate meaning through an extensive network of texts and allusions.[37] I draw on early dramatizations of nineteenth-century novels, which I discuss alongside paratextual evidence (including theater reviews, ephemera, memoirs, and letters). I am also interested in merchandise, new printings and special editions of books, sequels, spin-offs, parodies, novelizations, and so on—which I argue should also be included under the general umbrella of adaptation and appropriation, following more recent studies in transmedia storytelling, convergence culture, and fandom studies.[38]

---

36. Stam, *Literature through Film* (2005); Stam and Raengo, *Literature and Film* (2005); Corrigan, "Literature on Screen" (2007).

37. Moretti, *Distant Reading* (2013).

38. See Hutcheon, *A Theory of Adaptation* (2006); Sanders, *Adaptation and Appropriation* (2006); Leitch, *Film Adaptation and Its Discontents* (2007); Jenkins, *Textual Poachers* (2013), *Convergence Culture* (2006), and "Adaptation, Extension, Transmedia" (2017); Newell, *Expanding Adaptation Networks* (2017); Meikle, *Adaptations in the Franchise Era* (2019).

Two concepts anchor *Transmedia Adaptation in the Nineteenth Century* and inform my understanding of adaptation and other forms of extension through the twenty-first century: transmedia storytelling and convergence culture. These terms, coined by contemporary media theorist Henry Jenkins, help us rethink both the limitations and the possibilities that technology presents for critically aware cultural consumers as well as the future of art and entertainment. The first concept—transmedia storytelling—focuses on the narrative elements of storytelling and how single storyworlds unfold over multiple installments across media. In Jenkins's accounts, transmedia storytelling is a major model for storytelling today, built across technological platforms emerging at the turn of the millennium. *Star Wars* and *The Matrix* epitomize this practice as the transmedia storyworlds attached to them can be experienced through film, television, narrative games, and official tie-ins such as toys, novels, or novelizations of visual media. In all of the official sites of transmedia storytelling—those produced by the storyworlds' "owners" form only part of the whole—no single site is more authoritative than another. As Jenkins argues, even sites of "unauthorized" extension have significant cultural impact without enjoying "official" status. This includes fan fiction and the live-action role-playing that characterizes much of fan culture today. For Jenkins, these "participatory" sites of engagement form a substantial part of the whole storytelling experience and deserve serious recognition as parts of the cultural phenomenon of transmedia storytelling.

It's in the contested middle ground between creators and consumers that Jenkins theorizes convergence culture as

> the flow of content across multiple media platforms, the cooperation between multiple media industries, and the migratory behavior of media audiences who will go almost anywhere in search of the kinds of entertainment experiences they want. Convergence is a word that manages to describe technological, industrial, cultural, and social changes depending on who's speaking and what they think they are talking about.[39]

Convergence culture describes much more than stories and the forms they take; it goes beyond any specific medium or commercial industry. "More than simply a technological shift," Jenkins explains, "convergence alters the relationship between existing technologies, industries, markets, genres, and audiences. Convergence alters the logic by which media industries operate and by which media consumers process . . . convergence refers to a process not an

---

39. Jenkins, *Convergence Culture* (2006), 2–3.

endpoint."[40] Transmedia storytelling is a grounding technique for convergence culture. It provides shared narratives that extend well beyond any single site of consumption or type of engagement. It allows any story to extend itself infinitely. It includes authoritative prequels, sequels, and spin-offs that are notably referred to as part of the official "canon" of a storyworld. But transmedia storytelling in convergence culture also allows new creators to take the stories in new directions for different purposes, challenging strict, centralized models of commercial storytelling.

Jenkins's model marks consumers as creators as they write fan fiction or develop detailed online user communities. To media scholars, this may seem like a possibility that began with the Internet and similar modern technologies; however, we can apply this model in new historical contexts. What parallels might we draw between an anonymous Harry Potter fan tinkering with new technologies to create new Hogwarts adventures in the comfort of their home and William Blake experimenting with new painting and engraving techniques two hundred years earlier as he illustrated *Paradise Lost* and *The Divine Comedy*? Is it so widely different than an eighteen-year-old Mary Shelley remixing several literary texts to create a new monster story published in the new, popular form of the novel? In all of these examples, individuals use emerging technologies to create something new out of something old. Each is an artist. All are adapters.

Convergence culture differs from older models like Theodor Adorno and Max Horkheimer's "culture industry" by productively situating multiple sites of storytelling inside a larger cultural framework with many intersecting points.[41] Unlike Adorno and Horkheimer's centrally administered machine of cultural production, the only center in Jenkins's model of convergence culture is where multiple sites of production and consumption meet. Convergence culture includes industrial and commercial concerns, but it pairs them with audience reception, engagement, and participation. For Jenkins,

> Convergence... is both a top-down corporate-driven process and a bottom-up consumer-driven process. Corporate convergence coexists with grassroots convergence. Media companies are learning how to accelerate the flow of media content across delivery channels to expand revenue opportunities, broaden markets, and reinforce viewer commitments. Consumers are learn-

---

40. Jenkins, *Convergence Culture* (2006), 15–16.
41. Adorno and Horkheimer, *Dialectic of Enlightenment* (1944); Adorno, "Culture Industry Reconsidered" (1975).

ing how to use these different media technologies to bring the flow of media more fully under their control and to interact with other consumers.[42]

This model provides a more dynamic approach to transmedia storytelling, as well as art and entertainment industries. Convergence culture acknowledges that consumers can be active producers of meaning and content through various points of participation. Where Adorno and Horkheimer characterize audiences as passive consumers of prefabricated content, Jenkins provides a model that allows users opportunities to participate in the consumption and production of storytelling. Following Jenkins, my history of adaptation and transmedia storytelling in the nineteenth century presents a diffuse and dynamic cultural practice of determining what stories, texts, and authors get remembered for years to come.

Jenkins's models are grounded in twenty-first-century media and literacies, but he acknowledges the need for a more historical understanding of the ways that narratives unfold and how these histories may lead us to a better understanding of transmedia storytelling and convergence culture in the present. Matthew Freeman provides one historical account of transmedia storytelling, showing how even earlier texts like *The Wizard of Oz* and *Superman* also consisted of stories that unfolded over multiple books, as well as live performances, illustrated books, comic books, radio, film, television, toys, and more. However, Freeman's timeline begins at the turn of the twentieth century, the historical moment where my own project ends. Even though my work extends more than one hundred years farther back, Freeman and I arrive at similar conclusions about the cultural pervasiveness of transmedia storytelling across time and what history might teach us about the importance of these cultural practices.[43]

I sometimes adopt the language of contemporary media studies by referring to adaptations as spin-offs, off-shoots, sequels, and other words typically used to describe today's forms of pop culture, narrative extensions. The word I use regularly to refer to the phenomenon of transhistorical adaptation is "culture-text," a term coined by Paul Davis and developed by Brian Rose as a "body of adaptations extended over time that . . . has the potential of becoming a larger, reflexive body of narratological, performative, and cultural elements."[44] Davis's "culture-text" exemplar is *A Christmas Carol*, while Rose

---

42. Jenkins, *Convergence Culture* (2006), 18.
43. Freeman, *Historicising Transmedia Storytelling* (2017).
44. Rose works through another great example of nineteenth-century fiction that has eclipsed its author: Robert Louis Stevenson's 1886 novella *The Strange Case of Dr. Jekyll and Mr. Hyde*, which has more than one hundred dramatizations or appropriations to date. Geduld,

focuses on *The Strange Case of Dr. Jekyll and Mr. Hyde*; both nineteenth-century examples owe their widespread cultural visibility to regular adaptation and remixing. These characters and storyworlds exist primarily because they have been built through a vast network of adaptations over time. These numerous adaptations make up the culture-text, and the culture-text belongs to everyone (creators and consumers alike).

Instead of a "close-up" view of the ins-and-outs of specific adaptations, culture-texts ask us to zoom out for a "big-picture" view. From this position, we can better see adaptation and transmediation as a transhistorical phenomenon by following how major stories move across centuries. Throughout this book, I draw from a range of nineteenth-century writers and artists in England, France, and the United States, but older culture-texts like *Paradise Lost, The Divine Comedy,* and *Don Quixote* make several appearances. The theatrical, economic, and political contexts I draw on remain primarily situated in London but also reach out to other major industrial centers of art and culture. I avoid focusing on a single source in any given chapter, following recent trends in adaptation studies that complicate the traditional case study approach. Authors, texts, characters, and their many adaptations weave in and out of the chapters in this book. Some are mentioned in passing; others get a more extensive treatment.

The exception might be *Frankenstein,* which appears regularly in this book. What Dennis Perry and Dennis Cutcheon have termed "the Frankenstein Complex" (the collected notion of the novel and all of its adaptations and appropriations that exists in the cultural imagination) exemplifies almost all of the major arguments and claims throughout this book.[45] Julie Grossman sees Frankenstein as "an especially apt metaphor for film adaptation" because "the novel's own fascination with changing and reconstructed forms of being makes it a ripe source for theoretical discussions of adaptation."[46] Not only does the Frankenstein culture-text provide productive metaphors for understanding fragmentation and animation processes that fuel adaptation, it also troubles claims of authorial or textual "originality." The novel is an intertextual goldmine that asks us to reconsider the origins of creativity. Its history of reception, textual revision, and widespread cultural visibility since its publication two hundred years ago exemplifies the importance of adaptation in keeping stories alive. In driving interdisciplinary conversation, the Frankenstein

---

The Definitive Dr. Jekyll and Mr. Hyde Companion (1983) catalogs 136 film and television titles (including direct adaptation and loose retellings).

45. Cutchins and Perry, *Adapting Frankenstein* (2018).
46. Grossman, *Literature, Film, and Their Hideous Progeny* (2015), 17.

culture-text is one of the most accessible examples that literary scholars may draw upon when speaking to nonspecialists as well as the public.

Together, the pieces of this project paint a mural of nineteenth-century literature and popular culture that brings together authors, novels, plays, dramatists, theater personalities, advertisements, souvenirs, and other adaptation-focused products—all while tracing the period's relevance to contemporary models of adaptation and commercialization. Instead of a series of individual case studies, the book is organized around identifiable markers of the nineteenth-century culture industry (spectacle, celebrity, transmediation, world-building, and merchandizing). Beyond showing how adaptation informed or reflected contemporaneous historical, political, and social developments, I've chosen these topics because they continue to inform today's media and entertainment industries, helping us connect contemporary models of storytelling to those we've inherited from the past. This comprehensive, thematic organization also opens space for many more examples and provides a more robust picture of adaptation as a practice with a distinct cultural history.

CHAPTER OVERVIEWS

Chapter 1, "The Convergence of Censorship, Spectacle, Commercialism, and Aesthetics in the Nineteenth Century," outlines three contexts—political, industrial, and aesthetic—that facilitated the proliferation of commercial, literary adaptation in the nineteenth century. Censorship was rampant on the nineteenth-century European stage. Theaters were public spaces where the upper and lower classes intermingled, and large crowds sometimes led to violence, especially in times of political unrest as was common during the Age of Revolutions. Fears of inciting mobs through the emotional strength and affective nature of drama led to regulatory structures that shaped theatrical production. As the most popular medium for storytelling with the most diverse reach, changes to dramatic forms affected the way that old and new narratives circulated and necessitated a push toward stage spectacle and visual storytelling.

Technological innovation, rapid industrialization, and economic shifts led to a more consumer-based, capitalist economy that supported a commercialized culture of adaptation and storytelling across theatrical genres. Dramatic versions of the same story staged at rival theaters competed for ticket sales. Loose copyright laws fostered widespread borrowing and recycling. More adaptations followed, and these new productions often riffed off earlier adaptations. Spectacle became the real draw, with profit as the biggest motive.

Advertisements, playbills, and posters highlighted special effects. Technology and special effects not only featured prominently in all theaters but also supported related industrial economies (printing houses, skilled labor, materials for costuming, set design, etc.).

An aesthetic of self-awareness characterized many of these adaptations, as parody and pastiche permeated the nineteenth-century culture industry, playing a central role in dispersing stories, turning characters into popular icons and stories into culture-texts. The dialectical relationship between the London theater industry and the publishing industry during this period illustrates the convergence of politics, regulation, innovation, and commercialism. Together these contexts and arts-based industries shaped how stories circulated in nineteenth-century popular culture. Adaptation and transmedia storytelling provided cohesion in a commercial economy that professionalized writers and artists, bringing them closer to readers, audiences, and consumers than they had ever been before.

Chapter 2, "Professional Networks and Celebrity Culture: Authors, Actors, Adapters," considers celebrity culture at the historical moment when the arts shifted from a system of patronage to a commercial endeavor. Poets, novelists, dramatists, actors, painters, illustrators, and engravers all became professionalized in a burgeoning industrial economy, as did the management of each of these arts-based industries. My account of this history sees adaptation in the nineteenth-century culture industry as both a collaborative art and a business practice that was supported through several industries. Like film companies today, theater managers then made substantial investments in staffing, sets, and special effects to sell tickets, making the theater industry a large, entertainment-based businesses.[47] Adaptations were responsible for employing thousands of people on the stage, behind the scenes, and even back at the printing houses, where new print editions were brought out to capitalize on successful theatrical runs. Book sales turned writers into industrial-age authors—professionals whose careers depended on a network of adaptation for immediate visibility and future posterity.

Celebrity authors such as Lord Byron, Sir Walter Scott, Mary Shelley, Victor Hugo, and Charles Dickens populate this chapter alongside famous actors such as Thomas Potter Cooke, O. Smith, and Richard Mansfield (who were famous for their portrayals of literary characters on stage). However, the lesser-known but no-less-important characters in this chapter are the dramatists of the day. Critically acclaimed playwrights such as Dion Boucicault are

---

47. Murray, *The Adaptation Industry* (2012); Davis, *The Economics of the British Stage* (2000).

considered in conjunction with prolific professionals such as Richard Brinsley Peake, James Robinson Planché, Edward Fitzball, George Dibdin Pitt, and Andrew Halliday, most regarded as "hacks" in their day and largely forgotten now. I argue for rethinking the role of "hack" artists in perpetuating literature, art, and culture where they might be considered "auteurs," similar to how directors are seen in film studies. The connection reveals how much nineteenth-century adapters saw themselves as contributing to the arts in general as well as the individual careers of actors. Authors and actors found themselves recognizable to a growing audience that crossed gender, class, and national boundaries. Adaptations made this growth of celebrity possible, but also caused the biggest source of tension between authors and their adapters: licensing rights and payment. Modern copyright laws are derived from the legislation passed because celebrity writers like Dickens and Hugo fought for more control over their intellectual property and their financial rights to adaptations derived from their books. The concept of "derivative works" in copyright law was completely new legal territory at this time—and it remains a contested area of cultural production today as artists and companies struggle to deal with unlicensed uses of their works that simultaneously drive interest and profit.

Chapter 3, "Visual and Textual Adaptations in Fine Art Forms," focuses on the work of now-canonical poets and visual artists. A survey of nineteenth-century writers, painters, illustrators, and engravers shows the dynamic relationship between the "Sister Arts" of painting and poetry—a pairing that we see continuously at work (albeit regularly modified) throughout the Romantic period, and later extended through the Pre-Raphaelite Brotherhood in the latter half of the nineteenth century. The popularity of literary galleries at the turn of the nineteenth century provides a front-row seat to see how literature and culture was experienced through a fusion of textual and visual forms. In London, a customer could pay to view contemporary artists' paintings of scenes from canonical plays. She could purchase a print guide to the paintings, which included excerpts from the plays to understand the works of art hanging on the walls. She could also buy souvenir prints on-site or subscribe to have small-yet-skillfully adapted engravings of a gallery's massive oil paintings delivered to her home. The literary galleries were created and managed by printers, and the period's publishing industry played a central role in creating a demand for new versions of the same stories and innovating both their textual and visual presentations. It became common to see visual adaptations in both expensive books and penny publications, and this growing, for-profit industry in turn supported professional illustrators and engravers.

Demand for illustrated books drove the market for updated editions modernized for new audiences. The chapter shows how adaptation built the careers of several innovative artists who in turn shaped nineteenth-century visual culture and literary history. William Blake's various illustration projects functioned as forms of criticism, as he modernized Dante and Milton for the Age of Revolutions. Visual adaptations also crossed national boundaries and language barriers more easily than texts, and French artists such as Eugène Delacroix and Gustave Doré built careers on illustrating works of writers across countries and continents. Their transmediations of Dante, Milton, and Cervantes alongside contemporary writers such as Goethe, Byron, and Tennyson became part of a broader network of adaptations that shaped the receptions of their works into the next century. Today, Blake's, Delacroix's, and Doré's respective illustration projects remain widely available and important to literary and art historians alike, and their visuals continue to influence other visual arts such as theater, film, and television.

Chapter 4, "Culture-Texts and Storyworlds across Nineteenth-Century Media," shows how stories become culture-texts through various types of world-building using two especially fruitful nineteenth-century examples: the aggregate world that Dickens (plus his illustrators, adapters, and fans) built over the course of his writing career and the Camelot storyworld, especially as it expanded during the Victorian period. Dickens's career developed through a mixture of ekphrastic writing, textual expansions, serialization, and illustration. From the beginning, Dickens's writing career was supported by the visual and performing arts. Visual continuity between his texts occurred through illustrations, most notably those of his main illustrator, Hablot Knight Browne, who illustrated ten of Dickens's books.[48] And, of course, there was Dickens's never-ending complicated relationship with dramatists who produced stage adaptations of his works while the novels were still in serialization. But Dickens too participated in the ongoing adaptation and extension of his works. New projects sometimes expanded the work of previous ones, as Samuel Pickwick appeared in the frame stories of *Master Humphrey's Clock* (1840–41), a weekly periodical written entirely by Dickens. In fictional worlds, individual characters can establish continuity, but cohesion also occurs structurally through similar settings—in Dickens's case, London's growing urban landscape also took on a character of its own. The whimsical characters that inhabited his fictions were comical, grotesque, and memorable.

Seen through a historical lens, contemporary narrative world-building asks us to revisit the popularity of the medieval Arthurian tradition in the

---

48. Cohen, *Charles Dickens and His Original Illustrators* (1980).

Victorian period. The collective story cycles that make up the Arthurian tradition are among the most well-known and repeatedly adapted narratives. By approaching this culture-text through the mythic city of Camelot (as opposed to the singular character of King Arthur), I emphasize the world-building elements that create this culture-text. Instead of a specific story that can be traced down to an authoritative source text, the Camelot culture-text provides a transmedia storyworld populated by many iconic characters that many writers, artists, and performers have made their own. There are major textual sources including Malory's *Le Morte d'Arthur* (1485), but this fifteenth-century text collected and rewrote the stories found in dispersed medieval sources. Tennyson kicked off the Camelot-craze and the Victorian fascination with all things medieval, but was only one of many extensions and retellings that circulated in the second half of the nineteenth century. Poets such as Edward Bulwer-Lytton and William Morris drew from a combination of Tennyson and medieval texts in their new poetic adaptations. Musicians and artists adapted these stories into operas, paintings, and illustration using new technology and techniques. Women artists—such as the photographer Julia Margaret Cameron, who produced photographic illustrations of *Idylls* in 1874 at Tennyson's request to capitalize on this new technology—and later illustrators reimagined Camelot's women as active characters who could overturn gender ideologies by visualizing "iconic, passive femininity to have an articulate voice, expressed by women rereading and rewriting medieval legend."[49] Each individual, artistic contribution stood on its own merits, while also adding to the collective Camelot culture-text as it circulated in the new media ecology of the late nineteenth century.[50]

In Chapter 5, "Nineteenth-Century Tie-Ins, Commercial Extensions, and Participatory Culture," I analyze pulp fiction and toy theaters as early sites of adaptation-driven merchandizing. Souvenirs and related merchandise extended the reach of consumer engagement with popular narratives beyond text, illustration, and performance. Elegant gift editions, abridged chapbooks, pirated spin-offs, children's toys, housewares, consumables—any product could be turned into an additional site of storytelling for profit. I build on Diane Long Hoeveler's *Gothic Riffs* (2010), which traces the dispersed circulation of the gothic mode in nineteenth-century mass culture through a range of formats, from ballads to magic lantern shows.[51] From the beginning of the

---

49. Saunders, *Women Writers and Nineteenth-Century Medievalism* (2009).
50. I adopt the term "media ecology" here from contemporary media studies and nineteenth-century scholarship, including Fuller, *Media Ecologies* (2005); Mole, *What the Victorians Made of Romanticism* (2017); and Brylowe, *Romantic Art in Practice* (2019).
51. Hoeveler, *Gothic Riffs* (2010).

nineteenth century, the popularity of all-things gothic not only permeated literature, art, and theater but also drove the mass-market press. What David Jones calls the "gothic machine" crossed all available media platforms of its day.[52] Gothic stories in print, performance, and painting served up recycled plots infused with new-and-improved forms of terror. Multivolume novels were adapted into shorter, abridged chapbooks. Phantasmagoria and technology-driven spectacles drew from popular gothic stories, themes, and characters. These industries created jobs that contributed to the economy and provided new forms of income to the emerging middle class, especially for women. The gothic fictions churned out by the Minerva Press and other specialized publishing houses empowered women writers to earn a living, even when they were publishing anonymously or through pennames. Adapting content and materials provided a means for financially supporting themselves and their families at a time when women were not able to own property and were extremely limited in professional opportunities.[53]

Meanwhile, children's media emerged as a new, distinct market. The second half of the chapter showcases the popularity of toy theaters, perhaps the first mass-media, interactive storytelling form for children. These intricate play sets included abridged scenes and diverse characters from Shakespeare, Scott, as well as popular novels such as *Robinson Crusoe, Oliver Twist,* and *Uncle Tom's Cabin*. Publishers sold character sets for fairy tales and adventure novels, modeled after popular stage adaptations of the stories. Drawing on Jenkins's approach to participatory culture, I argue that toy theaters empowered young creators through active play, as they customized characters and wrote their own adaptations. The toys were popular because of their interactive and community-driven aspects. Children came together to prepare sets, and they staged their plays for live audiences of friends and family in the communal spaces of their homes. These tie-in products were active sites of storytelling—not passive consumer objects.[54]

Collectively, the chapters in this book map the many directions that adaptation took throughout the nineteenth century, informing the shapes of transmedia storytelling and convergence culture in the present. Through very specific practices of repetition, recycling, and remaking, adaptation affords us a better picture of narrative mobility across time, culture, and geography. The examples discussed in the following chapters turn our gaze back in time to

---

52. Jones, *Gothic Machine* (2011).
53. Neiman, "A New Perspective on the Minerva Press's 'Derivative' Novels" (2015).
54. I draw on several works by Jenkins, including *Textual Poachers* (1992); *Fans, Bloggers, and Gamers* (2006); *Reading in a Participatory Culture* (2013); *Participatory Culture in a Networked Era* (2015).

see the origins of today's commercial adaptation practices. Having a broader, historical view will better help us understand the cultural prominence of adaptations now and what cultural capital they may produce in the future—commercially, critically, and culturally.

The examples here position adaptation as central to literary history writ large and an equal player in the process of literary and artistic production. Continued adaptation and appropriation into a range of popular forms eventually ensured the place of many texts, writers, and artists in the canon—it might even be considered a prerequisite for inclusion. Approaching adaptation as an entry point to literature requires that we see adaptation not as a form of cultural afterlife, but as part of the ongoing history of culture-texts. Adaptations don't "raise texts from the dead"—they keep texts alive. Adaptations aren't the metaphorical ghosts of great literature that continue to haunt the minds of later generations. Instead, they are the active descendants of literature, the next generation that ensures continued cultural relevance, accessibility, and survival.

CHAPTER 1

Adaptation in the Nineteenth Century

or, the Convergence of Censorship, Spectacle, Commercialism, and Aesthetics

POSTMODERN THEORISTS have acknowledged that we can see prototypes for postmodern aesthetics and commercial practices in earlier periods, and cultural historians have established links between the rise of consumer culture in the eighteenth century and its steady intensification through the present.[1] The following chapter connects the past and the present through the rise of commercial adaptation and its continued influence on the art and entertainment industries of the present. Contemporary media theory is understandably immersed in the present; however, as Matthew Freeman argues, "Any attempt to historicise transmedia storytelling must account for consumer culture as a broad contextual backdrop; the consumerist ideology ingrained into [Henry] Jenkins' definition of transmedia storytelling suggests that its history is closely related to the rise of consumer culture."[2] And yet this historical emergence remains absent from contemporary accounts of the histories of adaptation and transmedia storytelling. Ann Bermingham blames "modernism's master narrative of culture" for "obscur[ing] the early history of consumption and its relationship to social and cultural forms, substituting in its place a history of culture focused on artistic production, individualism, originality, genius,

---

1. Bermingham and Brewer, *The Consumption of Culture* (1995); Mullins, *The Archaeology of Consumer Culture* (2011).
2. Freeman, *Historicising Transmedia Storytelling* (2017).

estheticism, and avant-gardism."³ In most of these discussions, a particularly noticeable tension exists between commercialism and aesthetics. As the following chapter argues, however, this tension has been dynamic and dialectical since the nineteenth century as the period's entertainment industry was driven by the convergence of commercialism and artistry in the form of plays, books, periodicals, illustrations, and a variety of merchandise—all of which continue to inform adaptation and transmedia storytelling in the twenty-first century.⁴

Whether viewed as a cultural practice, an artistic endeavor, or a commercial product, adaptation lies at the heart of cultural and artistic production, intensifying as capitalism has evolved and as art and culture have become increasingly industrialized. Adaptation even makes a cameo in Theodor Adorno and Max Horkheimer's conceptualization of the modern "culture industry" that "integrates all the elements of the production, from the novel (shaped with an eye to the film) to the last sound effect."⁵ Adorno and Horkheimer not only lament the way that a "Tolstoy novel is garbled in a film script" but also charge the culture industry with shaping the goals of novelists and thus controlling both the practice of adapting novels to the screen and the process of novel writing itself. Through repetition and recycling, "The machine rotates on the same spot," they write. "The movie-makers distrust any manuscript which is not reassuringly backed by a bestseller."⁶ On the surface, this critique of industrially produced art seems to mirror some of the more reactionary views of Romanticism's confrontation with industrialization and consumerism. However, from a historical viewpoint, Stana Nenadic suggests that the negative connotations associated with consumer culture can be reframed and renegotiated on Romanticism's own aesthetic terms and cultural practices where "consumption can be viewed as an act of the individual imagination," reminding us that as much as Wordsworth and other Romantics critiqued the commercial system around them, they still participated in it as both consumers and creators.⁷ The historical significance of this consumer model of cultural production and consumption intensifies once we remember that,

---

3. Bermingham and Brewer, *The Consumption of Culture* (1995), 3–4. I agree with Bermingham, seeing the rise of consumer culture as a distinctly democratic, if not always progressive, practice.

4. Aesthetically, postmodernism is characterized as an assemblage of chaotic and sometimes contradictory parts: minimalism and/or maximalism, intertextuality, metafiction, parody, pastiche, irony, skepticism, hyperreality, globalization, reader involvement, kitsch.

5. Theodor Adorno and Max Horkheimer, *Dialectic of Enlightenment* (1944).

6. Adorno and Horkheimer, *Dialectic of Enlightenment* (1944).

7. Nenadic, "Romanticism and the Urge to Consume in the First Half of the Nineteenth Century" (1999), 208.

as even Adorno and Horkheimer explain, "More than anything in the world, the culture industry has its ontology . . . from the commercial English novels of the late seventeenth and early eighteenth centuries" when "the profit motive itself . . . first gained its predominance over culture."[8]

Although I see popular culture and its cultural functions differently than Frankfurt School models, I invoke the "culture industry" conceptually here because the model still holds value in contemporary literary studies and theory, even as it has been subject to substantial criticism for its limited, totalizing view of commercial entertainment as an instrument of "mass deception."[9] Sameness and repetition are aesthetically devalued in Adorno and Horkheimer's culture industry, and they are yoked exclusively to conservatism and commercialism in ways that suggest no positive effects and no possibility for creativity or critique. However, today's media and adaptation theorists instead emphasize the critical artistry of creators and the participatory possibilities for audiences, sometimes even providing opportunities for those audiences to become creators themselves.

As many scholars have shown, repetition doesn't mean passive, derivative, or unoriginal; depending on one's vantage point, it can also be an active form of cultural criticism or collective memory-making.[10] Take for example parody and pastiche, two artistic practices defined through similarities to identifiable sources. Linda Hutcheon's approach to adaptation and parody characterizes these forms as "repetition with difference," making them both creative and critical acts of interpretation.[11] In Hutcheon's model, adaptation "does not lose its Benjaminian aura. It is repetition but without replication, bringing together the comfort of ritual and recognition with the delight of surprise and novelty. *As adaptation,* it involves both memory and change, persistence and variation."[12] Parody, pastiche, and transmedia storytelling are all intertextual forms of adaptation that create culture-texts. They fashion something new out of something old and, in the process of gesturing to an existing story, increase the chances that both versions of the story will be told again. They are central to the cultural fabric of storytelling, and they have artistic, historical, and commercial value.

Throughout the eighteenth and nineteenth centuries, the print, theater, and entertainment industries responded to one another, even if they were

---

8. Adorno, "Culture Industry Reconsidered" (1975), 13–14.
9. Nealon and Irr, *Rethinking the Frankfurt School* (2002).
10. Rigney, *The Afterlives of Walter Scott* (2012); Mole, *What the Victorians Made of Romanticism* (2017).
11. Hutcheon, *A Theory of Parody* (2000).
12. Hutcheon, *A Theory of Adaptation* (2006), 173.

not centrally coordinated or administered the way that popular entertainment is now through massive, multinational corporations. Theatrical censorship, international revolutions and war, continued imperial expansion, and the rise of commercial capitalism led to a new aesthetic that permeated literature, high art, and popular culture—categories that were more fluid in the eighteenth and nineteenth centuries. The most salient features of the contemporary culture industry are detectable in late eighteenth- and nineteenth-century popular entertainment, especially as it developed in London and Paris and was exported throughout the continent and across the Atlantic.

CENSORSHIP AND THE RISE OF HYBRID FORMS: A BRIEF HISTORY

The historical focus of contemporary adaptation studies on the early twentieth century obscures important connections between present and past regulatory and commercial structures. In the modern period, the cultural and industrial impact of the Motion Picture Production Code or "Hays Code" (enforced from 1933 to 1968) on the evolution of film as an artistic medium and form of storytelling is well documented. Timothy Corrigan cites the Hays Code as a major tool for the "cultural disciplining of film" whose effects have long outlived the regulatory system on which it was founded. His timeline of this cultural disciplining harkens to silent films and their "adaptation of material and practices from older literary or artistic heritage," specifically the narrative practices of nineteenth-century novels and theatrical melodramas.[13] Corrigan calls for a better understanding of how nineteenth-century cultural forms influenced the early development of film through the imitation of Victorian aesthetic practices that have "both economic and legal implications that are still operative today."[14] This connection is especially relevant with regard to the regulation of theater in the eighteenth and nineteenth centuries. Although theatrical censorship was common throughout Europe, the English stage provides a particularly fruitful example of the convergence of literature, art, and the separate industries that supported commercial culture over the following centuries.[15]

---

13. Corrigan, "Literature on Screen" (2007), 35. The Hays Code is largely understood as a backlash to several scandals and liberal attitudes of the 1920s.

14. Corrigan, "Literature on Screen" (2007), 34–35.

15. Goldstein, *The Frightful Stage* (2009); Hemmings, *Theatre and State in France* (1994); Goldstein, "Political Theater Censorship in Nineteenth-Century France in Comparative European Perspective" (2010).

Several factors shaped the development of English dramatic entertainment from the mid-eighteenth century until the Theatres Act of 1968 (passed the same year that the Hays Code was abandoned in the film industry). No study of the period's theater is complete without a discussion of theatrical regulation, yet the law's practical effects remain unknown outside of drama scholars and theater historians.[16] The Theatres Licensing Act of 1737 established strict regulation of the drama in London through two key dynamics that would permanently change the trajectory of the industry. First, only two theaters in London were "licensed" to stage spoken-word drama in the traditional genres of tragedy and comedy (which became referred to jointly as "legitimate" dramas). Drury Lane and Covent Garden were the chosen theaters, with the smaller Haymarket Theatre acquiring a third license in 1766 to operate during the summers. This system created a monopoly on sanctioned forms of entertainment that had class-based connotations—at least as they applied to "high" and "popular" culture—and it remained in place for more than a century. Competing theaters, the "minor" houses, were restricted to other genres: pantomime, opera, burlesque, farce, and other "illegitimate" forms. By the 1820s, the most dominant genre on the illegitimate stage was melodrama, which included significant spoken word parts but also relied heavily on music and song to drive a play's action and emotions. Importantly, the division between "legitimate" and "illegitimate" forms disproportionally favored the patent theaters, the only ones allowed to stage traditional drama. While minor venues were denied "legitimate" drama, patent theaters certainly included "illegitimate" forms in their repertoires because they were proven moneymakers.[17]

The second major dynamic of the Licensing Act was its requirement that all dramas receive a performance license, which had to be approved by the Examiner of Plays (a position under the direction of the Lord Chamberlain). The law applied to both "legitimate" and "illegitimate" dramatic forms, a point that often gets confused. Although minor theaters, music halls, and saloons often staged pieces that fell beyond the notice of the Examiner of Plays (or were intentionally ignored), all pieces produced on stage required licensing regardless of genre. In fact, the nonpatent or so-called "minor" theaters often relied on the official stamp of "respectability" afforded by the Lord Chamberlain's office when staging controversial pieces, which allowed them to simultaneously benefit from controversy while not having to worry about angering the censor or getting fined.

---

16. Liesenfeld, *The Licensing Act of 1737* (1984).
17. Burwick, *Romantic Drama* (2009).

One famous example of an adaptation staged at a minor theater using the "protection" of the Examiner of Plays was the controversial July 1823 premiere of *Presumption; or, The Fate of Frankenstein*. Steven Forry documents a group of protesters calling themselves "The Friends of Morality" who decried the melodrama as indecent and immoral, using the source novel as their main detraction against the play. The management at the English Opera House (later known as the Lyceum Theatre) responded to the complaints with an open letter published in the August 12, 1823, issue of the *Theatrical Observer*, reassuring potential patrons: "It is to be remembered that the *Right Honorable the Lord Chamberlain* sanctioned the Piece by granting his License, which License would certainly *have been withheld,* had the Drama been of an IMMORAL TENDENCY."[18] As might be expected from a good old-fashioned controversy, the public outcry proved profitable even as it was thwarted by the official protection of the Examiner of Plays. The play was enormously successful on many fronts, and it would continue to be revived and staged at other theaters for decades.

Presumption is one of hundreds of examples of censorship in the period's theatrical adaptations. In the nineteenth-century culture industry, if a novel was too political or its author too controversial, titles were changed and content was revised or removed to fit licensing requirements. Matthew Lewis's scandalous gothic novel *The Monk* (1796), for instance, was turned into a ballet titled *Raymond and Agnes; or The Castle of Lindenberg* (1798), focusing on a central love story, the only "sanctioned" relationship from the book. John Fawcett's pantomime *Obi; or Three-Finger'd Jack* (1800) became a sensational stage hit through its revisionist history of the real-life Jamaican rebel/bandit/folk hero on whom the story was based.[19]

Another well-documented example is George Colman "the Younger" who (at the request of theater manager Richard Brinsley Sheridan) reimagined William Godwin's *Things as They Are; or, The Adventures of Caleb Williams* (1794) as *The Iron Chest*. Staged at the Theatre Royale Drury Lane in 1796, the adaptation was sanitized for content, but it also raised general awareness of the book and generated additional sales of the original work, as well as new textual forms like the published play script. The play's 1796 print edition came with an "Advertisement to the Reader" where Colman carefully distanced himself from the radical philosopher Godwin, defending his adaptation choices:

---

18. Forry, *Hideous Progenies* (1990), 5–9.
19. Szwydky, "Rewriting the History of Black Resistance" (2011).

Much of Mr. Godwin's story I have omitted; much, which I have adopted, I have compressed; much I have added; and much I have taken the liberty to alter. All this I did that I might fit it, in the best of my judgment, to the stage. I have cautiously avoided all tendency to that which, vulgarly, (and wrongly, in many instances,) is termed Politicks; with which, many have told me, *Caleb Williams* teems. The stage has, now, no business with Politics: and, should a Dramatick Author endeavor to dabble in them, it is the Lord Chamberlain's office to check his attempts, before they meet the eye of the Publick. I perused Mr. Godwin's book, as a tale replete with interesting incident, ingenious in its arrangement, masterly in its delineation of character, and forcible in its language. I considered it as a right of Common; and, by a title which custom has given to Dramatists, I enclosed it within my theatrical paling.[20]

Colman detaches himself both formally and philosophically from Godwin, one of the most outspoken radical political philosophers of the day. *Things as They Are* is itself an adaptation—a novelization of Godwin's philosophical work *Political Justice* (1794), repackaged for a popular readership.[21] Knowing how much Godwin's work was synonymous with political radicalism, especially in the years immediately following the French Revolution and The Terror of 1794, Colman clears the air. Any apology for altering the text is surface-level and contrived. Note, however, the absence of backpedaling on his choice to adapt the work or evidence of regret for significantly altering Godwin's work. Colman doesn't second-guess himself at any point. The requirements of dramatic form get prioritized over concerns about fidelity to the novelist. This is business as usual in the theater industry, the standard practice of seasoned dramatists. Colman's account partially explains why even illegitimate forms, which are known to have resisted censorship and regulation, nevertheless typically supported conservative ideologies.[22]

The Licensing Act of 1737 set the tone of English theater for the next two centuries until the Theatres Act of 1968. As a result, "the damage to the drama and the theater," Robert Hume writes, "is incalculable."[23] Spoken-word drama in the traditional genres of tragedy and comedy took a major hit, as fewer writers were willing to write for the stage. That said, theatrical censorship created the cultural conditions for other types of work to flourish. Theatrical

---

20. Colman, *The Iron Chest* (1796), xxi.
21. Jellenik, "On the Origins of Adaptation, as Such" (2017).
22. Hadley, *Melodramatic Tactics* (1995); Worrall, *Theatric Revolution* (2006); Buckley, *Tragedy Walks the Streets* (2006); Williams, *Gilbert and Sullivan* (2010).
23. Hume, *Henry Fielding and the London Theatre* (1988), 253.

production, for instance, became much more diverse in its genres, audiences, and overall reach as spectacle became a centerpiece of theatrical experience, deemphasizing the written word—which was the major (though not the only) target of censorship under the English law. The shift toward spectacle, however, didn't necessarily mean a complete "dumbing down" of content nor an erasure of subversive possibilities or political critique, as both could happen in performance through a number of visual cues including body language, and theater historians have shown the power of performance as an act of political resistance.[24]

One of the most positive effects, in combination with rising literacy rates and the unprecedented expansion of the reading public, was that theatrical censorship further fueled the rise of print-based forms. The restrictive and commercial theatrical environment also led to new developments in poetry, including the invention of the Romantic dramatic poem or "closet drama," a form favored by Lord Byron and Percy Bysshe Shelley, as well as the popularity of the dramatic monologue in the Victorian period. The biggest and most immediate change, however, was the turn to prose fiction, which in turn allowed the novel to flourish as a popular form of storytelling, a point worth emphasizing. Philip Cox connects the shift between theater and fiction, pointing out that the period known for the "rise of the novel" runs concurrent with the "decline of the drama" in its previous form.[25] In other words, while a specific type of theatrical writing was absolutely stifled by the Licensing Act, the novel might not have taken off as quickly or effectively as it did in the eighteenth century. Over the next 100 years, the novel would become the dominant form of literary production, a cultural shift that had hugely impactful and immediately positive effects (commercially, socially, and aesthetically).

The career of Henry Fielding—among the most influential satirists of the 1730s, not to mention an established playwright and theater manager—is the clearest example of the immediate shift in cultural production between the page and the stage, as the political satire in his play *The Historical Register for the Year 1736* (1737) is widely seen as a primary reason for the Licensing Act. The 1737 legislation effectively ended Fielding's theatrical career, both as a dramatist and as the manager at the Haymarket Theatre. All was not lost, however. Fielding turned his attention instead to fiction, starting with his *Pamela* parody, *Shamela* (1741). He found huge success in prose fiction and became one of the earliest influencers of the novel as a form. (Not too bad for a dramatist who was run out of his previous profession!)

---

24. Hadley, *Melodramatic Tactics* (1995).
25. Philip Cox, *Reading Adaptations* (2000).

Fielding was not alone in finding the printed page more liberating than the regulated stage, a tension that would continue for a century. In 1807, the accomplished actress, dramatist, novelist, and essayist Elizabeth Inchbald provided the following warning "To the artist":

> [The writer of novels] lives in a land of liberty, whilst the Dramatic Writer exists but under a despotic government. Passing over the subjection in which an author of plays is held by the Lord Chamberlain's office, and the degree of dependence which he has on his actors—he is the very slave of the audience.[26]

According to Inchbald, the artist who wrote for the theater was a slave—a charged word to use, particularly two months after the Abolition of the Slave Trade Act 1807. This imagery comes from a writer who managed to effectively straddle the theater and print industries, while also maintaining a regular presence in the period's radical philosophical and literary circles, including a well-documented friendship with William Godwin. The political and economic dimensions are also clear; supporting herself financially as a dramatist would restrict her freedom to choose forms, genres, and thematic content.

Like Fielding and Inchbald, many writers adapted to these conditions by opting out of theatrical writing and turning their attention to novels, which although frequently the target of moral and aesthetic criticism, did not face the strict censorship of theatrical forms and provided a relatively flexible medium where artists and writers could engage in political and social issues in an array of print genres.[27] Yet despite the fact that some authors broke away from the stage, the relationship between literary and theatrical production regularly converged, especially by the 1790s when gothic novelists found a productive medium in the popular theater. At the height of the gothic's popularity, London's major and minor performance venues were staging theatrical adaptations of Ann Radcliffe, Matthew Lewis, and others across a range of theatrical forms and genres.[28]

Playwrights, actors, managers, designers, and anyone else involved in London theatrical life also adapted to theatrical regulation and censorship, which by the turn of the nineteenth century had become an efficient, commercial model. Theater managers became well versed in identifying crowd pleasers and, regardless of their personal politics, adhering to the censoring

---

26. Inchbald, "To the Artist" (1807), 14; quoted in Philip Cox, *Reading Adaptations* (2000), 25.
27. Burgess, *British Fiction and the Production of Social Order* (2000).
28. Saggini, *The Gothic Novel and the Stage* (2015).

regulations to protect their theaters from fines or other disciplinary measures. They understood that a play's profitability depended on its widespread appeal, which meant not offending crowds that might become agitated and violent.

This view of theaters as dangerous spaces was widespread across Europe in the nineteenth century following the French Revolution and Napoleonic Wars because, as Justin Goldstein explains:

> The stage was deemed more threatening than the press not only for its ability to reach even the illiterate, but also because it was generally perceived as more powerful and direct in impact, and because, unlike with the printed word, the audience was a collective one that, it was feared, might be stirred to immediate mob action. Print was perceived as "consumed" primarily by relatively educated people, often in private, who would not be immediately affected even by subversive material; therefore, if a publication proved dangerous, unsold copies could be confiscated before their ill effects were evident. The impact of subversive theater, however, could apparently be virtually instantaneous.[29]

Paranoia rose during times of political and social unrest, and theater reflected this cultural fascination with and fear of violence.[30] Class division fueled anxieties among the upper classes. As a storytelling experience with social and cultural power, popular theater had the power to stir the emotions of a large group ending in mob violence, fires, or other financially risky outcomes.

The Licensing Act chiefly aimed to regulate discourse in a network of large public spaces where large, diverse crowds would gather to ensure that the British Empire was represented in a positive light.[31] Yet despite the clear interest in promoting a carefully crafted image of nation and empire, the Lord Chamberlain's office rarely issued outright bans on most plays submitted for licensing. On the contrary, most plays received approval as long as the changes made to the text by the Examiner were reflected in their performances. As Matthew Kinservik argues, "The most important effects of the law were productive, not prohibitive," where this centralized office and its mechanism for processing and licensing plays "became an efficient censoring bureaucracy whose main objective was to make the play texts acceptable for performance. The emphasis was clearly on correcting texts, not punishing violators, even though there was no lack of violators to punish."[32] The procedure of writing scripts, acquiring

---

29. Goldstein, *The Frightful Stage* (2009), 6.
30. Crone, *Violent Victorians* (2012).
31. O'Quinn, *Staging Governance* (2005).
32. Kinservik, *Disciplining Satire* (2002), 98.

licenses, and producing plays was—like today—a "behind the scenes" process. Very little, if any, of the process was made public and as a result, theatergoers did not actively participate in debates about what was or was not appropriate material for public display and consumption. This procedural invisibility shaped an entertainment industry that suppressed radical political and social critiques overwhelmingly accepted by most patrons.[33]

The Theatres Regulation Act of 1843 eliminated the two-tiered system that divided "legitimate" from "illegitimate" forms in England, as well as the venues where they were staged. Deregulation of the patent system made all dramatic entertainment equal, following social changes such as the Reform Act of 1832 and growing enfranchisement movements such as Chartism. Yet because the censorship rules did not change, this new system meant that all dramatic forms were now equally under the purview of the Lord Chamberlain. As a result, what could have galvanized the stage suppressed by more than a hundred years of regulations barely caused a spark. Tracy Davis explains the event as follows:

> When . . . the drama was officially unshackled from the [patent theaters], nothing remarkable appeared to happen. London's theatrical business seemed to carry on very much as before, except that the patent houses and minor theatres alike could produce any genre they thought would turn a profit, legally unhindered by anything but market forces, uniformly under the supervision of the Lord Chamberlain.[34]

By 1843, spectacular entertainments that avoided controversial material had in fact become the norm in London theaters, and 110 years of continuous stage censorship produced and solidified the nineteenth-century so-called "taste for spectacle." When the Theatres Regulation Act opened the minor houses for full participation in the theatrical "free market," there was absolutely no need for managers to encourage the production of spoken-word drama that had long gone out of fashion. By the 1820s, melodrama (and all of its subgenres) was the most popular form on the English stage, and just about any story could be told in this form, including the most radical novels of the day.

Worth noting here is Adorno's later distinction between the "culture industry" (a centralized, or "top-down" production) and "mass culture" (dispersed, or "bottom-up" production); however, these differences weren't clear-cut in the eighteenth and nineteenth centuries. In England, government regula-

---

33. Winton, "Dramatic Censorship" (1980).
34. Davis, *The Economics of the British Stage* (2000), 18.

tion and censorship certainly produced a centrally driven, top-down model that needs to be understood more thoroughly for its direct impacts on cultural production for more than two centuries. At the same time, the theater industry—the artists and practitioners—pushed back against the regulatory model, finding ways to creatively circumvent the law. Pieces that had been licensed with one script might be altered when performed. New genres were created that highlighted music, song, dance, and spectacle. Even under the patent system, theaters found ways around the laws in order to stage whatever would draw interest and sell the most tickets. Despite regulatory attempts to curb its growth, popular culture saw massive growth and influence throughout the century, much like film, television, and new media today.

SPECTACULAR ENTERTAINMENT IN THE COMMERCIAL, INDUSTRIAL AGE

The most visible effect of the regulatory system was the immediate shift to a theater driven by spectacle. Popular theater continued to thrive, aimed at a new, broader audience who came more for the entertainment than for the politics. Detractors who saw the popular stage as a site of derivative entertainment and, therefore, mourned the "decline of the drama" were outnumbered by those with a more positive view. The variety of entertainments was a draw for many—theaters, music halls, waxworks museums, and fairs were spaces of innovation where the latest technologies were put on display to delight and awe. The stage, as an accessible and ubiquitous space for visually driven entertainment, became an exhibition arena for new developments in lighting, machinery, set design, costuming, and special effects, all of which required significant investment and supported several textile industries.

For today's reader, the rise of the spectacular nineteenth-century stage reads much like a prehistory of Hollywood blockbusters, and comparisons to contemporary cinema regularly show up in descriptions of nineteenth-century audiences' eagerness for spectacle and the theater industry's production of incredibly expensive, visually driven stage productions. Jeffrey Cox, for instance, likens early nineteenth-century dramas to contemporary action films: "Just as moviegoers today would prefer to go see the new installment of *Mission Impossible* . . . over the new film version of Shakespeare's *Titus Andronicus*, so audiences then flocked to the new drama of sight and sensation over the older theater of the word."[35] The present-day comparison is

---

35. Jeffrey N. Cox, "Theatrical Forms, Ideological Conflicts, and the Staging of *Obi*" (2002), par. 5.

supported by scholars studying the intersections between literary and film history, such as Timothy Corrigan, who takes a long-form view of how media and technology have shaped storytelling over time, "from theatrical spectacles and dioramas of the early nineteenth century to the photography, music halls, and cinema projections that followed."[36] Such a reliance on spectacle was commercially driven and necessary to the financial survival of forms in both high art and mass culture. In this regulated and commercial environment, popularity was prioritized, and the most popular technologies and special effects found their way into all genres and venues.

Special effects intersected with the latest literary fads on the popular stage. For example, in the 1820s, pirates were all the rage in print and performance across forms and media. Frederick Burwick and Manushag Powell have shown that, on stage and in print, literary and historical pirates were often portrayed as countercultural heroes who offered escapism for working-class audiences and the bourgeois classes, thereby serving as a popular incarnation of the Romantic rebel who defies repressive authority. Now-canonical authors added their pirate stories to the popular literary landscape in England and the United States, among them Lord Byron's narrative poem *The Corsair* (1814), Walter Scott's *The Pirate* (1821), and two novels by James Fenimore Cooper, *The Pilot* (1824) and *The Red Rover* (1828). All of these were adapted several times over for the London stage. Within two weeks of the publication of Scott's novel in December 1821, it appeared on stage at the Surrey Theatre in Thomas John Dibdin's *The Pirate; or, The Wild Woman of Zetland* (1822). Two additional plays premiered the following week: James Robinson Planché's *The Pirate* (1822, Olympic Theatre) and William Dimond's *The Pirate* (1822, Drury Lane).[37] The plays achieved varying levels of success, but all were praised for their scenery and spectacle-driven elements. Although he was a best-selling author at the time, Scott-the-novelist wasn't the draw here; rather, he was part of the larger popularity of pirate stories played out through various adaptations, extensions, mash-ups, and parodies across storytelling formats, media, and sites.

Written by experienced dramatists and portrayed by the day's leading actors, pirate plays drew on literary works, folk tales, historical sources, and other original dramatic pieces that featured adventures at sea, while participating in a popular theatrical subgenre known as nautical drama, naval drama, or aquatic drama. Beyond their ambiguous and often subversive politics in both print and performance, pirates made for grand spectacles. The stories on stage ranged from adaptations of recent novels to original plays imitating

---

36. Corrigan, "Literature on Screen" (2007), 42.
37. Burwick and Powell, *British Pirates in Print and Performance* (2015).

the popularity of the trope—all productions capitalize on the fad. Playhouses added spectacular water effects to their productions to draw theatergoers, and Sadler's Wells Theatre featured a large, custom-built water tank—the size of the entire stage—with additional tanks installed in the ceiling and back stage to simulate waterfalls or the rough waves of a stormy sea.[38] (See chapter 2 for further discussion of the genesis and staging of Edward Fitzball's adaptation of *The Pilot*.)

Melodrama included many subgenres—gothic, domestic, nautical—and literature spectacularly adapted for the stage was central to the development of all theatrical forms, with the visual aspects of a production determining success regardless of genre. For example, one reviewer who disliked Edward Fitzball's *Quasimodo; or, They Gipsey Girl of Notre Dame* (1836) nevertheless praised the piece as "extremely successful," evidently owing "its success, not to its merits as a drama, but to the excellence of the music, and the goodness of much of the singing and acting, the beauty of the scenery, and the general propriety which distinguished the manner in which it has been brought out."[39] While there were some critics who evaluated dramatizations based on their "fidelity" to source texts, most audiences had more flexible criteria, and wanted to see effective staging and production investment, as we see in a review of the ballet *La Esmeralda* staged at Her Majesty's Theater in 1844:

> Never did we see those parts of a long story that might be dramatically effective selected and arranged with such skill as in this new ballet. The catastrophe of the novel is altered, the incidents selected are greatly modified, but that tact with which five *tableaux* have been taken out of the romance, and combined into a neat pantomime of action, without a gap, deserves unqualified praise.[40]

Plays had to stand on their own merits and visual innovations. What's more, audiences were not usually comparing the theatrical version to the book. Because of the relative speed with which novels and current events were adapted for the London stage, it's reasonable to assume that with a few exceptions, most theatergoers were not familiar with the source texts being dramatized, or they didn't mind that plots or characters were altered for stage representation.

At times, stage adaptations were celebrated for changes made to their sources, which could even become a selling point for the production. One of

---

38. Burwick and Powell, *British Pirates in Print and Performance* (2015).
39. "Covent-Garden Theatre," *Times*, February 3, 1836: 5.
40. "Her Majesty's Theatre," *Times*, March 11, 1844: 5.

the first reviews of *Presumption; or, The Fate of Frankenstein*, published in the *Morning Post* on July 30, 1823, enthusiastically recommends the play no matter one's personal politics or morals or opinions of the book:

> Whatever may be thought of Frankenstein as a novel . . . there can be but one opinion of it as a drama. The representation of this piece upon the stage is of astonishing, of enchaining, interest. In the novel the rigid moralist may feel himself constantly offended, by the modes of reasoning, principles of action, &c.—But in the Drama this is all carefully kept in the back ground. Nothing but what can please, astonish, and delight, is there suffered to appear.[41]

Anyone who has ever wondered how Shelley might feel about the ways her monstrous story has become iconic through countless of film, television, and comic book adaptations can find their answer in a letter she wrote to Leigh Hunt in 1823 not long after attending a performance of Peake's play:

> The play-bill amused me extremely, for in the list of *dramatis personae* came——, by Mr. T. Cooke; this nameless mode of naming the unnameable is rather good. . . . The story is not well managed, but Cooke played——'s part extremely well: his seeking, as it were, for support—his trying to grasp at the sounds he heard—all, indeed, he does, was well imagined and executed. I was much amused, and it appeared to excite a breathless eagerness in the audience.[42]

Peake's *Presumption* was the first adaptation to remove the Creature's ability to speak. In line with the period's stage regulations on spoken-word drama versus "illegitimate" theatrical pieces, the popular stage actor Cooke played the Creature through pantomime. The physicality of the performance intrigued Shelley, and she enthusiastically describes the spectacle despite the fact that the "story is not well managed." Any artistic reservations are quickly glossed over to emphasize the power of spectacle. She is fascinated to witness her story sparking deep affective responses in a live audience—an experience only possible through the theatrical adaptation. Shelley clearly understands that stories work differently on stage than they do on the page. The powers of textual representation are not the same as those of visualization, an idea that is, fittingly, at the heart of Shelley's novel, even as it plays out very differently in most visual or dramatic adaptations of *Frankenstein*.

---

41. "Theatres: English Opera House," *London Morning Post*, July 30, 1823: 3.
42. Shelley, *Selected Letters* (1995), 136.

Even pieces that drew published praise in the periodicals for their depth of character and dramatic complexity needed to meet the visual demands of the day. A positive review of the Adelphi Theatre production of Andrew Halliday's *Notre-Dame; or, The Gypsey Girl of Paris* (1871), adapted from Victor Hugo, emphasizes the importance of combining masterful writing and impressive visual effect when adapting novels for the stage:

> Mr. Halliday embodies in his drama the entire substance of the novel . . . but he does not slavishly follow M. Hugo, and his work does not bear the least resemblance to those dramatized romances in which the merely external form of narrative is suppressed, without regard to internal structure. . . . While briefly sketching the course of incidents in Mr. Halliday's new drama we have assumed in our readers a reminiscence more or less distinct of M. Hugo's novel, our intention being to show the work actually done by the adaptor. The remark is too commonly made that anybody with the aid of scissors and paste can convert a long novel into a play, and that the performance of such a feat does not in the least entitle the performer to be called a dramatist. Several dramatized novels, the result of little more than mechanical abbreviation, have done much to justify this remark. . . . That it does not apply to [Halliday's] *Notre-Dame* we have sufficiently proved. . . . The public garden in Paris, and the bird's-eye-view of the French capital by night are excellent specimens of Mr. Lloyd's talent, and the eastern extremity of the Cathedral, built so as to cover a large portion of the stage, is one of those feats of scenic art by which modern audiences are so frequently surprised.[43]

The reviewer notably praises the dramatist both for his skill in adapting Hugo's novel and for the stage designer's spectacular visuals.[44] The adaptation is received as a collaborative piece combining the talents of many artists: performers, visual artists, musicians, and choreographers.

Special effects technicians and engineers were also among the many professional positions that the theater industry supported and financed substantially through adaptations of popular literature, folk tales, and classical sources. Adaptations not only made use of existing technologies of gaslight, limelight,

---

43. "Adelphi Theatre," *Times*, April 11, 1871: 9. Frederick Lloyds was one of several scenery designers and painters at the Adelphi throughout most of the 1870s.

44. Halliday's repertoire includes many dramatic adaptations, including several of Charles Dickens's novels. Halliday had also likely seen stage versions of *Notre Dame* before penning his version. Hugo's novel had been adapted several times including two separate melodramas written by Edward Fitzball in the 1830s, as well as a ballet and at least one farce. Szwydky, "Victor Hugo's *Notre-Dame de Paris* on the Nineteenth-Century London Stage" (2010).

and pyrotechnics but also inspired new mechanical stage effects, some of which remain in use today. The most well-documented example is the "vampire trap," later known as the "star trap." This special trap door in the stage, used to create the illusion that a supernatural character could instantaneously appear/disappear mid-stage, was developed for James Robinson Planché's *The Vampire, or The Bride of the Isles* (1820). Planché's successful play was an adaptation of the French play by Charles Nodier staged that year in Paris, and both plays were based on John Polidori's English novella *The Vampyre* (1819).[45] A similar spectacle-producing stage device, the "Corsican trap" (also commonly referred to as the "ghost glide" or "glide trap") made its stage debut at the Princess's Theatre in February 1852 as a feature of Dion Boucicault's *The Corsican Brothers; or, The Fatal Duel,* among the most successful nineteenth-century English stage adaptations of French writer Alexandre Dumas's popular 1844 novel.[46] Both *The Vampire* and *The Corsican Brothers* inspired further adaptations, each adding unique elements to these culture-texts in the making.[47]

Playbills and programs from the period emphasized the spectacular aspects of the plays. For example, in the program for Halliday's adaptation of Hugo's *Notre Dame* (see figure 1.1) we see how the document is designed using large, specialized type to catch the reader's eye and highlight the scenery and the climactic moments of the drama. The audience is treated to a "Grand Fantastic Ballet" during "The Festival of Fools"; "The Cloisters of the Cathedral" and "Roof of Notre Dame" will be the scenes that determine Esmeralda's fate as well as that of the "Goblin Monk."

What we would call "spoilers" today were hardly kept under wraps, and they were frequently part of marketing and advertising materials. What's more, if certain special effects proved dull or if popular effects lost their novelty, then plays might be restaged using new visual gimmicks. Later productions of Peake's *Presumption,* for example, replace some scenes—including its visually climactic ending—with scenes from other popular adaptations. In an 1830 production at Covent Garden, *Presumption*'s avalanche finale is replaced with a boating accident. The Playbill description, "Schooner in a Violent Storm / In which Frankenstein and the Monster are destroyed," announces the ending of the play as its new hook for audiences (see figure 1.2). The producers took the idea from another adaptation, stitching the finale of John Atkinson Kerr's *The Monster and Magician; or, The Fate of Frankenstein* (1826) to Peake's adaptation, which at this point had remained popular for seven years

---

45. Polidori's novella was an extension of Lord Byron's "Fragment of a Novel" (1819), its main character modeled on Byron's seductive appeal.
46. D'Arcy, "The Corsican Trap" (2011).
47. Stuart, *Stage Blood* (1994).

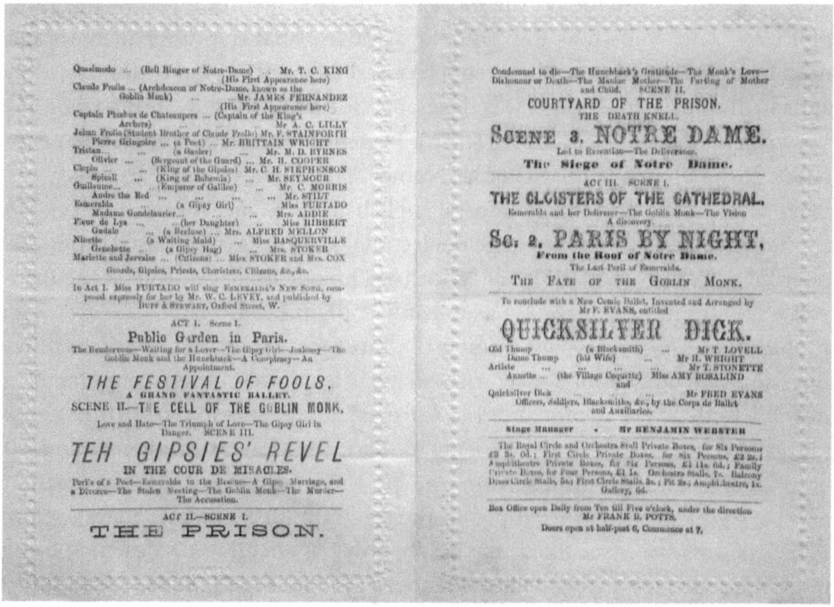

Quasimodo ... (Bell Ringer of Notre-Dame) ... Mr. T. C. KING
(His First Appearance here)
Claude Frollo ... (Archdeacon of Notre-Dame, known as the Goblin Monk) ... Mr. JAMES FERNANDEZ
(His First Appearance here)
Captain Phoebus de Chateaupers ... (Captain of the King's Archers) ... Mr A. C. LILLY
Jehan Frollo (Student Brother of Claude Frollo) Mr. F. STAINFORTH
Pierre Gringoire ... (a Poet) ... Mr. BRITTAIN WRIGHT
Tristan... ... (a Gaoler) ... Mr. M. D. BYRNES
Olivier ... (Sergeant of the Guard) ... Mr. H. COOPER
Clopin ... ... (King of the Gipsies) Mr. C. H. STEPHENSON
Spicali ... (King of Bohemia) ... Mr. SEYMOUR
Guillaume... ...(Emperor of Galilee) ... Mr. C. MORRIS
Andre the Red ... ... Mr. STILT
Esmeralda ... (a Gipsy Girl) ... Miss FURTADO
Madame Gondelaurier... ... ... Mrs. ADDIE
Fleur de Lys ... ...(her Daughter) .. Miss HIBBERT
Gudale ... (a Recluse) ... Mrs. ALFRED MELLON
Ninette ... (a Waiting Maid) ... Miss BASQUERVILLE
Genebette ... (a Gipsy Hag) ... Mrs. STOKER
Mariette and Jervaise ... (Citizens) ... Miss STOKER and Mrs. COX

Guards, Gipsies, Priests, Choristers, Citizens, &c., &c.

In Act 1. Miss FURTADO will sing ESMERALDA'S NEW SONG, composed expressly for her by Mr. W. C. LEVEY, and published by DUFF & STEWART, Oxford Street, W.

ACT 1. Scene 1.

Public Garden in Paris.

The Rendezvous—Waiting for a Lover—The Gipsy Girl—Jealousy—The Goblin Monk and the Hunchback—A Conspiracy—An Appointment.

THE FESTIVAL OF FOOLS.

A GRAND FANTASTIC BALLET.

SCENE II.—THE CELL OF THE GOBLIN MONK.

Love and Hate—The Triumph of Love—The Gipsy Girl in Danger. SCENE III.

TEH GIPSIES' REVEL

IN THE COUR DE MIRACLES.

Peril's of a Poet—Esmeralda to the Rescue—A Gipsy Marriage, and a Divorce—The Stolen Meeting—The Goblin Monk—The Murder—The Accusation.

ACT II.—SCENE I.

THE PRISON.

Condemned to die—The Hunchback's Gratitude—The Monk's Love—Dishonour or Death—The Maniac Mother—The Parting of Mother and Child. SCENE II.

COURTYARD OF THE PRISON.

THE DEATH KNELL.

SCENE 3. NOTRE DAME.

Led to Execution—The Deliverance.

The Siege of Notre Dame.

ACT III. SCENE I.

THE CLOISTERS OF THE CATHEDRAL.

Esmeralda and her Deliverer—The Goblin Monk—The Vision A discovery.

Sc. 2, PARIS BY NIGHT,

From the Roof of Notre Dame.

The Last Peril of Esmeralda.

THE FATE OF THE GOBLIN MONK.

To conclude with a New Comic Ballet, Invented and Arranged by Mr F. EVANS, entitled

QUICKSILVER DICK.

Old Thump (a Blacksmith) ... Mr T. LOVELL
Dame Thump (his Wife) ... Mr H. WRIGHT
Artiste ... ... Mr T. STONETTE
Annette ... (the Village Coquette) Miss AMY ROSALIND
and
Quicksilver Dick ... ... Mr FRED EVANS
Officers, Soldiers, Blacksmiths, &c., by the Corps de Ballet and Auxiliaries.

Stage Manager - Mr BENJAMIN WEBSTER

The Royal Circle and Orchestra Stall Private Boxes, for Six Persons £3 3s. 0d.; First Circle Private Boxes, for Six Persons, £2 2s.; Amphitheatre Private Boxes, for Six Persons, £1 11s. 6d.; Family Private Boxes, for Four Persons, £1 1s. Orchestra Stalls, 7s. Balcony Dress Circle Stalls, 5s.; First Circle Stalls, 3s.; Pit 2s.; Amphitheatre, 1s. Gallery, 6d.

Box Office open Daily from Ten till Five o'clock, under the direction Mr FRANK B. POTTS.

Doors open at half-past 6, Commence at 7.

FIGURE 1.1. Performance program for Andrew Halliday, *Notre-Dame de Paris,* Adelphi Theatre, Monday, April 24, 1871. Image courtesy of Matthew Lloyd (http://www.arthurlloyd.co.uk).

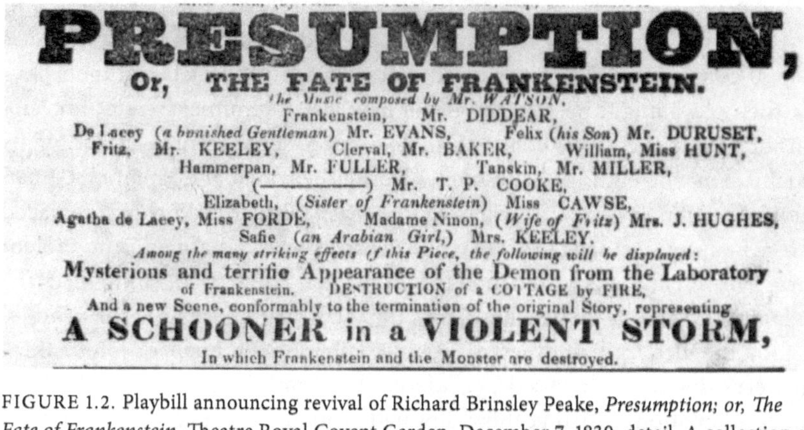

PRESUMPTION,

Or, THE FATE OF FRANKENSTEIN.

The Music composed by Mr. WATSON.

Frankenstein, Mr. DIDDEAR,
De Lacey (*a banished Gentleman*) Mr. EVANS, Felix (*his Son*) Mr. DURUSET,
Fritz, Mr. KEELEY, Clerval, Mr. BAKER, William, Miss HUNT,
Hammerpan, Mr. FULLER, Tanskin, Mr. MILLER,
(————) Mr. T. P. COOKE,
Elizabeth, (*Sister of Frankenstein*) Miss CAWSE,
Agatha de Lacey, Miss FORDE, Madame Ninon, (*Wife of Fritz*) Mrs. J. HUGHES,
Safie (*an Arabian Girl,*) Mrs. KEELEY.

Among the many striking effects of this Piece, the following will be displayed:

Mysterious and terrific Appearance of the Demon from the Laboratory of Frankenstein. DESTRUCTION of a COTTAGE by FIRE,

And a new Scene, conformably to the termination of the original Story, representing

A SCHOONER in a VIOLENT STORM,

In which Frankenstein and the Monster are destroyed.

FIGURE 1.2. Playbill announcing revival of Richard Brinsley Peake, *Presumption; or, The Fate of Frankenstein,* Theatre Royal Covent Garden, December 7, 1830; detail. A collection of playbills from Covent Garden Theatre, 1829–30. British Playbills, 1754–1882. © The British Library Board. Nineteenth Century Collections Online.

but could benefit from an innovative makeover. Much of the original cast and characters stayed intact; the novelty was seeing how the theater effects team would handle the new-and-improved spectacular climax. Special effects and mechanical innovation were the primary draw for restagings—playbills and newspaper advertisements announced "all new scenery," costumes, or musical numbers. The familiar story (if it was even familiar) served more as a narrative backdrop for a spectacle assembled from the parts of many others.

Spectacle already had a long history on the English stage at this point, but nineteenth-century theater thrived on audiences' ever-growing fascination with emerging technologies as industrialization rapidly changed entertainment in urban cultural centers like London, Paris, and New York. As the modern middle class emerged, the makeup of theater audiences changed. New audiences introduced a new set of expectations that theater managers had to consider in order to keep their business afloat. Despite the changing face of theater audiences, the most successful theater managers understood the nineteenth-century consumer's growing expectation for spectacular entertainment and thus employed the use of new technologies in order to ensure profits for always-more-expensive productions.[48]

NINETEENTH-CENTURY PARODY, PASTICHE, AND METATHEATRICALITY IN/AS ADAPTATIONS

Along with spectacle, so-called postmodern narrative techniques that we typically ascribe to twenty-first-century storytelling—including intertextuality, metafiction, and parody—find precursors in a wide range of traditional eighteenth- and nineteenth-century art and entertainment. Not coincidentally, they also form a series of narrative techniques frequently found in various forms of adaptation, which I explore in the following section.

In adaptations, self-reflexive engagement with other adaptations typically occurs through the direct importation of changes introduced (and repeated) in previous plays or films. Through deliberately emphasizing their relationships to various source texts (not just "original texts"), adaptations ask audiences to combine and collate new interpretations.[49] Although knowledge of all the parts isn't a prerequisite for enjoying an adaptation, the experience is layered (and arguably enriched) when the audience can identify these various

---

48. See the following by Booth: *English Melodrama* (1965); *English Plays of the Nineteenth Century* (1969–76); and *Victorian Spectacular Theatre* (1981).

49. This position is well established in adaptation studies, especially in Hutcheon, *A Theory of Adaptation* (2006) and Leitch, *Film Adaptation and Its Discontents* (2007).

intertextual references—frequently called "easter eggs" in contemporary transmedia storytelling and forms of postmodern narrative in both blockbuster superhero franchises and Oscar-winning films.[50]

For example, extensive intertextuality and hyper-self-awareness drive 2014's critically acclaimed, award-winning *Birdman or (The Unexpected Virtue of Ignorance)*, which has quickly established itself as a masterpiece of postmodern, cinematic storytelling. Michael Keaton stars as Riggan Thomson, a washed-up, big-screen superhero attempting to relaunch his career as a "serious" stage actor. *Birdman* critiques the film industry's fascination with adaptation, appropriation, sensation, youth, and celebrity on multiple levels. The film isn't itself an adaptation, yet adaptation is central to its thematic and narrative unfolding, as Riggan writes, directs, and stars in an artistic (i.e., not "commercial") stage adaptation of Raymond Carver's "What We Talk About When We Talk About Love" (1981).[51] *Birdman* blends the mundane and the sensational with the material reality (and anxieties) of cultural production in the twenty-first century. As Jane Barnett notes, through its metadiscursive framework and exposed backstage corridors, *Birdman* "reminds us that theatre is always already a kind of adaptation—each performance is different, adapting to its audience, and each time the same show is staged by different directors, it is adapted to suit different production concepts."[52] Like Spike Jonze's *Adaptation* (2002), *Birdman* adapts the idea of adaptation itself through its extensive metacommentary about the art and business of adaptation.[53] This self-reflexive approach to storytelling actualizes the formal, cultural, and commercial registers of adaptation and its ubiquity in the postmodern entertainment industry. The blending of film and theater also establishes a genealogical connection between the two primary arenas of the dramatic arts and entertainment. That is, if Riggan Thomson is ever going to make it back to the big screen, he will need to dominate the stage. The two sites work dialectically; adaptation binds them together.

Much of the film's metacommentary functions through intentional casting. In the film, the aging actor battles with the internal voice of his superhero alter ego, who insists they take on a fourth film in the "Birdman" franchise that made them famous. Birdman's voice and costume clearly riff on Batman,

---

50. Clarke, *Transmedia Television* (2013).

51. *Publishers Weekly* reports that in the first twelve weeks after *Birdman*'s opening, sales of Raymond Carver's collection *What We Talk About When We Talk About Love* more than doubled. The increased sales prompted Vintage to publish lesser known texts by Carver. Reid, "'Birdman' Drives Interest in Carver Collection" (2015).

52. Barnett, "How to Do Things with Birds" (2016), 131–34.

53. Directed by Spike Jonze; screenplay by Charlie Kaufman adapted from Susan Orlean's nonfiction book *The Orchid Thief* (1998).

the character that launched Keaton to super-stardom in the 1990s and is a culture-text in its own right. The highest level of metacritique in the film is also a form of self-parody: just like Riggan Thomson, Michael Keaton has aged out of superhero costumes and leading roles in big-budget action films. His acting career now depends on his ability to carry an artistic drama with the potential for critical acclaim (—and he did it!).[54]

Although *Birdman* is an exemplar of postmodern film, similar self-reflexive industry metacommentary was also found regularly on the nineteenth-century stage. As Katherine Newey explains, "Metatheatricality has always been an important feature of English theater. In the case of melodrama on the nineteenth-century popular stage, the genre as a whole is strongly marked by a metatheatrical awareness, and the self-referential nature of melodrama is one of its key modes of communication."[55] Barnett's observation regarding the film's propensity for melodrama also harkens back to the most popular dramatic genre of the nineteenth-century stage. The similarities don't end there. *Birdman*'s postmodern hero bears a striking resemblance to the Byronic hero, albeit an old, washed-out one.[56] Cultural historians might also recognize vestiges of Victorian theater in the film's full title, *Birdman or (The Unexpected Virtue of Ignorance)*, whose contrasting subtitle is reminiscent of the naming conventions of eighteenth- and nineteenth-century plays and fiction.

Nineteenth-century London theatergoers often saw similar, layered metanarratives unfold on stage, especially when attending comic entertainments like the harlequinade *Frankenstein; or, The Model Man* (1849). Like *Birdman*, the Victorian comedy is notable for its self-awareness, identifying itself as an adaptation with many "a trifling deviation / from Mrs. Shelley's marvellous narration" (*The Model Man,* Scene 1).[57] The play openly used plot points and props from previous adaptations of *Frankenstein*. For example, the Creature in *The Model Man* is calmed by music, a throwback to earlier melodramas from the 1820s. Through its rich intertextuality, *The Model Man* establishes itself as one of many "Frankensteins," which by 1849 included at least fifteen distinct dramatizations in England and France. Another example of a plot point taken

---

54. *Birdman* received nine Academy Award nominations, winning four awards including "Best Picture." At the Golden Globe Awards, Keaton won "Best Actor in a Musical or Comedy."
55. Newey, "Melodrama and Metatheatre" (1997), 85.
56. The self-centered protagonist struggles with celebrity, uncontrollable anger, substance abuse, and extreme fits of madness. Fulford, "What We Talk About When We Talk About *Birdman*," (2015).
57. Brough and Brough, *Frankenstein; or, The Model Man*, reprinted in Forry, *Hideous Progenies* (1990).

from previous adaptations is the use of alchemy, the animation method introduced in Peake's *Presumption* (1823) and other plays of the 1820s.[58]

The Model Man not only pieced together previous *Frankenstein* adaptations but also borrowed from other popular plays not attached to the Frankenstein culture-text to stitch together a new monstrous comedy. Some examples include the addition of characters, most notably Zamiel, a mystical being directly imported from Carl Maria von Weber's hit nineteenth-century opera *Der Freischütz* (1821), which was based on a classic German folk tale popularized in the early nineteenth century in a textual adaptation by Johann August Apel. *Der Freischütz* went through at least four English adaptations throughout the 1820s, as well as an unacknowledged translation by Thomas De Quincey titled "The Fatal Marksman."[59] Victorian audiences would have recognized the character, and *The Model Man* also makes explicit references to *Der Freischütz*'s most famous scenes. The mash-up asks audiences to see the similarities between the *Frankenstein* and *Der Freischütz* storylines, just as *Birdman*'s viewers see parallels between the film's main characters and their counterparts in the Carver play-within-the-film. The adaptation not only nods to its direct predecessors and source texts but also situates itself within a larger network of the period's popular stories.

Like *Birdman*, the 1849 *Frankenstein* comedy includes significant metacommentary, including in its casting. Zamiel was played by O. Smith, one of the Adelphi Theatre's most recognizable faces.[60] In the 1820s, Smith was the second-most famous actor to perform as Frankenstein's monster in London, taking the role in Henry Milner's *Frankenstein; or, The Man and The Monster* (1826) when Thomas Potter Cooke (the period's number one Frankenstein monster actor) was on the road. By *The Model Man*'s production in 1849, O. Smith was too old to play the physically demanding role of Frankenstein's monster, but the Adelphi knew they had a special gimmick and they put it to use, especially since Smith had also played Zamiel in a production of *Der Freischütz* adapted by George Soane and first staged at Drury Lane in 1824.[61] When *Frankenstein* was reanimated for the 1849 Christmas season, the actor who had made a career out of playing monsters and demons was cast in the special role of Zamiel, adding an additional ironic layer to the parody. *The*

---

58. See Forry, *Hideous Progenies* (1990). Frankenstein also receives the animating potion from a mystical third-party source in *Le Monstre et le Magicien*, as well as in its English translation by John Kerr, *Frankenstein; or, The Monster and the Magician* (1826).

59. Masson, "Introduction" to *The Collected Writings of Thomas De Quincey* (1897), 2–3.

60. (Richard John) Smith was famous for playing villains, monsters, and demons over the course of a nearly fifty-year career. He earned his stage name by playing the lead role in *Obi; or, Three Finger'd Jack*, a character he played at different venues for approximately a decade.

61. Soane, *Der Freischütz* (1825).

Model Man would fall flat without O. Smith precisely because he was famous for playing the monster in the 1820s; just as the metacommentary of *Birdman* wouldn't work without Michael Keaton, the most recognizable Batman of the 1990s for his role in two major film adaptations.[62]

Like the postmodern film, the 1849 harlequinade not only parodies its various source texts and stage influences, but also critiques industry pressures and the conditions of artistic labor. Where *Birdman* follows its characters off-stage to provide "behind-the-scenes" glimpses of what goes into a theatrical production, *The Model Man* frequently breaks the theatrical fourth wall to comment on the play's character changes, generic conventions, and technical elements.[63] In the following scene, Zamiel describes how stage effects shape audience experience:

> ZAMIEL: You'll see; to make what's coming more terrific
> I'll turn the lights down by a charmed specific,
> And when the business of the scene requires
> I'll heighten the effects with colored fires.
> *The room is darkened. All express terror.*
>
> . . . .
>
> FRANKENSTEIN: Oh dear what's coming, strange voices humming?
> The stage all dark too, with thunder hark too,
> Filling each headful—with notions dreadful.[64]

Both characters point out the contrived aspects of theatrical production. Zamiel comments on the theatrical use of lighting effects to scare the audience; Frankenstein pokes fun at the spooky singing and music. Yet, by not taking any of this seriously, the play carves out a space for critique that doesn't devolve into didacticism. Like *Birdman*, *The Model Man* achieves its greatest moments of drama by poking fun at its own artifice, as it merges the real and the surreal, as well as parody and pastiche, through a heightened self-reflexivity.

From a contemporary view, *The Model Man* of 1849 reads like a blueprint for the two most memorable *Frankenstein* film comedies of the twentieth century—*Abbott and Costello Meet Frankenstein* (1948) and *Young Franken-*

---

62. Keaton starred in *Batman* (1989) and *Batman Returns* (1992).
63. Similar "postmodern" strategies can be found in nineteenth-century novels, including Austen's authorial interruption in *Northanger Abbey* (1817) to defend the profession of novel writing, as well as the historical lessons Hugo provides throughout *Notre-Dame de Paris* (1831).
64. Brough and Brough, *Frankenstein; or, The Model Man* (1849), Scene 5. Reprinted in Forry, *Hideous Progenies* (1990), 243.

stein (1974)—but this comic tradition in the Frankenstein culture-text began immediately in its stage history. In what could serve as inspiration for an Abbott and Costello comedy or a Mel Brooks film, the same dramatist who wrote the first successful stage version of *Frankenstein* parodied himself. Peake followed *Presumption; or, The Fate of Frankenstein* (1823) with the aptly titled *Another Piece of Presumption* (1823), staged at the Adelphi Theatre just five months after the premiere of the first play at the English Opera House. The farce is a self-parodying sequel to the earlier play, and it includes sustained breaks of the dramatic fourth wall. A dramatic frame takes audiences backstage to witness the production of the play currently on stage. Throughout the dramatic framing, Dramaticus Devildum (a fictional playwright) discusses with Mr. Lee (the real-life manager at the Adelphi Theatre, played by himself) the ins-and-out of writing, selling, and staging the sequel to his successful *Frankenstein* adaptation:

> LEE: But Mr. Devildum—have I not heard that there is something of an immoral tendency in this story [founded on *Frankenstein*]?
> DEVILDUM: So much the better—every body will come and see it—The moment I told my wife of its being improper she went and laid out her last 2 shillings in the gallery—the children cried in bed all the evening, & I went without my supper!
> LEE: That piece, Sir—had a great deal of detraction—
> DEVILDUM: And a great deal of *attraction*—Bring my *Presumption* out, Sir—and you'll probably set the zealous friends of morality to work—. . . . That will make your fortune!—an abortive attempt to ruin the interests of a Theatre, or a performance is sure to add to its popularity—it sets all the world talking—it sets the Ladies all talking, and when the Ladies begin to talk, Mr. Lee, Heaven knows when or where it will end—.[65]

The exchange provides a glimpse into several business practices and social norms established by the early nineteenth century, including the famous adage that "all publicity, including bad publicity, is good publicity." Underneath the unapologetically sexist comment that controversy "sets the Ladies all talking" is an implicit acknowledgement that in order for a theater to be financially successful, it must meet the demands of all potential patrons, including one of the most influential consumer groups: women.

---

65. Peake, *Another Piece of Presumption* (1823), Act 1, Scene 1. Reprinted in Forry, *Hideous Progenies* (1990), 163.

The frame takes up the entirety of the play's first scene, and it reappears at least half a dozen times throughout the play as the two men regularly interrupt the action to discuss audience engagement, stage effects, plot development, and administrative logistics:

> LEE: But in your piece there are such abominable inaccuracies—Who taught that damn'd Demon to read?
> DEVILDUM: As I said before—he had a tailor's head on—and that Tailor subscribed to a Circulating Library!
> LEE: Yes, but are the Ladies and Gentlemen in the front to know it?
> DEVILDUM: How—why by instinct, to be sure—but I have depended a little too much on that Billy Burrowes's head—it is hazardous—but now my next scene—The house on fire—Carpenters!
> LEE: No, Sir—the County Fire Office won't stand it—that is doubly hazardous!
> DEVILDUM: Cut out my house on Fire—you've cut out the principle Engine in my piece—it is a burning shame—it would have drawn all the sparks in Town—
> LEE: Be cool, Sir—
> DEVILDUM: How can I be cool, Sir, when you won't permit the whole place to be burnt down. . . . Mr. Lee—you've ruined me—but I know the cause! It is jealousy because you are not in my piece—. . . . The last scene already—Why, Sir, there was two hours more stuff in my piece—
> LEE: Depend upon it—Sir—there is quite stuff enough.[66]

Like the Creature at the heart of this culture-text, Peake's dramatic double describes his second *Frankenstein* play as a fragmented assemblage of "stuff." Puns aside, the dramatic exchange above provides a glimpse into the art of comic appropriation and the material restrictions on nineteenth-century spectacle. From plot holes to fire codes, an irreverent playfulness permeates the play from beginning to end. Yet this playfulness simultaneously underscores very real frustrations for artists working in the nineteenth-century theater industry, providing opportunity to voice concerns through comedy. *Another Piece of Presumption* performs the ephemerality of theater while exposing the business side of stage production, including the writing, staging, and selling of dramatic entertainment adapted from various sources.

The farce also shows that adaptations drew as much (and perhaps more so) from previous adaptations as they did from the novel. Like Peake, Henry

---

66. Peake, *Another Piece of Presumption* (1823), Act 2, Scene 2. Reprinted in Forry, *Hideous Progenies* (1990), 174.

Milner (another dramatist who frequently adapted novels for the stage) wrote a now-lost drama, *Frankenstein; or, The Demon of Switzerland* (1823), which turned out to be a financial flop. However, his second attempt, *Frankenstein; or, The Man and the Monster* (1826), was much more successful because it drew on Peake's play, while adding its own original flourishes. Milner is responsible for staging the first creation scene in Frankenstein's adaptation history, and now this scene is a staple of any visual adaptation of the story. Victorian versions riffed off the plays of the 1820s, and the earliest twentieth-century films more closely resemble their nineteenth-century stage brethren than they do Shelley's novel.[67] The "Burlesque Extravaganza" *Frankenstein; or, The Vampire's Victim* featured singing and dancing monsters adapted from multiple sources, making it one of the original "monster mash-ups."[68] The first stage adaptation of the twentieth century, titled *The Last Laugh* (1915), also retold the story through a comic lens.[69]

By the time Mel Brooks parodied the novel's adaptation history in *Young Frankenstein*, the practice had already been attached to the novel's popular history for 150 years.[70] While there is no direct evidence that the cast and crew were familiar with *Frankenstein*'s earlier stage history, we know that Brooks saw himself as actively cataloguing the Frankenstein culture-text's early film history, and this film tradition was in turn heavily based on the theatrical tradition preceding it. Through endless acts of repetition (conscious or not), *Young Frankenstein* shares many plot points with the nineteenth-century comedies. The Creature learning to speak, for one, is a staple of Frankenstein's comic history and factors heavily into the plot of *Young Frankenstein*. The most famous scene from the 1974 film, where Frankenstein and the Creature perform Irvin Berlin's "Puttin' on the Ritz," is original to Frankenstein's film

---

67. Cutchins and Perry, *Adapting Frankenstein* (2018), particularly Szwydky, "*Frankenstein*'s Spectacular Nineteenth-Century Stage History and Legacy" (2018).

68. *The Vampire's Victim* was one of the Gaiety's most successful pieces of the 1887–88 season with at least 107 documented performances (a considerable run for this genre). This was the first stage adaptation to link the *Frankenstein* story to any vampire story, predating the publication of Stoker's *Dracula* (1897) by a decade. The monster mash-up is a staple of horror, from films such as *House of Frankenstein* (1944) to *Van Helsing* (2004), as well as the fictional universe of *The League of Extraordinary Gentlemen* created by Alan Moore.

69. Fisch, *Frankenstein: Icon of Modern Culture* (2009); Hitchcock, *Frankenstein: A Cultural History* (2007).

70. *Young Frankenstein* (1974) takes much of its visual cues from the films of the 1930s, most importantly in the recreation of Frankenstein's laboratory, which included machinery that was actually used in the 1931 film.

history; however, both the 1849 and 1887 comedies included singing and dancing monsters.[71]

Frankenstein's adaptation history is saturated with comedy, parody, and pastiche, showing how all play crucial roles in the transformation of texts into culture-texts. Hutcheon and Rose both see parody as a productive site engaging the issues that bind literature and history. Hutcheon defines parody as "repetition with critical distance."[72] For Rose, "Parody and meta-fiction . . . demonstrate critically the processes involved in the production and reception of fiction from within a literary text . . . [and] show how a literary work exists both within a particular social context and a literary tradition."[73] Parody and metafiction, that is, always contain an echo of history vis-à-vis literary tradition. Hutcheon argues that parody "is one of the ways in which modern artists have managed to come to terms with the weight of the past. The search for novelty in twentieth-century art has often—ironically—been firmly based in the search for a tradition."[74] Nineteenth-century adapters more easily situated themselves within an emerging popular history, particularly when it came to the adaptation of novels of the time. *Frankenstein*'s earliest stage versions demonstrate how dramatists involved in these adaptations intentionally wrote themselves into the cultural history of the novel, previous adaptations, and other popular entertainment.

Pastiche also played a part in this process of building cultural history, participating in the creation of "cultural memory and the merging of horizons past and present," according to Ingeborg Hoesterey.[75] Historical knowledge—whether literary, artistic, or political—is transferred through repetition in various genres and media, even if the imitation is simply repetition for the sake of repetition.[76] Though the two are somewhat distinct practices, parody and pastiche can also exist simultaneously within the same work. *Young Frankenstein* parodies the stereotypical depiction of the hunchbacked assistant in the Frankenstein culture-text. Igor (pronounced EYE-gore, remember!) steals the show repeatedly; Marty Feldman's physical performance is challenged (though never upended) only with the arrival of the Monster and his own antics.

---

71. Despite these similarities, I have yet to find any direct evidence that Mel Brooks and Gene Wilder (who wrote the script) had any familiarity with the early plays.
72. Hutcheon, *A Theory of Parody* (2000).
73. Rose, *Parody//Meta-Fiction* (1979), 66.
74. Hutcheon, *A Theory of Parody* (2000), 29.
75. Hoesterey, *Pastiche* (2001), xi.
76. Hutcheon echoes Genette's argument that parody transforms, while pastiche simply imitates. See Genette, *Palimpsests* (1997).

What's most interesting, however, is that *Young Frankenstein* never questions Igor's existence in the first place. The character is a direct pastiche-like import from the early films (which themselves copied the character from the stage tradition), and he continues to appear in *Frankenstein* adaptations, including films told from his perspective such as *Victor Frankenstein* (2015).

A similar reliance on pastiche explains how Frankenstein's Creature has been portrayed throughout much of this adaptation history. Today, depicting Frankenstein's Creature as a blue or green giant with a flat head and electrical nodes is a decision to explicitly engage with a popular history that has turned that image into an icon, a process that began in 1823 with the first stage adaptation of *Frankenstein*. The inverse is also true: *Frankenstein* adaptations that eschew the iconic image are making a conscious decision to part ways with established practices, whether by choice or due to the restrictions of copyright. Both choices are still deliberate practices that engage a range of earlier iterations of the story on page, stage, or screen. *Presumption* presented a blue-skinned monster and the adaptations that came after followed suit. By the mid-nineteenth century, *The Model Man* even poked fun at this convention in its creation scene, as Frankenstein narrates the finishing touches of his mechanical man by painting him with "a touch or two / Of red just here—and a tinge of blue," a nod to earlier plays that continued to stylize the Creature this way (see figure 1.7).[77] To date, the blue-green monster is one of the details most commonly associated with *Frankenstein*'s iconography, even as it has started to be eschewed in favor of more "realistic" physical portrayals of the Creature (see figures 1.3 through 1.6 and 1.8). Patterns of repetition (sometimes with and at other times without critical difference) turned Frankenstein's Creature into a cultural icon; pastiche made this possible both in performance and through reproductions of imagery from the plays in print culture like souvenir portraits and reviews in periodicals.

When situated within a particular culture-text's adaptation history, pastiche can transform an image into an international icon. The practice of painting the Creature blue on stage began in London but was repeated on Paris stages and everywhere else *Frankenstein* plays were performed. *Frankenstein*'s visual adaptation history helps us see the critical layers pastiche adds to repetition. It asks us to reconsider the nuance of pastiche against critics like Frederic Jameson who interpret pastiche as a "neutral practice . . . without any of parody's ulterior motives. . . . Pastiche is thus blank parody, a statue with blind eyeballs."[78] Instead of this dismissive view, my position is that pastiche

---

77. Brough and Brough, *Frankenstein; or, The Model Man* (1849). Reprinted in Forry (1990), 227–50.

78. Jameson, *Postmodernism* (1991), 17.

FIGURE 1.3. T. P. Cooke as Frankenstein's Creature in Jean-Toussaint Merle and Antony Béraud, *Le Monstre et le Magicien* (1826) in Paris. Cooke was the "original Frankenstein," first appearing as the Creature in Peake's *Presumption* (1823) in London. © National Library of France, Paris.

FIGURE 1.4. Set of miniature theatrical prints of characters from Jean-Toussaint Merle and Antony Béraud, *Le Monstre et le Magicien* (1826). © National Library of France, Paris.

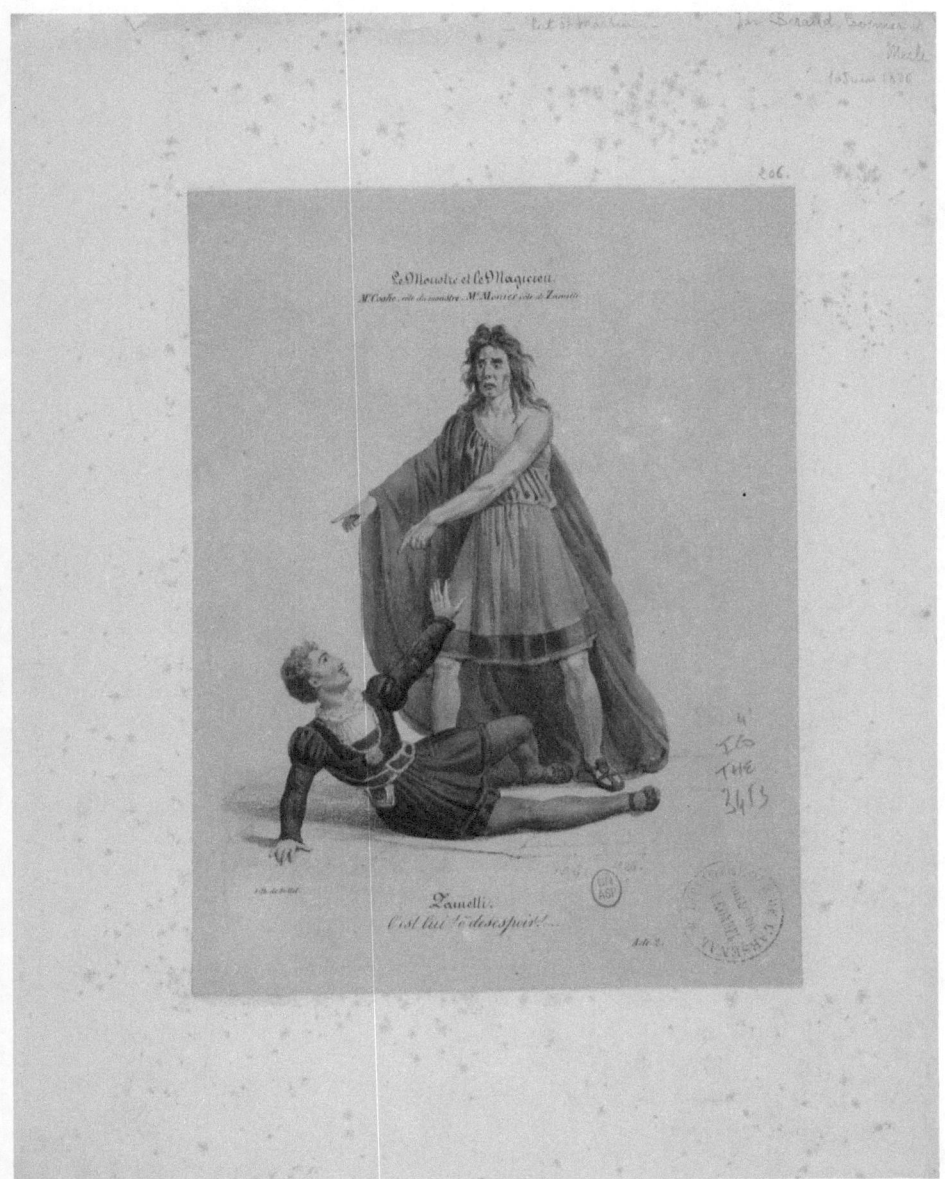

FIGURE 1.5. Green monster print from Jean-Toussaint Merle and Antony Béraud, *Le Monstre et le Magicien* (1826). © National Library of France, Paris.

FIGURE 1.6. Green monster print from Jean-Toussaint Merle and Antony Béraud, *Le Monstre et le Magicien* (1826). © National Library of France, Paris.

FIGURE 1.7. Creation scene from *Frankenstein; or, The Model Man* (1849) from the *Illustrated London News*, January 12, 1850. Image © The British Library Board. All Rights Reserved. Image reproduced with permission of the British Newspaper Archive (https://www.britishnewspaperarchive.co.uk).

FIGURE 1.8. Ferdinand Dugué, *Le Monstre et le Magicien* (1861), an adaptation of Merle and Béraud's 1826 play. © National Library of France, Paris.

and parody are pivotal in the making of culture-texts because they reinforce a narrative's reproducibility as well as the culture-text's iconography and recognition value where commercial successes support cultural longevity. Through such self-reflexive practices, these forms of adaptation reinforce the relationship between past and present (and perhaps possible futures). As adaptations, parody and pastiche not only acknowledge a history but also demonstrate a sophisticated signaling of themselves *as* history and, more importantly, as history *makers*. These adaptations and reiterations become part of a cultural lineage, as they have done with the *Frankenstein* culture-text and many others.

Texts survive over time through these patterns of repetition and adaptation.[79] As Simon Dentith explains, parody is a transhistorical, intertextual mode:

> Just as the specific techniques of the postmodernist novel have mostly been anticipated in the history of the novel, so too the parodic practices of contemporary popular culture can often be found in the systems of popular entertainment in the nineteenth and early twentieth centuries. What is different about the present moment is the dominance and scale of penetration of the culture industries, made possible by specific technical innovations.[80]

As we see in the cultural history of commercialized adaptation, what has changed is the extent to which technical innovations have made tried-and-true practices of imitation, recycling, and reinterpretation more dispersed and visible. The history of adaptation and similar imitative forms in the eighteenth and nineteenth centuries reveals that commercialism, spectacle, parody, and pastiche have driven cultural production from the eighteenth century to the present. The same critiques leveled at Hollywood films today were also made of the earliest novels, as a new form of popular literature gained a mass market and cultural capital. In this commercial environment, adaptation and other forms of repetition and imitation flourished.

LIKE HUTCHEON, Rose, and other theorists who see postmodern practices such as parody and adaptation as deliberative, creative, and critical practices, I see adaptation as a recuperative act, positioning it as a central force in cultural production and literary history. Practices of adaptation, repetition, and parody have shaped all areas of literary, artistic, and cultural production—from the

---

79. Bortolotti and Hutcheon, "On the Origins of Adaptation" (2007).
80. Dentith, *Parody* (2000), 184–85.

eighteenth-century novel to twenty-first-century transmedia storytelling. The forms of extension and array of imitations in the eighteenth and nineteenth centuries challenges the idea that postmodern aesthetics of parody, pastiche, intertextuality, and self-reflexive metafiction (including metatheatricality) are distinct phenomena of postmodern art or late capitalism. Specifically, early melodramas and stage comedies based on *Frankenstein* and other nineteenth-century novels show us that most of the aesthetic practices typically associated with postmodernism also characterized nineteenth-century popular culture in print and performance. A historical view allows us some critical distance from our own cultural moment while helping us better understand how we got here. In this light, adaptation may be seen as a requirement for cultural preservation, instead of as a simple by-product of consumer culture.

The dialectical relationship between the nineteenth-century London theater, art, and textual publishing industries certainly points to this conclusion, illustrating the convergence of politics, regulation, technological innovation, and commercialism. These political and industrial contexts led to a new aesthetics that was increasingly hybrid, self-aware, and explicitly discussed in print and performance. Through adaptation and other dispersed forms of transmedia storytelling, writers and artists consciously wrote their way into the nineteenth-century culture industry—and literary history. Writers rewrote old stories into newer, modern forms that resonated with audiences of their day. Artists visualized stories old and new, exhibiting narrative paintings in public galleries or designing illustrated books that would become common household items by the mid-nineteenth century. Theaters put novels on stage, widening their reach and increasing sales of the books and, as I discuss in the next chapter, helped to establish several art-based professions including authorship, professional playwriting, and acting, among others. In almost every example, the history of commercial adaptation challenges existing narratives about how literature and art circulated in the nineteenth century and reached later generations through additional adaptations. Seeing this process at work in the nineteenth-century culture industry helps us more clearly realize connections to today's trends in storytelling across forms and media, providing us with new models for predicting how commercial adaptations will continue to support a diversity of increasingly collaborative and dispersed storytelling models in the future.

CHAPTER 2

Professional and Celebrity Networks

Authors, Actors, Adapters

THE FOLLOWING CHAPTER traces a network of cultural production characterized by overlapping (if not always direct) relationships between authors, actors, and professional dramatists—three kinds of artistic celebrity produced and shaped by transmedia adaptation. This professional adaptation network includes people in the spotlight as well as those operating largely behind the scenes adapting literature for the stage, designing costumes, painting original scenery, choreographing dance and action scenes, and executing special effects. Although these professionals rarely get considered in the reception histories of novels and culture-texts, they had a significant hand in promoting and circulating stories through print, performance, or other visual forms.

While most writers understood the benefit of having their works adapted or imitated in various mediums, others were regularly at odds with adapters, accusing them of stealing and plagiarism. Certain grievances had some validity; however, claims of plagiarism asserted authorial originality and control at the expense of collaborative models that more accurately describe the creation and circulation of art in an industrial economy. Discrediting the important work of professional actors, dramatists, theatrical managers, and professional artists obscures their significant role in supporting arts and culture as both consumers and creators of content. Without these critical and commercial contributions to cross-media storytelling, I argue that literary celebrity would be less visible (perhaps impossible), and the stories that helped build their celebrity might be forgotten. Literary history has largely downplayed this intricate network of professional and commercial adaptation; however, the networks between authors, actors, and adapters, and the convergence of the arts and media industries, are responsible for the making of culture-texts and the rise of celebrity authorship as we know it today.

We see this convergence clearly illustrated in the early publication and adaptation history of *Frankenstein*. "But lo & behold! I found myself famous!" wrote Mary Wollstonecraft Shelley to her friend and fellow writer Leigh Hunt on September 9, 1823, after attending a performance of *Presumption; or, The Fate of Frankenstein*. The excited, descriptive paragraph she provides about *Presumption* stands out in a letter otherwise dominated by the solemn tone of a grieving widow struggling to keep herself "out of the gulf of melancholy." Recently returned from Italy where her husband Percy had drowned the summer before, Shelley determined to support herself and her only surviving son through her writing and editorial work. Her success depended on cultivating professional networks of writers and publishers, who in turn supported her financial independence with regular, commissioned work.

Although she was born into and lived almost exclusively within circles of literary celebrities, Shelley's return to England in 1823 marked the birth of her public, professional identity. On August 11, in order to capitalize on the momentum and visibility of Richard Brinsley Peake's stage adaptation, the second printing of *Frankenstein* was released. The 1823 printing of the novel identified the book's author for the first time and ultimately quadrupled the number of copies of *Frankenstein* in print. This new printing was arranged by Shelley's father, William Godwin, who accompanied her to *Presumption* on June 29, just four days after her arrival in London. In a letter to his daughter dated July 22, 1823, Godwin clearly expresses his personal and financial interest in the success of the stage adaptation of his daughter's debut novel:

> It is a curious circumstance that a play is just announced, to be performed at the English Opera House in the Strand next Monday, entitled *Presumption; or, the Fate of Frankenstein*. I know not whether it will succeed. If it does, it will be some sort of feather in the cap of the author of the novel, a recommendation in your future negotiations with booksellers.[1]

---

1. Unpublished letter. William Godwin to Mary Shelley. Huntington Library HM11634. Excerpts appear in Forry, *Hideous Progenies* (1990), 3; and Robbins, "It Lives!" (2017).

Godwin's prediction was correct: Shelley would continue to leverage *Frankenstein*'s success throughout her writing career. Although the novel never became a bestseller in her lifetime, she made more money on the second and third editions of *Frankenstein* than on the first edition.[2] The title pages of her later novels regularly identified her as "the author of *Frankenstein*," even if they had little in common with either *Frankenstein* or the many adaptations produced in subsequent decades. In more ways than one, *Presumption*'s popularity catalyzed Shelley's writing career. She would continue to publish novels, dozens of shorter works of fiction, and travelogues while editing her husband's poetry and memoirs in the shadow of *Frankenstein* and its many adaptations, which continued to be revived and newly adapted throughout her lifetime. Surprisingly, despite *Frankenstein*'s longevity, none of her other works appear to have been adapted for the stage or another medium, and she remains known primarily for her first novel. Its adaptations also helped establish other professional artists—actors who played the role of Frankenstein's Creature, such as Thomas Potter Cooke and O. Smith, went on to have considerable careers. The popularity of plays they starred in is the reason the Creature is usually referred to as "Frankenstein," a confusion already in place by the 1830s and driven by the success of the rising celebrities who embodied the monster on stage.

Godwin's foresight for *Frankenstein*'s financial potential through adaptation was hardly coincidental, as his own literary career included forays into adaptation in both print and performance. First, he adapted his philosophical book *Political Justice* (1793) into a more palatable, popular form as the gothic novel *Caleb Williams; or, Things as They Are* (1794). The gothic novelization of his philosophical tract was much more widely read and soon adapted for the stage by George Colman (the Younger) as *The Iron Chest* (commissioned by theater manager Richard Brinsley Sheridan and produced at Drury Lane in 1796), showing how even a radical, polemical work like *Political Justice* could prove interesting enough for cross-media adaptations in the period's emerging commercial entertainment industry.[3] As a staunch believer in the traditional model of patronage, Godwin resented the increasingly commercial nature of art and letters; yet he also acknowledged this cultural and economic shift in practical terms, imparting what he knew about the publishing and entertainment industries to his daughter. Future generations—biological and literary—would have to embrace adaptation in order to support themselves through their intellectual and creative labors, while also carefully cultivating social

---

2. St. Clair, *The Reading Nation in the Romantic Period* (2004).
3. Jellenik, "On the Origins of Adaptations as Such" (2017).

and professional networks for both immediate and long-term literary success. Godwin turned out to be a helpful professional mentor to his daughter in this regard, as *Frankenstein* continues to be one of the most frequently adapted novels of all time and showing no signs of slowing down in twenty-first-century art, culture, and entertainment.

Networked structures dominate today's art industries. Simone Murray maps the proliferation of contemporary adaptations across several media industries, as well as the networks of professionals converging around an expansive, adaptation-driven entertainment industry. Immersive storytelling happens across printed texts, film, television, video games, and comics. Media companies purchase individual licenses as well as the rights to full catalogs from authors, publishers, and production studios. This dynamic process moves in many directions, as print-based industries publish novelizations, compendia, and graphic novels based on films and popular televisions series that connect authors, literary agents, publishers, multimedia companies, book fairs, film festivals, awards, audiences, and fan culture. Murray explains:

> Contemporary literary adaptations are products of an intricate, hugely complex institutional and industrial system . . . [and a] detailed modeling of the adaptation industry allows us to see how the various contemporary media sectors are increasingly tightly converged into a single adaptation-industry network through conglomerate ownership structures, digital technologies and the ubiquity of the content rights economy.[4]

Few people would argue with Murray's networked model of the adaptation industry, but even fewer recognize how today's extensive, networked structures are inherited and modified from the nineteenth-century arts and entertainment industries driven by adaptations.

Various commercial trades that were becoming known *as* industries for the first time supported the nineteenth-century adaptation industry. As part of a larger network of professionalized cultural production, adaptation drove nineteenth-century celebrity culture at precisely the historical moment in which the arts shifted from a system of patronage to one that required artists to thrive in the commercial environment ushered in by a new, industrial economy. Adaptations employed thousands of people on the stage, behind the scenes, and even back at the printing houses, where new print editions were published to capitalize on the heightened cultural visibility of successful theat-

---

4. Murray, *The Adaptation Industry* (2012), 185–86.

rical runs.⁵ Book sales turned writers into industrial-age authors, professionals whose careers depended on a network of adaptation for both immediate visibility and future posterity.

For the first time in history, authors needed to learn how to negotiate with publishers, booksellers, and theater professionals, finding ways to leverage related arts-based industries to make their work appeal to larger audiences.⁶ Nineteenth-century artists thus needed to be equally skilled in both their craft and the professional side of cultural production, including establishing connections in the publishing and theater industries. Publishers and theater managers were in turn financially invested in the promotion and sale of literature, art, and culture across media. Drawing from fiction and narrative poetry, as well as historical and current events, the theater found an endless source of malleable material to adapt to its own forms. This inspiration came cheap, given that copyright laws did not apply across mediums and were also quite loose within the same formats, leaving abridgements and parodies to saturate the public sphere. Theater managers therefore paid very small amounts for resident dramatists to adapt stories for the stage, and they were under no obligation to acquire rights from publishers or pay royalties to living authors. Many writers, like Charles Dickens, explicitly scoffed at such unabashed and often unacknowledged profiteering, fighting instead for more control and financial rights to the use of their intellectual property. Others, like Lord Byron and Walter Scott, more readily embraced the practice for its commercial possibilities, adding their own adaptations to the mix to increase their celebrity in the present and ensure their continued cultural legacies.

BECOMING CULTURAL ICONS: AUTHORS AND ACTORS AS CELEBRITIES AND PROFESSIONALS

The nineteenth-century adaptation industry relied heavily on an emerging culture of celebrity that turned writers and artists into public figures. Poets, novelists, dramatists, actors, painters, illustrators, and engravers all became professionalized in the burgeoning industrial economy, which also marked the historical shift in the arts from a patronage system to a commercial one. Nineteenth-century celebrity involved many types of "fame," positioning individuals of historical or political significance alongside a range of cultural

---

5. See Davis, *The Economics of the British Stage* (2000) and Hemmings, *The Theatre Industry in Nineteenth-Century France* (1993).
6. Hamilton, *A Strange Business* (2015).

figures.[7] For the first time in history, artists became household names, and commercial culture turned them into celebrities. This new age of celebrity was supported by adaptations, parodies, remakes, and other forms of repetition and recycling that brought widespread recognition to artists across the public sphere. Adapters could use specific stories to create meaning in new forms such as painting or opera, two artistic mediums that themselves often tell stories through complex networks of adaptations and allusions. Adaptation enabled authors to widen their audience and recognition outside of the immediate context of their writing.

Through adaptation, a text or writer could also be resituated within new political and social movements, as well as within new historical and cultural contexts. Lord Byron is the period's most famous example. Often referring to him as the first literary celebrity, scholarly studies of Byron regularly tout the poet's fame (and infamy) in his own day; "Byromania," a term coined in 1814 by the poet's fiancée Annabella Milbanke, persists two hundred years later through several book-length reception histories dedicated solely to Byron's celebrity.[8] Byron's poetry earned critical praise, making him a major voice in British Romanticism and earning him a place in literary history, while his personality earned him infamy as one of the first countercultural celebrities, famously described by one of his lovers, Lady Caroline Lamb, as "mad, bad, and dangerous to know."[9]

Even greater than his critical and popular successes is the permanent impact Byron made upon literary and cultural history. By inventing the Byronic hero, a now-archetypal character that continues to appear in contemporary literature, film, television, and media, Byron became a household name.[10] From its debut in *Childe Harold's Pilgrimage* (1812), the character-type catapulted Byron into celebrity through its close association with the scandalous lifestyle the poet embraced and the related gossip in which he reveled.[11] Byron "awoke one morning and found [himself] famous," becoming an overnight sensation.[12] As one of the first writers to achieve this type of popularity and notoriety in his lifetime, he helped launch a new age of celebrity that finds immediate parallels in today's entertainment industry.[13] Byron broke

---

7. Mole, *Romanticism and Celebrity Culture* (2009); Berenson and Giloi, *Constructing Charisma* (2010).
8. McDayter, *Byromania and The Birth of Celebrity Culture* (2009).
9. MacCarthy, *Byron: Life and Legend* (2002).
10. Stein, *The Byronic Hero in Film, Fiction, and Television* (2004).
11. Tuite, *Lord Byron and Scandalous Celebrity* (2015).
12. Moore, *Life of Lord Byron* (1854), 2:137.
13. Marshall, *Celebrity and Power* (1997).

records as his poems sold more copies than those of his contemporaries, yet he became a celebrity because the theater industry, periodicals, visual artists, and personal gossip dispersed him across the period's mass culture. Adaptations of Byron—the man and the poet—amplified the reach of his works and celebrity through an endless network of cultural production, extending that reach well beyond the poet's lifetime.

Much of this transmedia storytelling came from Byron himself, as he constantly reworked his signature prototype/character while carefully crafting his image in the public sphere. He adapted the Byronic hero for new poems, reshaping the figure into new protagonists while situating them all in relation to his other works. Most of Byron's longer pieces include a variation of the Byronic hero, through either the semi-autobiographical guise of the young poet in *Childe Harold's Pilgrimage,* the world-weary Faustian figure in *Manfred* (1817), the rebellious antagonist of *Cain* (1821), or the satirical protagonist of *Don Juan* (1819–24). The Byronic hero, in all its permutations, was at the heart of Byron's public "brand."

Beyond adaptations of the brooding character-type by his own hand, Byron's work was also adapted by others. Despite being a lifelong patron of the theater, Byron famously refused to try his hand at drama, yet his dramatic poems—which he insisted were not intended for theatrical performance—were not only performed but often adapted into various theatrical genres. Sometimes these plays appeared in their original tragic or satirical modes, but they were just as likely reworked into lighthearted burlesques and other "illegitimate" genres.[14] The closet dramas he wrote for print publication weren't the only works to migrate to the stage. Byron's narrative poems were also dramatized, with *The Bride of Abydos* and *The Giaour* (1813), *The Corsair* (1814), *Mazeppa* (1819), and *Don Juan* each adapted into various theatrical genres.[15] This network of characters and associations was collectively built by Byron, his adapters, the actors who played his characters on stage, and the fandom that followed him across Europe, as he became one of the first celebrities to receive fan mail on a large, documented scale.[16] And these adaptations extended Byron's celebrity well beyond his own lifetime; indeed, there was a dramatic uptick in stage productions of Byron's works after his death in 1824.

Regardless of the genre and time in which his works appeared, Byron-the-celebrity was always imbricated. Actors played up the connection, not only to create the desired stage effect but also to increase their own celebrity by capitalizing on Byron's infamy. Through such imitation, Byron's celebrity con-

---

14. Tunbridge, "From Count to Chimney Sweep" (2006).
15. Burwick and Powell, *British Pirates in Print and Performance* (2015).
16. Throsby, "Byron, Commonplacing, and Early Fan Culture" (2009).

verged with the reputation of stage performers such as William Macready, as Burwick explains:

> Responding to the public celebration of the virtuoso performer, actors engaged a rivalry in performing Byronic roles. Much more was involved for the actors than simply the Byronic character; they must make it appear as if Byron himself were on stage performing that character. Parallel to the double role that Byron assigns himself as narrator and character in *Childe Harold* and *Don Juan,* the doubleness was also manifest in the stage performance.[17]

Similar forms of doubling conflated Byron and his characters in painting and illustration, such as the French artist Alexandre-Marie Colin's painting *Byron as Don Juan, with Haidee* (1831), which features the poet dressed as his satirical hero wooing (or being wooed by) one of several love interests from the mock epic (see figure 2.1). Colin's painting followed trends in French illustrations of Byron's poems that incorporated the author's likeness from the countless engravings and reproductions of Byron's image circulating in visual culture.[18] Both on stage and in visual art, the conflation of the poet with his protagonists emphasized the performative nature of nineteenth-century celebrity authorship—a new trend that permanently changed the relationship writers had to their works as they were publicly consumed and received.

European remixes of Byron's works into paintings and musical forms continued throughout the century. Among the most well-known nineteenth-century painters, the young French Romantic artist Eugène Delacroix returned regularly to Byron (alongside other authors) for sources of inspiration (see chapter 3). Mostly produced after the poet's death, these paintings extended the exoticized image that Byron solidified during his life.[19] Byron's poems also appeared as musicals, operas, and symphonies. The dramatic poem *Manfred* was adapted in Germany by Robert Schumann as *Manfred: Dramatic Poem with Music in Three Parts* (Opus 115), first performed in 1852, and in Russia as Pyotr Ilyich Tchiakovsky's *Manfred Symphony in B Minor,* Op. 58 (1886). Byron's closet tragedies published in 1821 (themselves adapted loosely from quasi- or authentic historical sources) were particularly prevalent as musical arrangements. For *Sardanapalus,* these included a cantata by French composer Hector Berlioz (1830); an unfinished opera by Hungarian composer

---

17. Burwick, "Staging the Byronic Hero" (2018), 4.
18. Soubigou, "French Portraits of Byron" (2008).
19. Johnson, "Delacroix and *The Bride of Abydos*" (1972).

FIGURE 2.1. Alexandre-Marie Colin, *Byron as Don Juan, with Haidee* (1831). Image © The Matthiesen Gallery, London.

Franz Liszt, who worked on his piece throughout the 1840s; an Italian opera by Giulio Alary (1852); and two operas in France by Victorin de Jonciéres (1867) and Alphonse Duvernoy (1882). Byron's *Marino Faliero* (1821), based on the tragic execution of the fourteenth-century Venetian aristocrat, was adapted into an 1835 opera by the Italian composer Gaetano Donizetti. The opera was immediately staged in Paris, London, and Florence, making its US premiere in New Orleans in 1842. Similarly, Byron's *The Two Foscari* (1821) provided the story for Giuseppe Verdi's opera *I due Foscari*, which premiered in Rome in 1844. Fredric Hymen Cowen's dramatic cantata *The Corsair* was composed for the Birmingham Triennial Festival in 1876, and sheet music was published and sold with the script.[20] Collectively, these adaptations dispersed Byron-the-poet throughout the world of music, while simultaneously making

---

20. Cowen, *The Corsair* (1876).

each composer more visible to poets and poetry readers through their associations with Byron.[21]

Operas, symphonies, and songs are rarely considered in reception histories and adaptation studies, making the array of musical forms in the adaptation of Romantic texts particularly notable. For a medium whose possibilities for political expression are highly contested, the use of radical or subversive stories or source texts—even as a backdrop—adds potential political dimensions to what many interpret as a neutral art form. Mary Ann Smart argues that despite historians' insistence on the relative impossibility of identifying explicit political meanings in much of opera's history, nineteenth-century Italian opera nonetheless "jolted audiences into more active and sympathetic modes of attention in the theater, fostering an engagement that . . . was a precondition for a more activist stance outside of the theater."[22] Adapting key Romantic tropes, themes, and texts for their grounding storylines situated musical forms within a larger context of artistic, political, and social revolutions. These adaptations layered complex meanings into new forms, producing a palimpsestic, intertextual exchange central to Linda Hutcheon's understanding of adaptation and its role in opera.[23]

Seeing the recurring role of adaptation in the cultural history of opera crystallizes adaptation's centrality to creative expression across fine art and popular culture, highlighting its primacy in the process of making artists celebrities and circulating literary works. Adaptation situated these individual works of art within a larger network of cultural production and literary history.[24] Most of Verdi's best-known operas were adaptations of successful plays in the European Romantic tradition. *Ernani* (1844) was based on Victor Hugo's *Hernani* (1830); *Il trovatore* (1853) and *Simon Boccanegra* (1853) were adapted from Antonio García Gutierrez's similarly titled plays of 1836 and 1843, respectively. I mention this larger network of adaptations by Verdi to counteract any growing notion that Byron was unique in his ability to inspire imitators. Networks of adaptation grew around various artists of the period and made them available to subsequent generations. This effect on immediate and long-term celebrity was reciprocal as well as dispersed. Adaptation increased Verdi's own stardom as much as it contributed to the celebrity of all of the poets and novelists whose works he adapted.

---

21. MacCarthy, *Byron: Life and Legend* (2002).
22. Smart, *Waiting for Verdi* (2018), 8.
23. Hutcheon and Hutcheon, "Adaptation and Opera" (2017).
24. Hutcheon, *A Theory of Adaptation* (2006); Hutcheon and Hutcheon, "Adaptation and Opera" (2017). The number of adapted titles included in *The Oxford Handbook of Opera* shows how much adaptation informs its history.

The international scope of these productions highlights adaptation's capacity to expand the geographical reach of artists by circulating their works across national borders in ways that a single medium alone could never accomplish. Byron, Dickens, Victor Hugo, and Harriet Beecher Stowe became celebrities both at home and abroad during their lifetimes, and their commercial success was tied to adaptations (by themselves and others) in various formats. By the 1840s, transatlantic reading and performance tours had become part of the professional life of artists, including authors and actors. Dickens became one of the earliest writers to participate in international reading tours, and he was embraced for his energetic, performative readings—a result of his lifelong interest in popular theater and early acting aspirations. Hugo, already successful in poetry, fiction, and drama, adapted *Notre-Dame de Paris* (1831) by writing the libretto for *La Esmeralda*, an opera collaboration with Louise Bertin and Hector Berlioz first staged in 1836. Stage actors increasingly went abroad. T. P. Cooke, Fanny Kemble, Ira Aldridge, Henry Irving, Ellen Terry, Richard Mansfield, and Sarah Bernhardt wowed audiences on both sides of the Atlantic by portraying well-known characters. A combination of adaptations and original dramas supported the rise of stage celebrity on a transcontinental scale.

Nineteenth-century celebrities became the first international celebrity-activists, using their fame and public appearances to promote causes personal and political. Dickens spent much of his first trip to the United States in 1842 advocating for stricter copyright laws (to his own benefit) and arguing for higher ethical standards for print and media industries. Hugo was one of the leading figures behind the Berne Convention of 1886, which established international copyright protections, and included language to cover adapted or derivative works for the first time.[25] The British actress Fanny Kemble and the American writer Harriet Beecher Stowe made the abolition of slavery in the United States a centerpiece of their celebrity activism, inviting comparisons to the humanitarian efforts of today's public figures.[26] Stowe's celebrity in particular was fueled not only through her best-selling novel *Uncle Tom's Cabin* (1852), but through its countless adaptations across forms and media.[27]

Achieving the celebrity status that afforded such activist possibilities depended on the widespread circulation, repetition, and reproduction of one's image and works. As Tom Mole explains, Byron's celebrity was largely supported through the period's growing visual culture, as authorized and unau-

---

25. See chapter 4 for discussion of Dickens's public performances and evolving copyright laws.

26. Clinton, *Fanny Kemble's Civil Wars* (2000); Morgan, "Crossing Boundaries" (2017).

27. Meer, *Uncle Tom Mania* (2005).

thorized images of Byron were "appropriated, altered, improved, rethought, varied or transformed" through a larger circuit of cultural production because "being a celebrity in the Romantic period meant seeing one's images proliferate, evolving or deforming as they suffused visual culture."[28] Heather McPherson locates the nexus of Romantic-period celebrity culture specifically in the convergence of media across high art and mass culture, where "more than anything else, it was the explosive, democratizing power of visual and print media—the rapid diffusion of news, books, pamphlets, portraits, and caricatures—that gave rise to modern 'international fame culture.'"[29] Technological advances in engraving and printing techniques intensified what McPherson refers to as "illusions of intimacy" by making mass produced images more prevalent in nineteenth-century homes. Authors became recognizable faces (not just names) as portraits were included as frontispieces to books, giving writers a new, public visibility within an emerging professional class with recognition surpassing the ruling elites.[30]

Celebrity faces also became recognizable through the work of professional painters, illustrators, and other visual artists who found their place within these growing networks of power and prestige—both as practitioners and participants. Visual artists built careers through commissioned portraits and illustrations, which in turn boosted celebrity culture. Public exhibitions and art galleries were filled with portraits of historical figures and political figures alongside contemporary celebrities, adapting the poses, costumes, and iconography of mythological, biblical, and literary characters and scenes—sometimes conflating all into a single painting. By the late eighteenth century, artists might themselves become famous, as did Sir Joshua Reynolds, whose own cult of celebrity came from a carefully crafted balance of critical acclaim and commercial success.[31] With a standard sitting fee from 150 to 1,000 guineas, Reynolds's subjects included writers, actors, and socialites, often posed in costume as allegorical figures or literary characters. Fred Inglis explains that Reynolds "was well aware . . . of his own power to confer status on the sitters in virtue of his agreeing to paint them," and he "made sure that the writers and actors he painted appeared in his canvasses as figures just as worthy of celebration and

---

28. Mole, *Byron's Romantic Celebrity* (2007), 81.
29. McPherson, *Art and Celebrity in the Age of Reynolds and Siddons* (2017), 8.
30. Kooistra, *Poetry, Pictures, and Popular Publishing* (2011); Elliott, *Portraiture and British Gothic Fiction* (2013).
31. Postle, *Joshua Reynolds* (2005), 17, 35.

public recognition as the *grands seigneurs* and their wives who owned and ran England and Scotland."[32]

This work was simultaneously political, critical, and artistic, and it included multiple levels of adaptation and interpretation. Reynolds brought the "grand style" of history painting to contemporary portraits, a form of adaptation that favored interpretive idealism over realism. The style's influence extended very directly to the performing arts and the theater industry. Stage actors were regularly depicted in the roles for which they were famous, or as allegorical embodiments of arts and culture, and these paintings could themselves inspire new imitations. For example, the famous Shakespearean actress Sarah Siddons was repeatedly painted and sketched in costume. Reynolds's allegorical painting *Mrs. Siddons as the Tragic Muse* (1784), a larger-than-life oil painting, was staged as a *tableau vivant* (living picture) at Drury Lane the following season starring Siddons as herself.[33]

In the nineteenth-century arts and culture industries, writers, artists, and actors became cultural icons through press coverage in paintings and illustration, in performance, and in the various offshoots and souvenirs available in an emerging commodity culture. Actors became famous for their starring roles, drawing equally or more so from adaptations than from "original dramas." Typecasting ensued, anticipating the ways that the earliest Hollywood stars of the twentieth century, such as Boris Karloff and Bela Lugosi, became synonymous with the nineteenth-century characters they portrayed on film. Similarly, the famous actor Thomas Potter Cooke had his breakthrough performance as Lord Ruthven in James Robinson Planché's *The Vampire; or, The Bride of the Isles* (1820), a melodrama based on both John Polidori's short novella *The Vampyre* (1819) and its French melodramatic adaptation by Charles Nodier's *Le Vampire* (1820).[34] Cooke would go on to log the most appearances as Frankenstein's Creature, credited with at least 365 performances by mid-century (see images in chapter 1), a conservative estimate considering how often Cooke performed the role in London, Paris, and other cities.[35] Aside from these notable roles, Cooke's celebrity coalesced around the figure of the British tar, and he played a long line of leading roles featuring sailors during the nautical melodrama craze of the 1820s, his height and athleticism making him a favorite choice for these starring roles.

---

32. Inglis, *A Short History of Celebrity* (2010), 55–56.
33. Asleson, *A Passion for Performance* (1999); McPherson, "Picturing Tragedy" (2000).
34. Polidori's novella was an extension of Byron's *Fragment of a Novel*, abandoned by Byron after it was unintentionally printed with the first edition of *Mazeppa* (1819).
35. Estimate from *The Illustrated London News* (October 15, 1853); Nichols, "The Acting of Thomas Potter Cooke" (1977).

Similar typecasting marked the career of Richard John Smith, known professionally as O. Smith, a name he earned for his 1807 performance in John Fawcett's *Obi; or, Three-Finger'd Jack* (1800), which adapted the story of the infamous Jamaican rebel-bandit-turned-folk hero but turned it into a colonialist pantomime.[36] Like Cooke, Smith specialized in sensational and action-driven roles. He was the second-most famous Frankenstein's Creature of the 1820s, a role he played for the first time in Henry Milner's *The Man and The Monster* (1826) while Cooke was starring in a different *Frankenstein* adaptation in Paris. At the end of his career, Smith's acting résumé boasted more than forty performances as Don Quixote in Fitzball's *Don Quixotte!* (1833), with just as many appearances the previous year in a dramatization of Washington Irving's "Rip Van Winkle" performed at the Adelphi Theatre.[37] Over the course of twenty-five years at the Adelphi (where he became a permanent fixture in 1829), Smith appeared in adaptations of at least eight Dickens novels.[38] He starred in at least three different adaptations of *Frankenstein* in the 1820s (in addition to his performance as Zamiel in *Frankenstein; or, The Model Man* in 1849). He played Claude Frollo in adaptations of Hugo's *Notre-Dame* during the 1830s. During the 1852–53 season, he appeared eighty-two times as Uncle Tom in *Slave Life* at the Adelphi. Smith's career consisted primarily of physical roles such as supernatural beings and rogue outlaws, with surviving portraits protraying him in popular action poses. Such poses were frequently used in souvenir portraits of popular actors sold at performances as well as in print shops and book stores, available for purchase at different prices in a range of sizes as well as in color or black and white. The image of Smith included here (see figure 2.2) is part of a series of theatrical portraits published by William West, who specialized in theatrical portraits and toy theaters (see also chapter 5).

Stage celebrities were produced by a mixture of sensationalism and adaptation, particularly in pantomime and the gothic tradition, the latter continuing through the film era's popular monster movies. One of the most well-documented nineteenth-century examples is the early adaptation history of Robert Louis Stevenson's *The Strange Case of Dr. Jekyll and Mr. Hyde* (1886) first staged in Boston within months of the novella's publication. Upon reading Stevenson's novella, the American actor Richard Mansfield wrote his friend Thomas Russell Sullivan, asking him to dramatize the story. With

---

36. Szwydky, "Rewriting the History of Black Resistance" (2011).

37. Fitzball's *Don Quixotte! Knight of the Woeful Countenance and the Humours of Sancho Panza* premiered at the Adelphi on January 7, 1833. William B. Bernard's *Rip Van Winkle* was first performed on October 1, 1832.

38. Nelson, Cross, and Donohue, *The Adelphi Theatre Project 1806–1900* (1988–2016).

FIGURE 2.2. O. Smith as Robert Baptiste in *Raymond & Agnes*, adapted from Matthew Lewis's novel *The Monk* (1827). Image Courtesy of The Billy Rose Theatre Division, The New York Public Library Digital Collections.

Stevenson's endorsement, the duo developed a play featuring Mansfield in the dual-lead role. Mansfield awed audiences with his ability to perform the Jekyll-Hyde transformation on stage using only bodily contortions and theatrical lighting. The breathtaking spectacle catapulted Mansfield to fame, and double-exposure photographs overlaying the two characters were used in promotional images and sold as souvenirs (see figures 2.3 and 2.4). Mansfield spent the following season at London's Lyceum Theatre in the company of

FIGURE 2.3. Richard Mansfield as Dr. Jekyll and Mr. Hyde (1888). Image courtesy of The Newberry Library, Chicago.

FIGURE 2.4. "December: Jekyll and Hyde," The Richard Mansfield Calendar for 1900 (1899). Public Domain. Digital image courtesy of The British Library.

the great late nineteenth-century actors Henry Irving, Ellen Terry, and Sarah Bernhardt, where his performances as Jekyll and Hyde were so chilling that they prompted gossip connecting him with the Whitechapel Murders (of "Jack the Ripper" infamy) occurring in London at that time. Mansfield would go on to play notable roles such as King Henry III and Shylock in Victorian adaptations of Shakespeare's plays. In 1892, he appeared as the Reverend Arthur Dimmesdale (a character he portrayed until the end of his career) in an adaptation of Nathaniel Hawthorne's *The Scarlet Letter.* He performed all of these roles while touring England and the United States through March 1907, stretching his Jekyll/Hyde fame across twenty years.[39] The souvenir calendar for the year 1900 illustrates how much these performances collapsed actor and character, as it features facsimile reproductions of Mansfield's handwritten notes to fans: "A Merry Christmas! Work never killed anybody but a fool!" plus lines from the play: "I have betrayed the balance of my soul, the evil power within me has the master, it is Hyde now that controls Jekyll—not Jekyll Hyde" (Act 4).

Despite the ephemerality of the stage, celebrity casting in adaptations could have long-term impact on the cultural history of a story. Adapters made artistic decisions based on practical needs, including creating characters for celebrity actors with primary associations at a theater (a practice dating back at least as far as Shakespeare's day).[40] This is precisely how the hunchbacked lab assistant entered the cultural history of *Frankenstein.* The character was introduced in Peake's *Presumption,* with the role of Fritz written specifically for the resident comedian Robert Keeley, one of the theater's featured performers.[41] The comic character of Fritz would morph throughout the ages, finding his way into James Whale's iconic film *Frankenstein* (1931) and eventually being replaced by Ygor/Igor in *Son of Frankenstein* (1939) and *Young Frankenstein* (1974). A similar change was introduced into the Jekyll/Hyde culture-text when Sullivan inserted a love interest for Jekyll into his 1887 script; the character of Agnes Carew became a near-permanent fixture in

---

39. Wilstach, *Richard Mansfield* (1909); Winter, *Life and Art of Richard Mansfield* (1910); Rose, *Jekyll and Hyde Adapted* (1996); and Danahay and Chisholm, *Jekyll and Hyde Dramatized* (2004).

40. Roy, *Plays by James Robinson Planché* (1986), 23.

41. From 1844–47, Keeley comanaged the Lyceum with his actress-wife Mary Ann Goward, where they regularly appeared in adaptations, especially of Dickens. Also known as a female impersonator, Keeley appeared in several cross-dressing roles, such as the nurse Mrs. Champ in *Martin Chuzzlewit.* The Keeleys performed together or individually in adaptations of the following books: Bulwer-Lytton's *The Last Days of Pompeii,* Dickens's *Nicholas Nickleby,* Harrison Ainsworth's *Jack Sheppard,* and Stowe's *Uncle Tom's Cabin,* alongside several Shakespeare adaptations. See Goodman, *The Keeleys On Stage and At Home* (1895).

later adaptations (albeit sometimes under a different name). Produced in 1920, 1932, and 1941, the first three major film adaptations of *Dr. Jekyll and Mr. Hyde* include variations on this new character, while more contemporary adaptations significantly add and expand roles for women in a story whose original form focused exclusively on male characters.

Adapting and reimagining familiar characters helped performers establish their credentials, not on an assumed "fidelity" to a role but instead based on their unique takes on characters. This point needs underscoring because it destabilizes the dominant perspective of literary reception history, shifting it from an author- or literature-focused model to one that spotlights the theater industry and its particular role in cultural history. Actors—not writers—became the headliners and main attractions, updating older roles and adapting them to suit their own needs and abilities.[42] To put this in perspective: the history of Shakespeare on the eighteenth- and nineteenth-century stage also doubles as a guide to the period's theater celebrities. Edmund Kean, William Macready, Ira Aldridge, Irving, and Mansfield—each celebrity had their share of signature Shakespearean roles.

These men shared the spotlight with tragic actresses who shaped their respective generations' gendered experience of Shakespeare's heroines, as Siddons, Kemble, and Ellen Terry reconceptualized these characters, gradually made them iconic, and pushed the boundaries of possibility when an old text met a new social context. For example, Terry updated the role of Ophelia, altering her costume to feature form-fitting, Victorian fashions (see figure 2.5). The French actress/theater manager/painter/sculptor Sarah Bernhardt broke new artistic ground as Ophelia's on-stage corpse when previous representations had only shown a casket to represent the character's death. Bernhardt played the male title role of *Hamlet* in both an 1899 stage production and a silent film produced in 1900 (see figure 2.6). Bernhardt's legendary, gender-bending performance (itself recently adapted for the stage in the 2018 play *Bernhardt/Hamlet,* written by Theresa Rebeck and starring Janet McTeer) connected her to several women in breeches roles who starred as Hamlet, a lineage started by Siddons more than a century earlier. Such identity-swapping techniques in adaptation continue to influence and challenge the creators and consumers of remakes and reboots today, especially regarding representational issues in media more broadly.[43]

---

42. Stephens, *The Profession of the Playwright* (1992), xiii.

43. Woo, "Sarah Siddons's Performances as Hamlet" (2007); Gold and Fizdale, *The Divine Sarah* (1992).

FIGURE 2.5. Ellen Terry as Ophelia (1878). Image © National Portrait Gallery, London.

FIGURE 2.6. Sarah Bernhardt as Hamlet (1899). Public Domain. Image courtesy of The Library of Congress Prints and Photographs Division Washington, DC.

"LITERARY GENTLEMEN" IN THE NINETEENTH-CENTURY ADAPTATION INDUSTRY

The theater industry provided lifelong careers, and many actors eventually transitioned into playwriting and theatrical management. George Colman (the Elder), for instance, began his career as a dramatist; his second play, *The Jealous Wife* (1761), partly founded on Henry Fielding's *Tom Jones* (1749), established his credibility as a playwright. He would go on to write other adaptations and original plays and then turn to theater management. After managing Covent Garden for seven years and selling his shares in 1774, he bought the Haymarket Theatre—one of the only venues to compete with the major playhouses. His son, George Colman (the Younger), would also pursue a theater career that began with writing adaptations at the Haymarket, notably

The Iron Chest (1796, based on Godwin's *Things as They Are*). He eventually inherited the theater from his father in 1794 and ran it until its sale in 1820. In 1824, the younger Colman became Examiner of Plays—the main licensor and censor under the Lord Chamberlain's office—a position he held until his death in 1836.

During Colman's tenure as Examiner of Plays, the most prominent literary celebrity on London stages was Walter Scott. Daniel Terry, actor-turned-dramatist-turned-theater-manager and close friend of Scott, regularly worked with the novelist on "authorized" stage adaptations, each of which became a sensational hit and a goldmine for the theater. Scott was fully on board, referring to Terry's dramatizations as "the art of *Terry-fying*" in his memoirs.[44] In a testament to the popularity of Terry's plays, spies from competing theaters would attend productions to get the latest scoop and audience reactions, and imitations would spring up within days, with theaters competing to produce the most popular and profitable versions of *Rob Roy* (1817), *Ivanhoe* (1820), and *The Pirate* (1822).[45] To date, Terry is best remembered for his connections with Scott and his professional expertise in adaptation. Beyond being Scott's go-to adapter, the relationship between the two was reciprocal. As Michael Gamer notes, when Scott wished to try his hand at popular theater without risking his reputation as an established novelist, he asked Terry to claim authorship for a gothic melodrama, *The Doom of Devorgoil* (1818), which Scott would eventually publish under his own name in 1830. These professional collaborations played a large role in the shaping of the gothic mode and the eventual canonization of many Romantic-period writers.[46]

In the 1820s, the man known as "the Great Unknown" proved to be one of the safest and most profitable theatrical investments across Europe and even in the United States, as Scott's historical romances broke sales records in bookstores, and theaters scrambled to compete for ticket sales by advertising "innovative" and "original" adaptations, with theater managers regularly commissioning adaptations from different writers. Philip Bolton has identified more than 4,800 distinct stage, radio, film, and television adaptations of Scott's work produced since 1810. Most of these are varied nineteenth-century theatrical entertainments, with roughly two-thirds concentrated on the following titles: *Guy Mannering, Rob Roy, Heart of Mid-Lothian, Bride of Lammermoor, Ivanhoe,* and *The Lady of the Lake*.[47] Like Byron, Scott's works were turned into

---

44. Lockhart, *Memoirs of the Life of Sir Walter Scott* (1837), 2:204.
45. Rigney, *The Afterlives of Walter Scott* (2012).
46. Gamer, *Romanticism and the Gothic* (2000); Scott, *The Doom of Devorgoil* (1830).
47. Bolton, *Scott Dramatized* (1992), 342.

operas, and this constituted a significant portion of the best-selling novelist's reception in England, Scotland, and throughout Europe.[48]

Professional and social networks extended in many directions, and much theatrical output depended on established relations or chance meetings between professionals. One of Terry's first managerial decisions at the Adelphi Theatre was to purchase Edward Fitzball's adaptation of James Fenimore Cooper's *The Pilot* (1824). At the time, Fitzball was an emerging dramatist, and he approached this project reluctantly on the suggestion of T. P. Cooke (recently of *Frankenstein* fame), who wanted to play a sailor in a nautical drama and thought Cooper's novel would make for a solid, dramatic story. As Fitzball explains in his memoirs, the playwright didn't even like Cooper's novel on his first reading, but agreed to the adaptation based on Cooke's assurance that it would make them money. The major obstacle in Cooper's American novel—the unfavorable portrayal of British sailors—was quickly fixed by swapping the characters' nationalities. Starring Terry and Cooke in the lead roles, Fitzball's adaptation premiered on October 31, 1825, and was the season's greatest hit, "being played to crowded houses and having a run of more than one hundred nights," a number rarely reached in a single season's performance. Fitzball estimates that the play brought in upwards of £7,000 for the Adelphi that season.[49] His adaptation of *The Pilot* continued to be staged for the next three seasons at the Adelphi and was revived again in 1831, 1839, and 1856. *The Pilot*'s success eclipsed Fitzball's earlier hit adaptation at the Adelphi, a melodrama based on Scott's *Waverly* staged in 1823, which had solidified Fitzball's career. Cooke also benefited from the exposure, becoming famous for his nautical roles.

Most novelists, dramatists, actors, and other professionals saw stage adaptation as a mutually beneficial practice throughout the Romantic period. By the end of the 1830s, however, this relationship would become more contentious. Although adaptations played a large part in the rise of celebrity culture, they also caused major tensions between authors and their adapters—especially around payment and copyright laws, as Dickens and other writers became increasingly interested in controlling the circulation of their works, fighting for royalties and other authorial rights to works derived from their publications.

This tension notwithstanding, stage adaptations impacted Dickens's literary career immediately. By the late 1830s, serial publication was on the rise, and Dickens pioneered the new format not only artistically but also commercially through constant negotiation with publishers. But this new profitable

---

48. Pittock, *The Reception of Sir Walter Scott in Europe* (2007).

49. Fitzball, *Thirty-five Years of a Dramatic Author's Life* (1859), 2:162; Fitzball credits *The Pilot* to Cooke in 1:136–38.

form of publishing came with unanticipated challenges: his novels-in-progress were adapted for the stage while they were still in serialization, undercutting any idea that the "greatness" of these texts served as the primary reason behind decisions to adapt them. William Rede's *The Peregrinations of Pickwick; or, Boz-i-a-na The Pickwick Papers* was first staged at the Adelphi on April 2, 1837, while Dickens's first novel was only one-third completed.[50] Likewise, Dickens's second novel, *Oliver Twist*, began its theatrical "afterlife" six months before its serialization was complete. Dickens paid close attention to stage versions of his novels and was often in attendance at the theater. Sue Zemka suggests that "Dickens might have been inspired to kill Nancy by the lackluster performances of *Twist*, as there were two produced in London playhouses before November 1838, and both failed for want of a stirring climax."[51] The stage adaptation, thus inspired a climactic scene in the novel and even became a highlight of Dickens's dramatic readings, causing people in the audience to gasp and even faint as the aging author energetically described the violent murder, adapted for this public storytelling platform.

Despite these positive effects on his career, Dickens had an antagonistic relationship with his earliest adapters, and he grew increasingly frustrated when adaptations of his third novel began appearing in November 1838, halfway through the novel's serialization. Dickens attended the production of Edward Stirling's farce *Nicholas Nickleby; or, Doings at Do-the-Boys Hall* (1838) at the Adelphi, and he immediately started planning how to strike back. In the May 1839 installment of *Nicholas Nickleby*, Dickens included a critical portrait of a "literary gentleman who had dramatized in his time two hundred and forty-seven novels as fast as they had come out—some of them faster than they had come out—and who *was* a literary gentleman in consequence." The dialogue between Nicholas and the literary gentleman turns combative, summing up the tensions building between authors and adapters in the industrial age's network of literary celebrity and cultural production:

> "When I dramatise a book, sir," said the literary gentleman, "*that's* fame. For its author."
>
> ". . . you take the uncompleted books of living authors, fresh from their hands, wet from the press, cut, hack, and carve them to the powers and capacities of your actors, and the capability of your theatres, finish unfinished works, hastily and crudely vamp up ideas not yet worked out by their original projector, but which have doubtless cost him many thoughtful days

---

50. Koger, "Calendar for 1836–1837" (2012).
51. Zemka, "The Death of Nancy 'Sikes'" (2010), 29.

and sleepless nights; by a comparison of incidents and dialogue, down to the very last word he may have written a fortnight before, do your utmost to anticipate his plot—all this without his permission, and against his will; and then, to crown the whole proceeding, publish in some mean pamphlet, an unmeaning farrago of garbled extracts from his work, to which you put your name as author, with the honourable distinction annexed, of having perpetrated a hundred other outrages of the same description. Now, show me the distinction between such pilfering as this, and picking a man's pocket in the street."

"'Men must live, sir,' said the literary gentleman, shrugging his shoulders."[52]

The confrontation shows that Dickens's major objection to the practice of dramatization is financially driven, as he compares the adapter to a common pickpocket. Dickens understood novel writing and stage adaptation as business practice more so than an abstract, aesthetic act, and he worked tirelessly to situate himself within the period's growing professional networks (see chapter 4).[53] The message coming from the theater industry was similar given the sheer number of adaptations produced, emphasizing quantity and novelty. By 1840, London theaters had staged sixty distinct plays based on Dickens's first three novels, making theater professionals money while turning Dickens into a cultural icon.[54]

For Dickens, the speed of adaptation was a double-edged sword. Dramatists were creating scenes and climatic endings that had little to do with authorial intent, but they were also simultaneously promoting his works through adaptation and extension. Being a lifetime patron of the theater contributed to his respect for the theater's power to increase visibility, drive sales, and secure recognition.[55] However, he wanted to be involved, credited, and—most importantly—paid for these works. As his career developed, Dickens was able to exert more influence over how his stories were adapted, and he even guided the dramatist Andrew Halliday (who had worked as a staff writer for Dickens's periodical *All the Year Round*) on an adaptation of *David Copperfield* staged in 1869 and other plays.[56] Yet none of this was likely possible without the proliferation of adaptations that catapulted Dickens to fame in the late 1830s. Although Dickens grew to admire some adaptations later in his career, the

---

52. Dickens, *Nicholas Nickleby* (2003), ch. 48, 597–98.
53. John, *Dickens and Mass Culture* (2010), 54–55.
54. Bolton, *Dickens Dramatized* (1987).
55. Glavin, *After Dickens* (1999).
56. Laird, *The Art of Adapting Victorian Literature* (2016), 101.

disdainful caricature he paints in *Nicholas Nickleby* remains a model for how adapters (historical and contemporary) are often seen by literary scholars: as second-rate hacks, plagiarists, and thieves.

Yet such negative portrayals fail to account for the productive impact that professional dramatists and artists contribute to literary reception and cultural history. Dickens may have targeted dramatist William T. Moncrieff (or Edward Stirling) as his "literary gentleman," but most professional dramatists worked in the same way, adding to the network of adaptations. A brief roster of playwrights from the 1820s through the 1870s includes James Robinson Planché, Edward Fitzball, George Dibdin Pitt, Dion Boucicault, and Andrew Halliday—all wrote hundreds of plays and were best known for their adaptations. Like proto-film auteurs, they were artists in their own right as well as important cultural mediators.[57] Adapters kept texts in circulation beyond their primary audience and initial print runs, which catapulted nineteenth-century writers into literary celebrity. Knowing the nuances of the profession, adapters made significant artistic and economic contributions to theatrical life, cultural production, and literary history. As Larry Stephen Clifton explains, "The Victorian theatre prospered because, as in Shakespeare's day, theatre and drama were left to professionals in the field. The shoddy and inept writer quickly faded through commercial pressure. The hack, for all of his hurry and insecurities, kept the theatre solvent, stressing that the theatre was as much an economic concern as it was an artistic one."[58] Despite how Dickens saw them, these dramatists belonged more to the professional ranks of novelists, journalists, and illustrators than they did pickpockets. However, instead of being remembered as artists who explored and extended a story's potential into a new form or medium, they have been primarily reduced to footnotes in literary history.

Nineteenth-century adapters saw themselves as positive, active contributors to the arts in general as well as to the individual careers of writers and actors. They saw the practice of adaptation as a reciprocal relationship that primarily benefited poets and novelists. The prolific playwright James Robinson Planché spends considerable time defending adaptation in his 1872 memoirs, describing his experience dramatizing Thomas Love Peacock's novel *Maid Marian* (1822) into *Maid Marian; or, The Huntress of Arlingford*, which premiered at Covent Garden on December 3, 1822.[59] According to Planché, the only objection at the time came from Peacock's "short-sighted publisher, who could not perceive how greatly the value of his property would be increased

---

57. Leitch, "The Adapter as Auteur" (2005).
58. Clifton, *The Terrible Fitzball* (1993), 12.
59. Planché, *Maid Marian* (1822).

till the gold began to jingle in his own pocket—some of it, I trust, finding its way into that of the amiable author."[60] The success of this adaptation opened the floodgates for more of the same, Planché explains:

> After the success of "Maid Marian," I had piles of novels sent me, not only by authors, but by their publishers, requesting my acceptance of them for that purpose. They knew it was the finest advertisement for a book in the world; and I have been even offered money by some to obtain for them that advantage. The author was especially on the safe side; for if the adaptation was good, and the piece successful, he had the chief glory, and a brisk sale for his book; while if it failed, the dramatist was the sufferer in purse as well as reputation.

According to Planché, novelists need dramatists to fully realize their story's potential: "The great mass of writers of fiction are not dramatists, and if they desire, as to my knowledge they nearly all do, to see their works transferred to the stage, they must be indebted to the playwrights." Planché explicitly mentions the friendship and partnership between Scott and Terry, presenting it as an ideal professional and artistic relationship in which "the talent of the novelist is displayed in elaboration; that of the dramatist is condensation." Planché points out that "no one can deny that it has been the practice of the greatest dramatists in every age and every country to found their plays upon the popular tales of their own or of former times" and "question[s] if any author felt otherwise than flattered by [it]." Growing commercialization pulled writers and adapters apart, casting them as competitors more than complementary agents in storytelling. Reflecting on these tensions at the end of his own career, Planché maintains that the "complaint of injury" to novelists was overexaggerated.[61]

Indeed, history shows that novelists saw their celebrity increase exponentially more through adaptation than did the fame of the dramatists adapting the work. Playwrights also made much less money and had to keep a steady output of new works to make a decent living. Legitimate dramas such as tragedies and traditional comedies could earn a writer up to a £500 upfront payment at the turn of the nineteenth century, and some playwrights even managed to negotiate percentages of ticket sales. However, these payments were far from the norm and only for established dramatists. Melodramas, farces, pantomimes, and other illegitimate, popular forms made up the vast

---

60. Planché, *Recollections and Reflections* (1872), 47–50.
61. All excerpts in this paragraph are from Planché, *Recollections and Reflections* (1872), 47–50.

majority of any theater's repertoire and rarely fetched more than a £50 standard payment, and sometimes as low as £5, with prices fluctuating over the century as economic conditions changed.[62] Professional playwrights had to produce a lot, and the most prolific dramatists (especially those employed as "stock authors" or "house dramatists") might produce 150–250 plays over the course of their careers. In order to produce this many plays, all dramatists resorted to liberal adaptation from various sources.

In addition to working with the written content of plays, theater professionals—whether dramatists, actors, choreographers, scene painters, or managers—also needed to be skilled in several areas of theatrical production, including the financial and material limitations of particular theaters. When one of Fitzball's early plays was rejected by Terry, Cooke assured him that the manager didn't hate his work and that he should simply try writing a piece better suited for the physical dimensions of the Adelphi's smaller stage, and then recommended adapting *The Pilot* instead.[63] In addition to providing scripts, Fitzball found himself making regular recommendations about scenery and special effects. One of his most successful pieces, an adaptation of the legend of *The Flying Dutchman; or, The Phantom Ship* (which premiered at the Adelphi in 1826), might not have been produced if not for the playwright's technological ingenuity. When Terry complained that timber to construct the ship would be an expensive £200, Fitzball proposed that they project the ship with "magic-lantern" technology at a small fraction of the cost and even recommended a technical expert to create the effect. The piece became one of Fitzball's most frequently staged plays, with the dramatist claiming more than (a rather unheard of) 10,000 performances in his memoirs.[64] Fitzball's popular adaptation of the legend even sparked new versions of the story in print and performance, including the opera *Der fliegende Holländer* by Richard Wagner in 1843.[65]

Specializing in popular forms (as did many of his contemporaries), Fitzball was dubbed "The Terrible Fitzball" for his penchant for gothic, burlesque, adventure, and true-crime melodramas. His formula was straightforward: write spectacle-driven pieces that update existing stories for new audiences, while recycling or repurposing scenery, costumes, and props to keep costs down for the house. Fitzball's repertoire drew heavily on adaptation, including

---

62. Stephens, *The Profession of the Playwright* (1992).
63. Fitzball, *Thirty-Five Years of a Dramatic Author's Life* (1859), 1:137–38.
64. Fitzball, *Thirty-Five Years of a Dramatic Author's Life* (1859), 2:13–15.
65. For a description of the technology used to create the effect in Fitzball's play and Wagner's opera, see Cruz, "The Flying Dutchman, English Spectacle and the Remediation of Grand Opera" (2017).

novels, poems, news stories (especially sensational crimes), historical retellings, international myths, or translations of foreign plays and operas. One of his earliest plays was *Giraldi; or, The Ruffian of Prague* (1820), an adaptation of Amelia Opie's story "The Ruffian Boy" (1818) at the Theatre Royal Norwich. Opie admired the play and the two developed a friendship, with Opie serving as a professional mentor to the young playwright.[66] Throughout the 1820s, Fitzball would go on to adapt Robert Southey's *Thalaba the Destroyer*, as well as several of Scott's works, including *Marmion*, *Waverly*, *The Fortunes of Nigel*, and *Peveril of the Peak*. In 1855, he provided the libretto for a new version of the operatic ballet *Raymond and Agnes*, based on one of the many subplots in Matthew Lewis's gothic novel *The Monk*, which by this time had a fifty-year history on the stage.

Fitzball's adaptations crossed national boundaries, bringing to the London stage a burletta based on Cervantes's *Don Quixote*, as well as two different melodramas founded on Hugo's *Notre Dame de Paris* (premiering in 1834 and 1836). During a three-month span in 1852, he also wrote three distinct versions of Stowe's *Uncle Tom's Cabin* during a period of intense demand. Fitzball's memoirs provide a snapshot from a productive midpoint in his career:

> The publication of "Uncle Tom's Cabin" . . . set all of the managers mad to produce it on the stage. . . . I was engaged by three managers to write three distinct pieces, which I did to the best of my abilities: indeed, it did not require any remarkable ability, as it was only to select scenes and join them together. My pieces were produced: one at the Olympic . . . one at the Eagle . . . and one at the Theatre Royal Drury Lane. The crowd to witness the representation . . . at the latter house was so immense, that many accidents occurred from the pressure outside. In the theatre, not a word was heard, from those who could not obtain seats stamping . . . and kicking up the most appalling noises in the gallery. Mr. James of the Queen's Theatre . . . after the run of the Drury Lane "Uncle Tom's Cabin," although he had already played a piece on the same subject, did me the honor to revive mine at his theatre with the greatest care and attention; and being a first-rate artist . . . painted some beautiful scenery himself, especially the Sea of Ice, which contributed immensely to the run of this piece.[67]

---

66. Opie's "The Ruffian Boy" was published in 1818 as part of the collection *New Tales*. Opie's story was also adapted for the stage in 1820 by Thomas Dibdin, discussed in *The Reminiscences of Thomas Dibdin* (1837).

67. Fitzball, *Thirty-Five Years of a Dramatic Author's Life* (1859), 2:261–62.

This brief anecdote illustrates the range of Fitzball's reach. At different points, Fitzball was employed as house dramatist; when he wasn't tied to one manager, he operated as a free agent, and his plays could be seen at different theaters both in and outside of London. Pieces were revived at different theaters—new scenery, props, costumes, and other spectacular embellishments extended the theatrical life of any play, while also making money for managers and employing actors, dancers, musicians, painters, and skilled tradesmen.

During a fifty-six-year career spanning 1817 through 1873, Fitzball wrote more than 175 theatrical pieces for major and minor venues. He was most associated with the Surrey, the Adelphi, and the Coburg—and the sensational, spectacle-driven fare for which they were known. Fitzball wrote nearly all genres: comedy, tragedy, opera, burletta, ballet, and of course melodrama in all of its incarnations. The work was exhausting at times, and Fitzball describes being "wearied and worn out" by "continued mental exertions" and being "somewhat disheartened by, if not disgusted with, the selfishness of managers, who were never satisfied with *me,* unless I brought them a *fortune.*"[68] The picture he paints with characteristic melodramatic flair conjures professional dramatists under constant pressure to produce financial blockbusters over critical acclaim.

Adding to this stress, professional dramatists were subject to scathing reviews in the periodicals, sometimes quite personal, as Fitzball regularly experienced firsthand. One reviewer unimpressed with an Adelphi production of Fitzball's *Esmeralda; or, The Deformed of Notre Dame* (1834) writes: "All the peculiarities [of] the leading characters of Victor Hugo . . . [Fitzball has] covered with the melodramatic mantle . . . generalized into a lewd monk and a tenderhearted hunchback; and Esmeralda . . . is converted into a mere Gipsy dancing-girl."[69] Despite this criticism, the adaptation was commercially successful. Fitzball's simplification of the characters and plot of a long novel such as *Notre-Dame* followed the necessary conventions of the stage. He stuck fairly close to this style two years later when he adapted Hugo's story again as *Quasimodo; or, The Gipsey Girl of Notre Dame* (1836) for Covent Garden. Another reviewer calls the drama "but a feeble shadow" of Hugo's novel, taking personal shots at Fitzball's skill as a dramatist:

> Indeed, he who could condense the interesting scenes which are contained in Victor Hugo's volumes, and bring them forward prominently in a dramatic form, must possess powers infinitely beyond those which have fallen

---

68. Fitzball, *Thirty-Five Years of a Dramatic Author's Life* (1859), 2:1.
69. "Adelphi Theatre," *Times,* November 19, 1834: 3.

to the lot of Mr. Fitzball, the concoctor of the new piece. . . . Mr. Fitzball was evidently unable to grapple effectively with the abundance of materials which were placed at his disposal; and instead of availing himself of them to the most ample extent, he frequently fell back upon his own resources, which are of a very meager description.[70]

These critiques of melodrama are hardly representative of theatrical tastes of theatergoers at large. Tickets continued to sell and plays in the same style continued to be produced, in part because of the excellent scenery and production value praised in these otherwise negative reviews. More so than their colleagues who wrote for print publication, professional dramatists permanently straddled the worlds of artistic and commercial production. They admired Shakespearean drama and many aspired to produce philosophical dramatic works, but they also understood the necessity of filling the theater.

Fitzball's contributions (and shortfalls) cannot be separated from the demands of a growing mass culture and the increasing professionalization of the playwright; still, there was more at stake than commercial demands. Popular adaptations had democratic and educational dimensions. Melodrama, in particular, was birthed by the Revolution in France, and by the time it made its way to England at the turn of the nineteenth century, there was no denying its appeal to the masses. Peter Brooks highlights the populism of the genre: "While its social implications may be variously revolutionary or conservative, [melodrama] is in all cases radically democratic, striving to make its representations clear and legible to everyone."[71] In spite of censorship and other political restrictions, Fitzball and other theater professionals were engaged in the social turn of art and culture in the Revolutionary Age.

The period's prolific dramatists demonstrated a deep love of literature, spending considerable time immersed in books old and new, searching for stories well-suited for stage representation. Writing for the stage not only involved navigating a strict regulatory system and sensitive political contexts but also required adapters to be up-to-date on their knowledge of classics as well as contemporary works. Although they were rarely described as learned individuals, nineteenth-century "literary gentlemen" had to be extremely well-read in order to meet production demands, and their learning was structurally interdisciplinary. In England, Planché was an elected fellow of the Society of Antiquarians and critically recognized as a scholar. He also spearheaded trends in historical costuming, including emphasizing period-specific dress

---

70. "Covent-Garden Theatre," *Times*, February 3, 1836: 5.
71. Brooks, *The Melodramatic Imagination* (1976), 15.

in plays.[72] In France, the prolific René-Charles Guilbert de Pixerécourt had a very similar reputation.[73] Of Pixerécourt, Maurice Disher writes:

> Some critics were surprised that the people's playwright should be so ardent a bibliophile—. . . . Having picked a subject, he would consult learned books of ethnology or archæology in order to claim erudite accuracy for everything. . . . Resenting a critical contempt for popular entertainment, he acquired, and aired, vast quantities of historical and geographical facts; these he exploited in scenes of other times and other places, for which he claimed scholarly and unnecessary exactitude.[74]

Pixerécourt and Planché, and dramatists like them, embraced the potential of popular culture as an accessible, educational tool that could promote history, heritage, and literacy. Professional playwrights regularly produced new plays based on Greek mythology, medieval legends, and folk tales, as well as newer fictions, all of which could be adapted into any theatrical genre. Melodrama in particular offered a theatrical form that through "cultural circulation and adaptation" built a "continent-wide network of people, objects, and ideas that enable the rapid spread of a new form of musical theater," especially in cultural centers such as London, Paris, Vienna, and Berlin.[75] Professional dramatists like Planché, Fitzball, and Pixerécourt spent considerable time researching and incorporating new archeological findings or reading travel narratives in order to infuse their melodramas with more "realistic" or "authentic" settings, regional customs, or historically accurate dress.

Even if dramatists could not produce radical or revolutionary interpretations due to stage censorship or other limitations, conservative adaptations made texts and their "original" authors more relevant by increasing the cul-

---

72. Roy, *Plays by James Robinson Planché* (1986).

73. Pixerécourt established his playwriting career with *Victor, ou l'Enfant de la forêt* (1798, *Victor, a Child of the Forest*) and *Cœlina, ou l'Enfant du mystère* (1800, *Celina, or the Child of Mystery*), melodramatic adaptations of popular novels by François Guillame Ducray-Duminil, published in 1796 and 1798. Pixerécourt's *Cœlina* was in turn adapted by Thomas Holcroft as *A Tale of Mystery* (1802), a play credited with importing the genre of melodrama to England. François Guillame Ducray-Duminil was an author of young adult novels. Hoeveler, "The Temple of Morality" (2003).

74. Disher, *Blood and Thunder* (1949), 67. I omit Disher's description of native peoples as "savages" in theatrical productions like *Robinson Crusoe*. Although my research emphasizes the progressive potential at the intersections of adaptation and melodrama in the nineteenth century and today, the nineteenth-century culture industry undoubtedly included systemic racism and cultural imperialism, and Disher's commentary exemplifies the lack of diversity that continues to impact diversity and representation in media and adaptations.

75. Hambridge and Hicks, *The Melodramatic Moment* (2018), 2.

tural capital of these stories. In these ways, professional dramatists influenced the early reception histories of now-canonical figures and paved the way for later adapters to repeat these stories through new remakes. Since minor theater venues targeted working class audiences, these theatrical trends had significant democratic and educational functions. In essence, hacks like Fitzball served as public humanists by promoting cultural literacy and general education among an expanding public. For many theatergoers, adaptations were the only—or at least the primary—point of contact with authors like Byron, Scott, Dickens, and Stowe. Adapters thereby created opportunities for a shared experience of any given "text" that was remediated, repackaged, and resold while cutting across class and national boundaries.

All of the period's professional dramatists discussed in this chapter adapted foreign plays, novels, history, and even the news, as did Thomas Dibdin (the Younger), William Henry Murray, Edward Stirling, John Brougham, Colin Henry Hazlewood, George Dibdin Pitt, Andrew Halliday, Thomas Russell Sullivan, and numerous others. Yet despite their prolific and extensive output and substantial contributions to nineteenth-century theater, literature, and cultural history, very few adapters have full-length studies dedicated to them, even though most published their own memoirs in the nineteenth century.

Even dramatists who weren't considered "hacks" underscore the role that adaptation played in the development and trajectories of their careers. Dion Boucicault stands out as an exemplar actor-dramatist who earned critical acclaim and commercial success for both his original plays and his adaptations, even spearheading a new model of profit sharing during the 1860s. Stephens calls him "the prime example of the dramatist as entrepreneur," who was "intensely aware of the immense power he could exert on managers through his ability to create a desirable commodity." Boucicault acted as not only a playwright but also an attorney and literary agent. Unapologetically negotiating higher compensation for his labor, Boucicault

> reversed the terms of the traditional relationship between manager and author and exerted a profound and lasting, though not immediate influence on the general economic status of the late Victorian playwright.... His negotiating strength with theatre managers helped to turn the theatre from the habitat of the amateur, the hack, and the gentleman-dramatists into [a] lucrative, commercial theatre.[76]

---

76. Stephens, *The Profession of the Playwright* (1992), 53.

Although the theater industry was commercial, few professional dramatists became wealthy from their writing. Whether in the form of flat fees paid upfront, additional payments for purchase of copyright, benefit nights for dramatists, incremental payments based on number of performances, royalties based on ticket sales, or a combination of these payment formats, compensation was determined largely by the dramatist's negotiation ability.

While Dickens complained about getting pickpocketed by the "literary gentleman," he failed to see that these adapters were merely at the very human front line of a large, commercial machine. Professional dramatists served as skilled intermediaries who navigated the complexities of censorship laws, licensing requirements, audience interests, and the emerging market of commercial entertainment. They popularized the works of contemporary writers, transforming the authors and their characters into household names and cultural icons. Instead of characterizing the relationship between novelists and theatrical "hacks" in antagonistic terms, we should reconsider theirs as a productive exchange that extended and expanded the cultural reach of many now-canonical texts. Nineteenth-century adapters played key parts in the cultural life of stories that continue to thrive through further forms of recycling. They occupied unique positions in this ongoing media matrix of adaptations; simultaneously consumers and creators, they contributed to an intricate web of literary reception and cultural history making.

In the nineteenth-century culture industry, multiple media industries converged around adaptation as a sound business practice. The period's networked system of cultural production connected producers and consumers from all directions. Just as hired content creators or fans write for production studios or online communities in the digital age, established and struggling artists adapted stories for consumption across multiple sites of storytelling. The proliferation of adaptations by multiple creators was an early form of participatory culture, an audience-focused practice that Jenkins stresses as crucial to participatory democracy. Indeed, through shared storytelling across forms and media, nineteenth-century art and culture became more accessible to a wider range of audiences, with more people consuming stories through print, performance, and visual culture at an unprecedented rate.

Though structurally different from their twenty-first-century counterparts, nineteenth-century entertainment industries formed complex networks of production and circulation that were central to England's commercial and industrial economies. Authors, dramatists, actors, theater managers, and publishers saw their artistic, professional, and commercial interests converge through the period's own adaptation industry. The eighteenth and nineteenth centuries saw the steady professionalization of all of these players, with the tradition of artistic patronage all but extinct by the turn of the nineteenth century. Art-focused trade unions, writers' guilds, and other professional societies formed alongside other nineteenth-century labor movements, establishing ethical standards, influencing labor practices, and protecting the rights of writers and artists. A growing popular demand for entertainment and leisure turned forms of cultural production, including literature and art, into commercial commodities. And, for the first time, artists found themselves officially in the ranks of the professional class, regularly interacting with publishers, managers, and other professionals to purchase and distribute their work. Negotiation itself became an artistic talent.

Although the networked, industry-based approach I am proposing for the nineteenth-century culture industry has been largely shaped by my understanding of the contemporary media landscape, my approach complements critical models that have grounded British cultural studies for decades. Raymond Williams, for example, argues that at the turn of the nineteenth century "at this very time of political, social and economic change there is a radical change also in the ideas of art, the artist, and of their place in society," at a time when "the production of art was coming to be regarded as one of a number of specialized kinds of production, subject to much of the same conditions of general production," and that these factors are "clearly very closely interrelated . . . as to render a clear division impossible."[77] Artistic production, even in its most individualistic modes, became a more collaborative process across mediums just as society was entering the first phases of more egalitarian models of political engagement and commodity consumption alike. Through their new, emerging status as professionals, artists and writers changed their relationship to their art, to audiences, and to other artists. Artists created a network of cultural production in an economic environment requiring a strong grasp of both artistry and commercialism, as well as a network of well-trained professionals to keep the engine running and all of its moving parts connected.

---

77. Williams, *Culture and Society* (1958), 32.

CHAPTER 3

Visual and Textual Adaptations in Literature and Fine Art Forms

BEYOND ITS IMPACT behind the scenes of theatrical production, industrialization and commercialization transformed the creation and consumption of both high and mass culture. The performing, literary, and visual arts became accessible to a growing audience that was more socially and geographically diverse. Visualization was key in this process. Experiencing the same story with shared iconography across multiple forms and media nurtured widespread consumption of art and culture, intensifying as society became increasingly democratic and participatory during the Romantic period. Adaptations in literature, painting, and illustration crossed traditional boundaries, supporting social mobility for artists, authors, and audiences by providing a shared language that could be experienced and commercialized in various artistic forms. Technological advancements of mass reproduction further facilitated the creation of new cultural capital for artists while also expanding opportunities for creators and consumers alike. These aesthetic and commercial developments simultaneously shaped and mirrored cultural and political contexts by providing mediums through which to channel both progressive positions and conservative reactions to the changing sociopolitical landscape.

Scholars of nineteenth-century painting and illustration stress the importance of understanding the relationship between the period's literary and visual arts. Martin Meisel's foundational work demonstrates how the visual, performing, and literary arts converged as complementary sites of cultural production, where the "shared structures in the representational arts helped constitute not just a common style, but a popular style." Meisel terms the process "realization," connecting the representational arts of literature, drama, and picture where "each form and each work becomes the site of a complex interplay of narrative and picture" and storytelling.[1] As Meisel thoroughly documents, illustration was understood by visual artists in the nineteenth century as carrying "a sense of enrichment and embellishment beyond mere specification; it implied the extensions of one medium or mode of discourse by another, rather than a materialization with a minimum of imaginative intervention."[2] Whether in the mediums of painting or print, illustration was understood as a creative process characterized by critical intervention and interpretation, not a derivative form of mere visual translation.

Meisel's defense of nineteenth-century realizations anticipate similar arguments circulated in contemporary adaptation studies, found especially in the work of Kamilla Elliott and Kate Newell. Elliott illustrates how nineteenth-century book illustration paved the way for silent film adaptations and later cinema, linking contemporary media studies to eighteenth-century theories of poetry and painting. Focusing on the aesthetic and rhetorical connections between these forms of cultural production from the nineteenth century through the present, Elliott's close readings of the dynamic "points of interchange between words and images and other verbal and pictorial forms" reveals a "lively exchange . . . in which categorical differentiations [unravel] and new interdisciplinary dynamics [emerge]" through interart exchanges.[3] More recently, Newell has shown how illustration and ekphrastic traditions converge around the practice of adaptation, especially in contemporary print-based forms that appeal to both fine art critics and mass-culture consumers.[4] In the following two chapters, I extend the work of these scholars to situate adaptation's centrality to transmedia adaptation in the nineteenth century, showing how its groundbreaking experiments in fusing textual and visual forms—particularly through various forms of illustration—continues to influence participatory and immersive storytelling today.

Nineteenth-century creators used many forms of intertextual engagement and adaptation as writing, performing, painting, drawing, and engraving became professional fields that opened social possibilities to writers and artists from merchant or working-class backgrounds. The careers of William Blake, John Keats, and Charles Dickens all reveal substantial indebtedness to

---

1. Meisel, *Realizations* (1983), 4, 3.
2. Meisel, *Realizations* (1983), 30.
3. Elliott, *Rethinking the Novel/Film Debate* (2003), 16.
4. Newell, *Expanding Adaptation Networks* (2017).

adaptation across forms and media. For example, Grant F. Scott suggests that ekphrastic writing served Keats "as a means of access to cultural and class status" that his more affluent contemporaries were likely to have inherited from their social standing. Born to a working-class family who could not afford a classical education, Keats used ekphrasis as a social "means of acquiring status and legitimacy by quoting cultural references."[5] Keats's work prominently features ekphrastic writing as a form of intertextual adaptation based on fine art and literature. Poems such as "On First Looking into Chapman's Homer" (1816), "On Seeing the Elgin Marbles" (1817), and "Ode on a Grecian Urn" (1819) consciously situate the speaker within a history of writers, translators, sculptors, and illustrators, because "ekphrasis is never about mere copying; it is as much recreation as re-creation" of both the subject and the self.[6]

Much of Keats's poetry rewrites myths, legends, and folklore, drawing in particular from well-known sources—both visual and print. His abandoned epic *The Fall of Hyperion: A Dream* (1820) blends Greek mythology with Milton's literary expansion of the Book of Genesis in *Paradise Lost*. His narrative poem *Isabella; or, The Pot of Basil* (1818) was adapted from Giovanni Boccaccio's fourteenth-century text *The Decameron*. His gothic poem *The Eve of St. Agnes* (2019) fuses the medieval legend of the patron saint of virgins with a story of star-crossed lovers reminiscent of *Romeo and Juliet*. The literary ballad "La Belle Dame sans Merci" (1819) takes its title from a fifteenth-century poem by Alan Chartier, with a total disregard for fidelity in plot and a healthy dose of remixing from folk ballads, mythology, and medieval images of chivalry. Through print-based forms of adaptation, Keats wrote his way into literary history while the idea of "history" was developing an entirely new meaning, as the rise of art galleries and public museums provided access to ancient artifacts like the Elgin Marbles and Grecian urns.

Just as Keats borrowed from earlier writers and artists, nineteenth-century painters borrowed from him. Keats's posthumous reception was largely shaped by visual adaptations, particularly appropriate given his strong interest in the visual and performing arts.[7] His own textual adaptations of medieval themes and characters inspired painters and illustrators in the Victorian period, most notably the Pre-Raphaelites, whose "Representations of [Keats's] work are key to our understanding of the Pre-Raphaelite aesthetics and the respective fortunes of its founder members."[8] As Wootton notes, Keats did more than

---

5. Scott, *The Sculpted Word* (1994), 20.
6. Scott, *The Sculpted Word* (1994), 19.
7. Scott, *The Sculpted Word* (1994); Mulrooney, *Romanticism and Theatrical Experience* (2018).
8. Wootton, *Consuming Keats* (2006), 42.

FIGURE 3.1. John William Waterhouse, *La Belle Dame sans Merci* (1893). Public Domain. Wikimedia Commons.

influence the original members of the Pre-Raphaelites and their followers; adaptations helped boost their earnings and success through critical contests and the commercial sales of visual art.

At the same time, Keats's impact was significantly amplified (long beyond his lifetime) because his works were adapted into visual forms. Visual art provides a way to understand how nineteenth-century audiences received and interpreted Keats's poetry. Several painters took up the theme of "La Belle Dame sans Merci"—including Dante Gabriel Rossetti and Elizabeth Siddal—working against the narrative laid out in Keats's poem by portraying the lady as a sympathetic figure instead of a femme fatale. These interpretations were

FIGURE 3.2. Frank Dicksee, *La Belle Dame sans Merci* (1901). Public Domain. Original held at Bristol Museum and Art Gallery.

further adapted in response to social anxieties posed by the New Woman and other movements aimed at women's independence in the later Victorian period. Building on both Keats and the original Pre-Raphaelites, works of John William Waterhouse and Frank Dicksee reimagined the lady as an active seducer (see figures 3.1 and 3.2). Regardless of the interpretation, repetition through adaptation kept the tale relevant and recognizable. Individually and collectively, these artworks contributed to the "La Belle Dame sans Merci" culture-text and the femme fatale archetype as they developed into the next century.[9] Through painting and illustration, "La Belle Dame sans Merci" became Keats's most culturally impactful poem as adapters repeatedly returned to the poem's hauntingly erotic imagery. Similarly, William Holman Hunt's painting situates Keats's Isabella in the pantheon of Pre-Raphaelite heroines using the elaborate, ornamental style and vivid colors characteristic of his peers; on the other hand, the American painter John White Alexander's rendering serves as a striking contrast in its use of simple lines, minimalism, and muted shades used to highlight sensual silhouettes (see figures 3.3 and 3.4). Different paintings of the same story highlight the role of the visual in creating culture-texts. In transmedia storytelling, visual iconogra-

---

9. Scott, "Language Strange" (1999).

FIGURE 3.3. William Holman Hunt, *Isabella & the Pot of Basil* (1868). Public Domain. Original held at Laing Art Gallery, Newcastle upon Tyne, England.

FIGURE 3.4. John White Alexander, *Isabella and the Pot of Basil* (1897). Image © Museum of Fine Arts, Boston.

phy establishes crucial continuity between adaptations, through what Newell calls "hinge moments," while also serving as the most directly transferrable language across cultures and history.[10]

Treating the textual rewrites of ekphrasis, painting, and illustration as early examples of collaborative transmedia storytelling and convergence culture demonstrates the central role that adaptations played in the circulation and reception of old and new stories alike. Such rewrites permeated both high and mass culture in the nineteenth century, from exclusive art galleries to cheap illustrated periodicals.[11] Reframing these visual forms of adaptation connects them at multiple sites of storytelling, each with its own set of influences on cultural production and popular literacy. At these intersections, painting and illustration work alongside textual adaptations and dramatic forms to update stories to meet the needs of modern audiences.

The following chapter traces a network of nineteenth-century textual and visual adaptations that together illustrate an early history of transmedia storytelling tied to multiple visual art–based professions and industries. The rise of literary art galleries and the establishment of public museums in the nineteenth century created physical sites for storytelling as an immersive experience. The rise of illustrations in books and periodicals also influenced new reading practices that were both textually and visually constructed. The careers of English and French artists like William Blake, Eugène Delacroix, and Gustave Doré demonstrate how visual artists saw themselves simultaneously as artists, adapters, and critics. These artists not only translated textual works into visual forms but also reimagined their accessibility for new audiences. Tracing various forms and media of storytelling across the spaces in which they circulated in the nineteenth century shows us the convergence of multiple art-based industries that were central to the period's artistic innovations and their relationship to the literary marketplace. The most-adapted stories remained in the public imagination to be eventually canonized in academic circles and to create blueprints for today's immersive experiences of transmedia storytelling.

A visual history of adaptation troubles some of the underlying scholarly assumptions about literature, particularly the primacy of text and the derivative, "unoriginal" nature of remediation. Reconnecting multiple early sites of remixing and recycling shows us how transmedia storytelling helped stories and authors exist over time and across cultural borders. Together the examples reveal a dynamic network driving the creation, circulation, and recep-

---

10. Newell, *Expanding Adaptation Networks* (2017).
11. Melot, *The Art of Illustration* (1984).

tion in the nineteenth century and in our own day. Among the most notable takeaways in the varied examples that follow is the way adaptation unites the seemingly disparate worlds of fine art and popular culture.

LITERARY GALLERIES AND THE CONVERGENCE OF HIGH ART AND INDUSTRY IN THE PUBLIC SPHERE

As Meisel and others argue, the Romantic "Sister Arts" tradition, where painting and poetry were seen as complementary storytelling sites, functioned as a dynamic exchange with dialectical influence on practices of reading and seeing. Luisa Calè and, more recently, Thora Brylowe have shown how the Sister Arts tradition—especially around the rise of the English literary art galleries, which fused the literary and visual arts—grounded the production of engraving and printing in a commercialized model of leisurely entertainment and cultural education. Brylowe's detailed archival research, close readings of the period's art, and theoretical contribution to visual literary history highlights the professional and industrial tensions between the period's painters, engravers, publishers, and booksellers. Particularly useful is her careful illustration of how painters repurposed print culture to gain the artistic and cultural authority writers sought to secure their own critical legitimacy and canonical status.[12] In the section that follows, I explore the literary gallery phenomenon and its legacies for adaptation studies and the commercial history of transmedia storytelling, participatory culture, and immersive storytelling experiences.

The demand for spectacle that characterized eighteenth- and nineteenth-century theater also found its way into music halls, fairs, waxworks, and other sites of popular and mass culture. Spectacle-driven technological displays and multisensory trends similarly dominated the venues of high culture such as museums and art galleries. At the turn of the nineteenth century, a visit to London's commercial and fashionable Pall Mall district might include a visual tour of the collected works of William Shakespeare, John Milton, and other writers. The rise of literary-inspired art galleries reflected several turning points in the history of literature, art, and culture: the rise of museums as public sites of knowledge production; the commercialization of culture; increased literacy facilitated by visual culture; and the convergence of text and image in print culture through illustrated books and periodicals.

---

12. Calè, *Fuseli's Milton Gallery* (2006); Brylowe, *Romantic Art in Practice* (2019). Brylowe uses variations of the word "adaptation" throughout her study; however, her book understandably focuses on the cultural function of the Sister Arts in the Romantic period and not in explicit conversation with contemporary media studies or adaptation studies.

The first of these literary galleries was the Boydell Shakespeare Gallery (in operation 1789–1805), a commercial venture launched by the engraver and publisher Alderman John Boydell. The Shakespeare Gallery launched as a multimodal experience featuring three main products (each sold separately): a public gallery where visitors could see paintings and sculptures inspired by Shakespeare's works; a souvenir book of engraved prints made from the paintings and sculptures housed at the gallery; and an illustrated edition of Shakespeare's plays, printed, of course, by Boydell's publishing company. Despite driving Boydell to the brink of bankruptcy at the end of his career, the fifteen-year experiment made immediate and permanent contributions to visual and print culture by adapting Shakespeare for nineteenth-century viewers and readers, and modernizing those works for mass public viewing and consumption.

Boydell's walk-through gallery of paintings featured the work of contemporary artists influenced by combinations of print sources, imitations of classical art, and performances.[13] All the works were new, commissioned by Boydell because part of the project's intention was to generate a fresh wave of historical painting in England that celebrated British culture and created a public willing to pay for the experience. Calling the Shakespeare Gallery "at once a business venture, an assertion of national pride, and an artistic declaration of independence," A. E. Santaniello notes how "the project unfolded with a display of energy and fanfare that captivated attention and still leaves us with questions about the complex motivation of its originators."[14] Already a successful printer, Boydell extended his social, cultural, and historical influence through this single ambitious, multipart project intended to make him money, spark public support of the fine arts in England, and create an innovative venue for entertainment and socialization. Boydell's Shakespeare Gallery was simultaneously a space of commercial consumption and of public engagement. Francis Wheatley's watercolor depiction of Boydell's Shakespeare Gallery (see figure 3.5) focuses on the space's social function. Wheatley's painting foregrounds the crowds (the paintings in the Gallery are reproduced only as barely-there outlines), showing how Boydell's Shakespeare Gallery was a place to see and be seen.

The Shakespeare Gallery also combined textual and visual experiences of reading and interpretation. Patrons could purchase an exhibition guide that included information about each work of art, the play upon which it was based, as well as excerpted passages detailing the scenes in the paintings. The

---

13. Hawkins and Ziegler, "Marketing Shakespeare" (2018).
14. Santaniello, *The Boydell Shakespeare Prints* (1979), 5–6.

FIGURE 3.5. Francis Wheatley, "View of the Interior of the Shakespeare Gallery" (1790). Image © Victoria and Albert Museum, London.

paintings and sculptures in the walk-through gallery were best experienced with a copy of this catalog (sold on site). Running over 180 pages in length, the catalog also doubled as an anthology (not to mention word-of-mouth advertising). Individual engravings of the Shakespeare Gallery's paintings were sold as souvenirs. Patrons who could afford it purchased subscriptions that included new engravings of the paintings. Also for sale was a large picture book with minimal textual embellishment. In 1803 a two-volume folio edition featuring engravings of the gallery's large paintings and sculptures was priced at sixty guineas, affordable only to England's most elite.[15] For customers who preferred their Shakespeare in a textual format, Boydell also commissioned a distinct set of smaller designs adapted for the new, nine-volume edition of Shakespeare's works and lavishly illustrated with images from the Boydell Shakespeare Gallery (completed in 1802). The venture was advertised as a collaborative, multimodal experience. Boydell's family name featured prominently, but the contributions of painters, engravers, and printers were credited as evidence of the project's innovation.

---

15. Santaniello, *The Boydell Shakespeare Prints* (1979).

In its fifteen-year run, Boydell's Shakespeare Gallery grew from three dozen paintings to more than 160 pieces, plus three sculptures displayed in three large exhibition rooms under a single roof. Despite this growth, the project failed commercially. The paintings were sold by lottery in 1805 and later dispersed in auction.[16] Today, most of the paintings that hung in the Shakespeare Gallery have been lost; others exist only as fragments. However, this turn-of-the-nineteenth-century, London-based transmedia experience was reproduced in the twenty-first century as a virtual adaptation visually modeled after Wheatley's painting, an endeavor only made possible due to the transmedia nature of the original project.[17]

Boydell invested more than £100,000 between payments to painters and engravers, printing costs, and real estate. Artists were paid well for their work, typically £100–300 but up to £1,000 per painting based on canvas size and artist prestige. Even higher payments went to those who engraved the works for print reproduction. The project eventually bankrupted Boydell as subscriptions slowed after a few years, having exhausted a smaller than expected market. The gallery opened one month before the start of the French Revolution and subsequent wars are believed to have cut substantially into the potential for international tourism and intercultural exchange that the gallery would have attracted during a time of peace and political security. In other words, the timing wasn't right for this type of high-art, transmedia venture, but the idea itself was transformative.

Boydell's Shakespeare Gallery emphasized the relationship between the textual and the visual by amplifying the role of visual culture in circulating literature. Visitors to the Shakespeare Gallery might be more interested in seeing the massive oil paintings and sculptures, but the exhibition nonetheless familiarized them with the textual versions of the plays through excerpts printing in the catalog. The large folio edition of prints only (similar to a contemporary coffee-table art book) did not include excerpts from Shakespeare but nonetheless organized the images for narrative continuity. By contrast, the nine-volume illustrated edition of Shakespeare's works was meticulously edited to serve as an authoritative edition heightened by the visual elements. Painting presented interpretive and representational possibilities unafforded to the theater. Whereas nudity was prohibited on any nineteenth-century stage, in painting the artistic nude was an accepted norm. For the Shakespeare Gallery's original patrons, the different standards of each medium would have been obvious and striking.

---

16. Burwick, "Introduction" in *The Boydell Shakespeare Gallery* (1996a).

17. "What Jane Saw," a virtual tour of the Boydell Shakespeare Gallery from the Liberal Arts Development Studio at The University of Texas at Austin.

Boydell's Shakespeare Gallery also had a long-lasting effect on art, literature, performance, and criticism. Frederick Burwick notes:

> The paintings/engravings altered subsequent staging and acting; they influenced, throughout the century, the manner and matter of illustrations to Shakespeare's plays. Too, they were the subject of elucidation and criticism in the contemporary reviews. Images from the Gallery haunted [Samuel Taylor] Coleridge's Lectures on Shakespeare and [William] Hazlitt's dramatic criticism. Even Mary Lamb's *Tales from Shakespeare* was illustrated in elegant Victorian editions with plates from Boydell's Gallery.[18]

Boydell's Shakespeare Gallery promoted intersections between artistic, cultural, and academic industries, influencing each of these forms for decades to come.[19]

Imitators were also inspired. The Swiss-born artist Henry Fuseli had nine paintings featured in Boydell's gallery, and the venture motivated him to launch the short-lived Milton Gallery (1799–1800). Another publisher to join in on the multiform, literary-inspired venture was Thomas Macklin, who proposed The Poets' Gallery in 1787 as a primarily print-based project featuring an annual art exhibition that ran until he was forced to sell off the painting collection (by lottery, like Boydell) in 1797.[20] Similarities notwithstanding, Macklin's celebration of British literature and culture modified Boydell's business plan to include multiple authors, past and present, including Chaucer and Spenser alongside contemporary writers such as Anna Barbauld. Macklin also expanded the thematic scope by including in his cross-media business an extensively illustrated Bible, which made up more than half of the Macklin's printed guide to the gallery under the heading "Scripture Pictures." Macklin's Bible became the standard for illustrated editions during the Victorian period.[21]

The literary art galleries marked the convergence of several social, cultural, and political ideologies. Blurring the boundaries of high and popular culture, they provided opportunities for historical, academic painting to be reimagined through contemporary, popular artists. The nineteenth century

---

18. Burwick, "The Romantic Reception of the Boydell Shakespeare Gallery" (1996b) 144–45.
19. Ritchie and Sabor, *Shakespeare in the Eighteenth-Century* (2012); Marshall, *Shakespeare in the Nineteenth Century* (2012).
20. Groom, "Art, Illustration, and Enterprise in Late Eighteenth-Century English Art" (1992).
21. Boase, "Macklin and Bowyer" (1963).

marked the birth of public institutions aimed at promoting culture and supporting mass education, largely in the service of cultural imperialism and commercial industrialization. Combining antiquarianism, nationalism, technological innovation, and spectacle, art galleries and museums celebrated a convergence of history, literature, art, and industry.[22] This convergence of culture and industry supported broader trends in the democratization of culture that accompanied the Age of Revolutions both politically and industrially, as well as the Reform movements that followed.[23] In response to revolutionary upheavals at the end of the eighteenth century—the establishment of democratic governments, the start of antislavery legislation, women's movements, and political representation for a greater number of British men—literature and art took a notable public turn. Exclusive works of art once housed privately were curated and opened to the public. Many art collections were nationalized, with major European cities targeting the rise of international tourism.[24] Galleries and museums were arranged to tell stories about the rise of civilization, and works of art served as genealogical links to the past.[25]

In these spaces, art converged with archeological discovery, and this new knowledge found its way back to contemporary sites of cultural production. One example of the convergence of literature, art, archeology, and theater in this regard is Charles Kean's 1853 adaptation of Byron's historical closet-drama *Sardanapalus* (1821). Shawn Malley explains that "Kean billed and built his show on [English archeologist Sir Austen Henry] Layard's recent excavations" and "offered his audience a rich expression of archeological knowledge" through props, costumes, and scenery that "were carefully replicated or inferred from artifacts available to the public view in the sculpture galleries of the nation's museum."[26] The play sought to entertain and educate, mirroring the objectives of galleries and museums in the production of cultural heritage and public knowledge. In this way, these disparate sites converged around the practice of transmedia storytelling by adapting works into formats best suited for their own space and purpose.

The Boydell, Fuseli, and Macklin multimodal gallery projects brought together the worlds of high-art and commercial entertainment. This disruptive union was radical and intentional on Boydell's part, directly challenging the authority of the Royal Academy of Arts, which continued to uphold exclu-

---

22. Waterfield, *The People's Galleries* (2015).
23. Whitehead, *The Public Art Museum in Nineteenth-Century Britain* (2005).
24. Meyer and Savoy, *The Museum Is Open* (2014).
25. Ian Jenkins, *Archeologists and Aesthetes* (1992).
26. Malley, *From Archaeology to Spectacle in Victorian Britain* (2012), 77–78; also Meyer and Savoy, *The Museum Is Open* (2014).

sionary views of art under a system of patronage. Boydell's goal of giving historical painting greater accessibility mirrors the goals of Romantic art and its support of Revolutionary, democratic ideals. The galleries provided new ways of understanding cultural heritage and literary history while also transforming practices of reading and methods of interpretation by exposing an emerging middle class to fine art and high culture. As Luisa Calè explains:

> The reconstitution of great British literature in the form of galleries of paintings had a dual cultural function. The galleries made a claim to be a new, narrative form of high art, yet they also circulated celebrated examples of the national literature in the commercial form of visual attractions. Indeed, the galleries were commercial outlets for the sale of illustrated books and prints, offering readers a visual entertainment for advertising and marketing purposes. Material conditions such as the galleries' mode of production, circulation, and marketing suggest the mutual influence of reading practices and ways of seeing.[27]

Calè stresses that the convergence of multiple forms and sites gave rise to new literacies that were dialogically constructed through the dynamic interchange between text and image. This fusion would become central to nineteenth-century print culture, manifested in periodicals, serialized fiction, novels, gift books, and instructional materials, all of which were illustrated.[28] Twentieth- and twentieth-century artists and media producers would continue these practices, further adapting and extending their scope, forms, and media as new technology and trends created demand for storytelling in media such as film, radio, television, comic books, and eventually interactive, digital forms.

Given the centrality of the illustrated book to the evolution of print culture since the nineteenth century, Boydell's and Macklin's insistence on diversifying their projects across multiple forms and mediums proved prescient, even if they didn't find long-term success themselves. The print formats ensured their broader cultural and historical impact. Because many of the paintings commissioned for the literary galleries have been lost or destroyed over the last two centuries, the engraved prints now serve as a primary archive, allowing access to nineteenth-century adaptations that would have otherwise been lost. One notable example is Fuseli's original oil painting picturing Prospero, Caliban, Miranda, and Ariel from Shakespeare's *The Tempest,* which today only exists in fragments. The published engraving is the only way to access

---

27. Calè, *Fuseli's Milton Gallery* (2006), 6.
28. Curtis, *Visual Words* (2002).

FIGURE 3.6. Engraving of Henry Fuseli's painting, *The Enchanted Island before the Cell of Prospero*. Illustration of a scene from Shakespeare's *The Tempest*. Engraved by Peter Simon for the Boydell Folio of images housed in the Shakespeare Gallery (published 1803). Gertrude and Thomas Jefferson Mumford Collection, Gift of Dorothy Quick Mayer, 1942. Public Domain. Image courtesy of The Metropolitan Museum of Art, New York.

what the full painting presented in the Shakespeare Gallery looked like, making the multimodal dimension of the project crucial to its historical legacy (see figure 3.6).

Beyond their immediate push to democratize elite culture and create a new visual archive for preserving literature, art, drama, and culture, the Shakespeare and Macklin Galleries funneled money back into the printing and engraving industry, where Boydell had established himself over five decades and Macklin had entered as a new investor. Evidencing the value of printed illustrations to these business ventures, engravers on these projects earned more than the painters—and without a market for the engravings, the paintings may not have been commissioned at all.[29] Like theatrical

---

29. Gage, "Boydell's Shakespeare and the Redemption of British Engraving," (1996); Lennox-Boyd, "The Prints Themselves" (1996).

hacks who adapted novels for a wider popular audience that did not typically include readers and book buyers, Boydell, Macklin, and Fuseli served as cultural intermediaries who bridged fine art and popular culture, text and image, aesthetics and commerce. The convergence of these industries birthed a new economy sustained by an influx of new consumers of culture. As Gloria Groom explains:

> In their intermediary role between artist and consumer, these two entrepreneurs [Boydell and Macklin] encouraged the public's taste for painting and fine prints while financially assisting both artists and engravers. Through public exhibitions of the paintings, followed by their publication as engravings, in portfolio or book form, they were able to open up the market for a new type of patron.[30]

This new patron, drawn from the emerging professional and middle classes, supported the emergence of professional artists—writers, painters, illustrators, and engravers—all of whom served as cultural creators and influencers, earning a living from their art. At the time of his death, Boydell had "succeeded in contributing to the overall importance of the printmaker's position through the extension of well-paid commissions."[31] This multiform approach to literature and art anticipated a growing interest in the fusion of these forms. As the nineteenth century progressed, the combination of textual and visual arts and the convergence of their respective industries strengthened through the rise of illustrated books. Supported through innovations in printing technologies, illustrated books became a staple of cultural production and a standard object in the Victorian home.[32]

Important to note here is the additional convergence of public and domestic spheres around the democratization of art and literature. Not only did illustrated books and embellished gift editions provide access to literature and art at home, they also provided a source of income for women writers, including Mary Shelley, Leticia Elizabeth Landon, and Felicia Hemans, among others—as well as repackaged male writers for women readers through a highly visible publishing venue.[33] Nineteenth-century painting and illustration were notable

---

30. Groom, "Art, Illustration, and Enterprise in Late Eighteenth-Century English Art" (1992), 129.
31. Bruntjen, *John Boydell* (1985), 245.
32. Kooistra, *Poetry, Pictures, and Popular Publishing* (2011); Elliott, *Rethinking the Novel/Film Debate* (2003).
33. Hoagwood, Ledbetter, and Jacobsen, *L. E. L.'s "Verses" and* The Keepsake *for 1829* (1998).

for emphasizing gender, which was not as readily reflected in the period's popular theater and was often obfuscated in textual forms. Literary heroines' roles were heightened in the period's visual art, from Shakespeare's female characters to the women who dominate Pre-Raphaelite painting and illustration.[34]

The rise of the literary galleries and the publication industry that turned them into an early site of commercial popular culture provides a crucial point for rethinking the history of transmedia storytelling and convergence culture. Specifically, they upend the myth that culture-texts are built or owned by a select, centralized few because fine art and popular culture equally influence cultural production and the marketplace. Through various forms of adaptation, these early commercial forms of transmedia storytelling and convergence culture created more fluid boundaries between high and mass culture, setting the conditions for new forms to follow. Literary galleries and illustrated books were presented as high culture but were no less commercial than the popular stage. Although these galleries were historically short-lived, the convergence of visual and print culture would only continue to intensify as the nineteenth century progressed, and the "literariness" of this convergence would expand into mass culture as literacy rates increased and the cost of books decreased. Overall, fusions between the textual, visual, and performing arts proved the most important cultural development as it created a shared language that incorporated multiple media around the more general practice of storytelling through adaptation.

ILLUSTRATORS AS ADAPTERS, TRANSMEDIA STORYTELLERS, AND LITERARY CRITICS

Although literary scholars don't always think of illustrations as adaptations, the relationship between text and image parallels the function of adaptation in other forms. Among the print-based forms that Newell includes in *Expanding Adaptation Networks,* illustrated editions get extensive treatment due to their centrality to reception and interpretation histories:

> Illustrated editions contribute to a work's adaptation network multiple visual interpretations that create (in collusion with film, television, and stage adaptations) a particular cultural impression of the work. Comparisons of successive sets of illustrated editions of canonical works will quite often show the

---

34. Ashton, *Shakespeare's Heroines in the Nineteenth Century* (1980); Pearce, *Woman / Image / Text* (1991).

same moment or scene being illustrated again and again. The data from such comparison indicates what "counts" in a particular work and which aspects of a work mold the popular imagination around certain "hinge" points.[35]

Illustrated editions mediate text, image, and performance by guiding interpretation and connecting texts to new visual contexts. As Newell notes, illustrators select key scenes in a longer work that serve as "gateways," not only aiding in textual comprehension but also situating the text within a larger network of cultural meanings that "illuminate tension and nuances of a work not evident in a prose reading alone and ... the reiterative process by which the cultural knowledge and memory of a particular work is constructed."[36] Charting a history of the similarities between illustration and other forms of adaptation is particularly well suited for transhistorical adaptation studies, given the explosion in production and demand for illustrated books during the nineteenth century.

Throughout this period, illustrated texts increased in popularity as technology made the reproduction of images financially accessible for more people—and more profitable for publishers—in a range of printed media. Whether novels, gift books, or illustrated newspapers, the proliferation of pictorial texts broadened the consumption of print-based forms, as the demand for illustrated texts supported a new class of commercial artist: the professional book illustrator and engravers who could make a living by focusing on the fusion of text and image in print-based forms.[37] The commercial nature of this work unfortunately situates nineteenth-century illustrators on the margins of art history and literary history alike, despite the fact that they played central roles in book history and the history of visual art, while also facilitating the development of a wider cultural literacy. Illustrated books were one of many sites of cultural remediation that brought novelty to old works and marked new ones as distinctly modern. Literary scholars typically approach illustration as secondary to texts (with a few exceptions, like Blake's paintings and illuminated manuscripts); however, in the eighteenth and nineteenth centuries, illustrations had more fluid meanings and were more readily understood as forms of criticism.[38]

In particular, adaptation through modernization played a central role in determining which texts were read by later generations and which ones fell

---

35. Newell, *Expanding Adaptation Networks* (2017), 93.
36. Newell, *Expanding Adaptation Networks* (2017), 93–94.
37. Golden, *Book Illustrated* (2000).
38. Cohen, "Literary Criticism and Illustration of *The Seasons*" (1964); Meisel, *Realizations* (1983).

from visibility. Tom Mole has recently shown how Victorian editions of the works of Romantic writers featuring "retrofitted illustrations" (i.e., illustrations for works that had not been previously illustrated) "offered a way to naturalize [the Romantics] in a new media ecology and renovate them for a new generation of cultural consumers."[39] As Mole shows, this update could happen through the restylizing of dress, as we see in Charles Daly's 1852 edition of Byron's *Don Juan*, with characters shown wearing mid-nineteenth-century clothing and hair styles that weren't fashionable until centuries after the cultural birth of the Don Juan character and decades after Byron's death.[40] This practice of modernizing characters and settings is closely analogous to contemporary techniques, especially neoclassical adaptations that displace characters temporally or overhaul characters and situations in order to help readers imagine their continued relevance in the present.[41] Illustrations could bridge generational divides in this way. The cultural refashioning that Mole describes certainly helped revitalize and update the Romantic poets in the Victorian period, keeping them relevant for the next generation of readers—and adapters.

Unlike the ephemerality of stage performances, print illustrations and textual forms created permanent objects in nineteenth-century homes, to be experienced again and again. Illustration informed the century's dominant artistic practices, crossing historical and national boundaries. Tragedies from Ancient Greece through the Early Modern period inspired Romantic and Victorian poets from Blake to Tennyson, and visual artists across Europe also adapted literary works into paintings, sculptures, and engravings. Historical and fictional persons were reimagined or reinterpreted as tragic subjects or heroic rebels, with different media industries converging and turning fashionable figures into cross-cultural icons across Europe. Refashioning characters according to Romantic aesthetics or Victorian social mores, illustrators became critics and transmedia storytellers at the same time.

As poet, painter, and engraver, Blake was among these early transmedia storytellers, exemplifying Romanticism's investment in intertextuality, allusion, hybrid genres, and extension. He fused textual and visual culture and used his technical experience as an engraver to produce art that took advantage of technological advancements in printing. Blake's works drew heavily on biblical and mythological allusions to create a new, interconnected, vision-

---

39. Mole, *What the Victorians Made of Romanticism* (2017), 45. Mole dedicates three chapters to illustration as a form of remediation and modernizing, but he does not use the term adaptation to describe this process.

40. Mole, *What the Victorians Made of Romanticism* (2017), 57.

41. Leitch, *Film Adaptation and Its Discontents* (2007).

ary mythology of his own, where Eric Pyle explains, "Blake would adopt and adapt the symbols from the ancient and more difficult tradition as he went about constructing his own imaginative world."[42] At times, Blake recycled parts of his earlier works, adapting and expanding them into new stories as he borrowed from more established storyworlds and mythologies. Blake's own poems rely so much on allusion—classical, literary, self-referential—that they function as an early example of high-art, transmedia storytelling in the modern world. His visionary poetics resemble world-building techniques that underscore today's transmedia franchise system, each iteration adding a new piece to the whole storyverse.[43]

Blake's illustrations to his own poems additionally situate the author-artist as a critical intermediary of textual and visual literacies, each with a unique language. As scholars have documented, Blake's illuminated books blend poetry and illustration, highlighting and expanding one another with sometimes complementary and sometimes contradictory takes on the same subject. In his best-known short poem, "The Tyger" from *Songs of Innocence and of Experience: Shewing the Two Contrary States of the Human Soul* (1794), the mature and disillusioned speaker's ruminations about religion and the animal's ferocity are juxtaposed with an illustration showing the tiger in a calm and natural state of existence. Text and image work together, as they do elsewhere within this multimodal work, to illustrate the project's central thesis. Blake pairs simple verse with intricate visuals to draw on both the imaginative and visual literacies of the reader-viewer, where text and image occupy equal roles in storytelling.[44] Joseph Viscomi explains that "Blake realized very early . . . that *rewriting texts* was also an act of visual invention, and thus that the medium could be used for production rather than reproduction," as he arranged all of the elements into individual plates that were "invented only during execution" and sold only in expensive, limited sets.[45]

Such textual-visual fusions were also central to Blake's artistic vision of several eighteenth-century writers. Known for their critical sophistication, these illustration projects complement the achievement of his own intertextual poetry and illuminated works, in which "allusion becomes an act of criticism when it situates received material in a new context."[46] Among Blake's most radical adaptations are his illustrations to John Gabriel Stedman's memoir *The Narrative of a Five Years Expedition against the Revolted Negroes of*

---

42. Pyle, *William Blake's Illustrations for Dante's Divine Comedy* (2015), 113.
43. Jenkins, *Convergence Culture* (2006); Meikle, *Adaptation in the Franchise Era* (2019).
44. Viscomi, *Blake and the Idea of the Book* (1993).
45. Viscomi, "Blake's Illuminated Word" (2010), 108.
46. Youngquist, *Madness and Blake's Myth* (1990), 78.

Surinam (1796), where, as Esther Lezra notes, "Blake's interpretive adaptations of Stedman's scenes of colonial violence offer images of what that violence of subjection could look like if it could be turned to the favor of the subjected and become a successful force of revolution."[47] Blake's illustrations thus reflect and extend his own philosophical views and visionary art, especially with regard to his political and humanistic opposition to slavery and other forms of tyranny, extending the use of the original text and redeploying it to align with his own worldview.[48]

Blake's illustration projects ranged from the work of contemporaneous writers like the eighteenth-century poets Edward Young and Thomas Gray to more historically established culture-texts such as the Bible, Dante's *The Divine Comedy*, and several works by Milton, each showing significant variety in approach and form. His illustrations for Young and Gray, for example, appeared within or alongside text in illustrated editions, whereas the plates and paintings developed for Milton omitted the text and assumed audience familiarity with the scenes. The range of topics covered in his illustrations and engravings for others—most of which were produced as commercial projects—spans literature, history, science, and visual arts.[49] In all of these projects, Blake saw himself as both illustrator and critic. Pamela Dunbar explains, "Emphatically held beliefs and a strong creative personality inevitably led Blake in his designs for the works of others to 'correct' those works in the light of his own acquaintance with the one Truth," as was the case in his illustrations to Young's *Night Thoughts* and Gray's *Poems*, "where he had concentrated simply on exposing the 'errors' of his authors by altering or directly contradicting their message."[50] When illustrating Milton, "he confined himself to releasing the insights which he considered to lie hidden beneath them . . . through the unobtrusive omission or addition of 'minute particulars,' the subtle alteration of emphases, and the intermittent interpolation of another 'layer' of significance that bring a detail or a whole passage into harmony with his own 'system.'"[51]

---

47. Lezra, "Monsters in Motion" (2006), 6.
48. Gallant, "Blake's Coded Designs of Slave Revolts" (2011).
49. Bindman, *Blake as an Artist* (1977); Essick, *The Separate Plates of William Blake* (1983); Essick, *William Blake's Commercial Book Illustrations* (1991).
50. Dunbar, *William Blake's Illustrations to the Poetry of Milton* (1980), 5. Behrendt and Dunbar both note marked differences in Blake's illustrations of Milton versus his illustrations of the eighteenth-century poets Edward Young's *Night Thoughts* (first published 1745 and illustrated by Blake in 1797 with more than five hundred watercolor page illustrations) and Thomas Gray's poetry (more than one hundred illustrations). See also Saklofske, "A Fly in the Ointment" (2012).
51. Dunbar, *William Blake's Illustrations to the Poetry of Milton* (1980), 5.

Blake was doing more than appropriating Milton for his own art—he was also updating Milton to better suit a post-Enlightenment, post-Revolutionary age. Julie Sanders calls Blake "Milton's eighteenth-century commentator and adapter," as he was the first to radically imagine the poetic epic tradition on behalf of the Romantics in both textual and visual forms.[52] This illustration project required Blake to grapple with both the cultural status of Milton and the culture-text of *Paradise Lost*, the most significant expansion/adaptation of the Book of Genesis to date. Despite the deep respect he felt for Milton as a poet, Blake still brought his own interpretive framework and radical beliefs to the seventy-six plates and twelve paintings produced over the course of seventeen years.[53] Through his Milton illustrations, Blake remediated nearly a century and a half of commentary, criticism, and other artistic engagement separating the Romantic revolutionary from his Puritan predecessor. As Stephen Behrendt clarifies, with *Paradise Lost* in particular, "The conscientious illustrator . . . consider[ed] not only the text itself [but also how it] had blended with that of Genesis illustrations to the extent that by 1800 it was often difficult to ascertain whether a particular depiction of . . . the Garden of Eden was derived from Milton or the Bible."[54] To these sources one could add an array of other possible influences (either intentional or consequential) from textual, visual, or performance traditions, as well as "classical statuary, the figure-drawing of Michelangelo and Raphael, medieval manuscript illumination, and the Miltonic paintings and drawing of his friends and contemporaries."[55]

Blake's vision of Milton's Satan (see figure 3.7) blends multiple sources of influence reimagined through Romanticism's modern ideologies. Satan stands in a prideful, rebellious stance that invokes the period's theatrical poses and dramatic conventions. The characters are arranged to resemble a theatrical *tableau vivant*, a popular dramatic moment where all characters would pose on stage to form a "living picture" at the end of an act or finale (a practice that

---

52. Sanders, *Adaptation and Appropriation* (2016), 159. Sanders revises the language in the second edition to "commentator and adapter" from her original "reader and commentator" published in 2006.
53. Blake illustrated the following works by Milton: the companion poems *L'Allegro and Il Penseroso* (a single series of twelve illustrations); *Ode on the Morning of Christ's Nativity*, a.k.a. the *Nativity Ode* (two sets of six illustrations); *Comus* (two sets depicting similar scenes of eight plates); *Paradise Lost* (multiple sets of twelve images); and *Paradise Regained* (twelve images). Most of the projects are comprised of twelve illustrations, though sometimes in multiple sets with revised versions of the same scene. Dunbar, *William Blake's Illustrations to the Poetry of Milton* (1980).
54. Behrendt, *The Moment of Explosion* (1983), 66.
55. Dunbar, *William Blake's Illustrations to the Poetry of Milton* (1980), 7.

FIGURE 3.7. William Blake, *Satan Arousing the Rebel Angels*. Illustration to Milton, *Paradise Lost* (1808). Image © Victoria and Albert Museum, London.

finds a contemporary equivalent in the "freeze frame"). Satan and his fellow rebels are framed in fire and action, invoking a forceful, sublime energy characteristic of Romantic literature and art. In Blake's adaptation, Satan is bold, brave, and beautiful. Blake's modernization would dominate the Romantic imagination for decades, making the earlier writer a "True Poet and of the devil's party without knowing it" decades before Percy Shelley and other second-generation Romantic poets embraced the figure of Satan as a poetic ideal.[56]

Blake brought the same critical energy to his Dante illustrations, a project loaded with the cultural baggage of a long line of adaptations, appropriations, and interpretations.[57] The Dante series is comprised of more than one hundred drawings, mostly for the *Inferno*, all infused with the poet-artist's signature style and personal beliefs, as Blake's illustrations "embody his own ideas at the same time as they portray the events of Dante's poem."[58] Blake's illustrations to *Paradise Lost* and *The Divine Comedy* are intentionally independent works, adapting and not faithfully translating the literary texts on which they were based. These adaptations situate the visual over the verbal using illustration as a form of simultaneous critique and homage.

More broadly, Blake's approach to illustrating Dante and Milton resonates with the challenges that contemporary adapters negotiate when recreating nineteenth-century culture-texts with long adaptation histories, such as *Frankenstein*, *A Christmas Carol*, or *Alice in Wonderland*. Whether illustrating works dating back centuries or those closer to his own day, Blake engaged in a two-way dialogue with these texts through his visual designs. Blake's relationship with Milton was dynamic, "as nearly a reciprocal relationship as it can be possible to attain with the dead."[59] Later artists grappled with the same challenge, now adding Blake to the long line of adapters whose interpretation of the source material shaped how the work was received and remembered.

Two illustrations by different artists of the same story from Canto 5 of Dante's *Inferno* demonstrate how adaptations create a chain through time, with earlier adaptations influencing newer ones (see figures 3.8 and 3.9). In the first, Blake engages in a dialogic exchange with Dante, adapting him with the new tools of the present. Forty years later, Gustave Doré illustrates the same scene. There are many new elements here, but there is also continuity—an extension of vision that strongly mirrors Blake's earlier design. Both artists share a similar conceptual image, visualizing the Circle of Lust as a continuous swirl of bodies embracing, melting into one another in an infinite cycle of desire. Doré draws on Blake as much as he does Dante, and each becomes

---

56. Blake, *The Marriage of Heaven and Hell* (1790–93). For Shelley on the poetical nature of Milton's Satan, see *A Defense of Poetry* (1821) as well as the Preface to *Prometheus Unbound* (1820).
57. Klonsky, *Blake's Dante* (1980).
58. Roe, *Blake's Illustrations to the Divine Comedy* (1953), v.
59. Dunbar, *William Blake's Illustrations to the Poetry of Milton* (1980), 1; Behrendt echoes this point in *The Moment of Explosion* (1983).

FIGURE 3.8. William Blake, *The Circle of the Lustful: Francesca da Rimini*. Illustration to Dante, *The Divine Comedy* (c. 1825–27). Public Domain. Image courtesy of The Metropolitan Museum of Art, New York.

FIGURE 3.9. Gustave Doré, *Paolo and Francesca* (1861), engraved by Ausman. Illustration to Dante, *The Divine Comedy: The Inferno*. Public Domain. Courtesy of The Victorian Web.

a new node in the network of adaptations that make up the culture-text of *The Inferno*.

Here it's helpful to invoke dynamic approaches proposed by contemporary adaptation scholars to articulate both the firsthand process of adapting texts and their long-term effects on reception. Regina Schober understands adaptations as a "complex assemblage of cross-influences rather than a seemingly unidirectional procedure between two media."[60] Jørgen Bruhn supports a similarly dynamic approach, proposing a dialogical model for adaptation studies where "adaptation . . . ought to be regarded as a two-way process instead of a form of one-way transport."[61] Blake's illustrations epitomize these views as they both incorporate and extend these two-way models: his illustrations to Milton not only speak back to Milton but also position both poets in conversation with adaptations that follow. These subsequent adaptations included contemporary art that Blake viewed in Fuseli's Milton Gallery exhibitions; he and the Swiss-born painter were friends and regularly discussed art and poetry.[62] Blake's illustrations thus form a major node in a far more complex network of adaptations and associations across time, forms, and mediums that grew and expanded as new artists added their own versions to the mix, extending the cultural history—and ongoing life—of these culture-texts.

Like other visual artists, Blake's approach to illustration should be contextualized in the larger network of cultural production emerging in the nineteenth century. Because of his clear interest to literary scholars, his illustrations have received a considerable amount of scholarly attention and close reading. However, seen alongside other nineteenth-century illustrators, Blake's visual adaptations function as one of many entry points into nineteenth-century transmedia storytelling and convergence culture through the rise of visual print culture. Albert Roe echoes other Blake scholars in emphasizing the importance of situating all of Blake's individual projects within the larger body of the poet-artist's collected works, both textual and visual, "to discern the counterpoint of Blake's own beliefs as they blend with the dominant theme provided by the incidents and personalities of the *Divine Comedy*," and the same can be said for other texts he illustrated.[63] Blake's illustrations are not closed relationships between illustrator and author but part of a larger transtextual and cross-media network of allusions, ideas, texts, and images drawn from the complete body of Blake's work and from an array of influences work-

---

60. Schober, "Adaptation as Connection—Transmediality Reconsidered" (2013), 92.
61. Bruhn, "Dialogizing Adaptation Studies" (2013), 73.
62. Wittreich, "A Note on Blake and Fuseli" (1969).
63. Roe, *Blake's Illustrations to the Divine Comedy* (1953), v.

ing together to produce meaning and remake familiar stories into versions that spoke to Romantic-era concerns.

Although he didn't achieve celebrity or commercial success in his lifetime, Blake's radically modern illustrations and engravings influenced later artists and solidified his reputation as an artist in his own day.[64] When he died in 1827, Blake left behind more than 1,200 designs illustrating texts written by other writers, in addition to designs illuminating nearly four hundred pages of his own work.[65] His multiple illustration projects reflected an understanding of illustration as a type of literary criticism that took many intertextual forms, from direct quotation to radical revision.[66] His career exemplifies the relationship between creative output and literary criticism mediated through textual and visual print culture. Blake was an early multimedia artist, negotiating not only the relationship between textual and visual literacies but also the shift from artistic production under a system of patronage (historically associated with high art) to commercialism (typically understood as the driver of mass culture).

Parallel practices informed nineteenth-century painting and engraving in France, where several visual artists built careers by adapting literary sources from around the world. Central to French Romantic painting and sculpture, for example, were the shared stories of classical mythology, translated into visual forms in which "mythic subjects and interpretations [became] a central mode of meditating upon modern mores, culture, and the human condition."[67] French artists frequently turned to literary illustration in both painting and engraving as a form of transnational cultural exchange; between the two of them, Eugène Delacroix and Gustave Doré produced thousands of illustrations of literatures in French, English, German, Spanish, and other languages.

From the 1820s until his death in 1863, Delacroix produced more than nine thousand works of art in a combination of paintings, pastels, and drawings, many of which were adaptations from mythology and literature, both old and new. Making use of his classical education, Delacroix "read a great deal, and because, like many of the young artists of his time, he wanted to break with

---

64. Viscomi, "Blake's Illuminated Word" (2010).
65. Figures reported in Dunbar, *William Blake's Illustrations to the Poetry of Milton* (1980), 7.
66. Kooistra, *The Artist as Critic* (1995). Kooistra proposes a "bitextual" relationship between text and image through five dialogic models: quotation, impression, parody, answering, and cross-dressing. Although Kooistra's focus is the Victorian illustrated book starting with the Pre-Raphaelites, her models are also helpful for the first half of the nineteenth century, prior to the mass-produced illustrated books of the latter half of the period.
67. Johnson, *David to Delacroix* (2011), 2.

FIGURE 3.10. Eugène Delacroix, *La Morte de Sardanapale* (1827), after Byron's tragic closet drama *Sardanapalus* (1821). Public Domain. Wikimedia Commons.

David's school, he chose the subjects for his pictures from the poets in favor with the use of the time, such as Dante, Shakespeare, Byron and Goethe."[68]

He adapted Byron's works into massive oil paintings, such as Delacroix's *The Execution of the Doge Marino Faliero* (1825), which was inspired by Byron's closet drama *Marino Faliero, Doge of Venice: A Historical Tragedy* (1821). One of Delacroix's best-known works continues to be *La Mort de Sardanapale* (1827), adapting his subject from Byron's closet drama *Sardanapalus: A Tragedy* (1821), a fictionalized account of the quasi-historical last Assyrian king (see figure 3.10). The painting caused considerable scandal when it was first exhibited at the Paris Salon of 1827–28. Today, however, the massive oil painting, measuring 154 in. x 195 in., is one of Delacroix's best known and most reproduced works.[69] *The Death of Sardanapalus* was the first visual adaptation of Byron's 1821 tragedy. (It was first staged six years later on April 10, 1834, at Drury Lane in London.) Delacroix was an Orientalist, regularly painting East-

---

68. Fosca, *French Painting* (1960), 51.
69. Jobert, *Delacroix* (1997), 78–83.

ern themes and cultures and favoring exoticized depictions, and there was no lack of source material from Byron, including *The Giaour* (painted by Delacroix in 1826) and *The Corsair* (painted in 1831, see figure 3.11), as well as at least four different paintings based on *The Bride of Abydos* produced between 1827 and 1857.

Delacroix continued adapting literature into visual art throughout his career. In addition to oils and watercolors, he produced several illustrations for print publication. His illustrations and engravings for the 1828 French translation of Goethe's *Faust: Part 1* included seventeen full-page illustrations (plus a portrait of the author), receiving wide critical acclaim and praise from Goethe himself as having "surpassed" his own imagined vision for the work.[70] Importantly, Delacroix's images were inspired in part by watching a theatrical adaptation of the German opera by George Soane and Daniel Terry staged in London's Drury Lane Theatre in 1825.[71] The form of visual print media, however, allowed artistic license unavailable on stage, including more explicit depictions of sex (see figure 3.12).

Like Blake before him, Delacroix's illustrations create critical commentary in a new medium that situates visual artists not only in art history but also as cultural mediators in literary history. Adaptation in the form of illustration provided both occasions to celebrate via imitation and opportunities to create new interpretations of literature and to modernize art. Fosca notes that "Delacroix found it necessary to free reality from the trivial and the commonplace, by moving back in time and space. . . . He found in books satisfactory subjects for his experiments in form and color, and which gave them a foundation and a meaning."[72] Delacroix relied on literary subjects to provide viewers with a grounding framework to offset and highlight what was unique in his own artistic approach to recognizable subjects. Allying himself with fellow radical Romantics in Germany (Goethe) and England (Byron), Delacroix painted himself into an emerging, international literary canon. He forged a hybrid aesthetic that sought to create literature and art reflecting the political ideals of a world impacted by major political and social revolutions. While adaptations could ground the careers of artists across the political spectrum, it was an instrumental practice for those who wanted to align themselves politically or aesthetically with radical ideals.

---

70. Goethe, *Faust* (1828). This illustrated edition is available online from the National Library of France. For Goethe on Delacroix's illustrations, see *Conversations of Goethe with Eckermann and Soret* (1850), 298.

71. Mellby, "Delacroix's *Faust*" (2009).

72. Fosca, *French Painters* (1960), 55.

FIGURE 3.11. Eugène Delacroix, from Byron's *The Corsair* (1831). Watercolor. Public Domain. Digital image courtesy of the J. Paul Getty Museum Open Content Program.

FIGURE 3.12. Eugène Delacroix, "Faust in the Prison with Marguerite" (1828). Lithograph illustration to Johann von Goethe, *Faust* (1825). Image courtesy of The National Gallery of Victoria, Melbourne.

Other artists focused on the more commercial aspects of illustration and transmediation but still strongly influenced the visual-cultural history of major culture-texts. Doré achieved both commercial and critical success in France and England by illustrating an extensive list of texts from the medieval period through his contemporary moment, including *Paradise Lost, The Divine Comedy,* and several works by François Rabelais, Byron, and Edgar Allan Poe. Doré's illustrations to Miguel de Cervantes's *Don Quixote* (1601; illustrated in 370 images in 1863) and Samuel Taylor Coleridge's *The Rime of the Ancient Mariner* (1798; illustrated in 1877) are still regularly reproduced and widely anthologized (see figures 3.13 and 3.14). Although he produced nearly two thousand paintings (including oil, watercolors, charcoal, and chalk) and approximately thirty sculptures over the course of his career, Doré became famous for his book illustrations—and he continues to be remembered today almost exclusively for these visual literary adaptations.[73]

Similar to Blake and Delacroix, Doré was drawn to major culture-texts, though he also produced hundreds of illustrations for European contemporary popular works like the German novel *The Adventures of Baron Munchausen* (first published in 1785 and illustrated by Doré in 1862), as well as major fairy tales and legends like the collected works of the seventeenth-century French author Charles Perrault, for which Doré published eleven illustrations in 1862. His illustrations include a long list of frequently adapted works: *A Christmas Carol* (1843; illustrated by Doré in 1861), Alfred Lord Tennyson's *Idylls of the King* (1859; illustrated by Doré in 1867), and Poe's *The Raven* (1845; with twenty-six steel engravings published in 1884, soon after Doré's death).[74] Doré's memorable images have become part of the reception and adaptation histories of all of these works, establishing iconography that has been reproduced in later editions, inspired new illustrations, or informed visual styling for adaptations in film and new media, from classic Hollywood films to animated children's movies.[75]

Like other notable nineteenth-century illustrators such as George Cruikshank (see chapter 4), Doré began as a professional caricaturist in the 1840s while still in school, creating cartoons on demand as commissioned

---

73. Zafran, Ronsenblum, and Small. *Fantasy and Faith* (2007); Davidson, *The Drawings of Gustave Doré* (2014).

74. See Davidson for representative illustrations to *Idylls of the King, The Raven, The Divine Comedy, The Adventures of Baron Munchausen, Fables, Don Quixote, Paradise Lost,* and *The Bible*. Doré's least-known classics illustrations are those for Dickens's *A Christmas Carol*, which appeared in an illustrated magazine, not published in book form like most of his illustration projects. See Malan, *Charles Dickens'* A Christmas Carol *with 45 Lost Gustave Doré Engravings* (1996).

75. Robert, "Cinema and the Work of Doré" (2014).

"A world of disorderly notions, picked out of his books, crowded into his imagination."—p. 3.

FIGURE 3.13. Gustave Doré. Illustration to Miguel de Cervantes, *Don Quixote* (1863). Public Domain. Image courtesy of Wikimedia Commons.

Und in des Schiffes Schatten sah
Ich große Wasserschlangen.

FIGURE 3.14. Gustave Doré. Illustration to Samuel Taylor Coleridge, *The Rime of the Ancient Mariner*, German edition (1877). Public Domain. Digital image courtesy of The British Library.

by publishers.⁷⁶ In addition to illustrating literature, he was one of the earliest experimenters in sequential art—the nineteenth-century precursor to the graphic novel. His first attempt at the form adapted the story of Hercules into *Les Travaux d'Hercule* (*The Labors of Hercules,* 1847), a parody of the Greek hero in a series of 104 panel cartoons over forty-six pages of pen lithographs, whose short captions emphasized visual storytelling over textual.⁷⁷ Doré completed his first major literary illustration project in 1854, publishing more than one hundred illustrations for François Rabelais's *Gargantua and Patagruel* (1532–64). Within two years he also completed major illustration projects for works by nineteenth-century French writers, such as Honoré de Balzac's *Drôlatiques* (*Droll Tales*; first published in 1832, illustrated by Doré in 1855) and Pierre Dupont's poetic adaptation of *La Légene du Juif Errant* (*The Legend of the Wandering Jew*; first published in 1856 with twelve illustrations by Doré), as well as shorter works by Victor Hugo and Alexandre Dumas. These projects solidified his reputation as an illustrator throughout Europe, making him one of the highest paid artists of the century.⁷⁸

Looking at the collective illustration projects of prominent nineteenth-century artists such as Fuseli, Blake, Delacroix, and Doré shows that each artist wove a web of adaptation that foregrounded his own aesthetics and interpretations, creating original works of art that were also adaptations. Fuseli used stories from Shakespeare and Milton to scaffold the nightmarish visions central to his own visual oeuvre. Blake saw Milton and Dante through a revolutionary lens that guided his adaptations. Delacroix modernized art by using literary texts to ground storytelling, experimenting with new techniques in color and highlighting to provide a visual depth that could not be captured through textual description alone. Doré demonstrated that literature could turn a profit when it was repackaged in a medium that combined text and image to expand not only readership but also (and more importantly) the potential market of book buyers. All of these visual artists used past and contemporary literary sources to participate in the process of visual and textual canon formation, essentially influencing which stories would remain consumable in multiple formats. Like the multiform gallery projects of Boydell, Macklin, and Fuseli, illustrated editions inspired new editions of texts featuring new illustrations, with every later artist contributing yet another piece to these culture-texts produced across generations. Victorian writers and artists would continue this

---

76. Houfe, *The Dictionary of 19th Century British Book Illustrators and Caricaturists* (1978).

77. For a full reproduction of this early graphic novel, see Kunzle, *Gustave Doré: Twelve Comic Strips* (2015).

78. Davidson, *The Drawings of Gustave Dorè* (2014).

work, though they often found a new set of stories to adapt—stories that more accurately reflected their own social mores.

The substantial bodies of work produced by all of these visual artists demonstrate adaptation's centrality to painting, illustration, and translation in the nineteenth century, including its role in international cultural exchange and the intergenerational ways that literature could be revamped through the fusion of text and image. Whether adapters chose to revise political contexts, update social mores, or modernize settings and character fashions, writers and artists used existing culture-texts or created new ones as a means of redefining literature and art for their contemporaries. Sometimes the primary motivation for new adaptations was tied to homage of authors or texts. In other cases, the novelty of the illustrations and their commercial interest centered more on the illustrators themselves, as in the case of celebrated visual artists such as Doré. The interest might come from the popularity of a new technologically driven medium, such as photography and later film. No single driver of interest is more important than another, as each created an economic market for art and culture animated by adaptation, appropriation, and transmedia extension. Nineteenth-century visual culture—whether in painting, book illustration and engraving, sculpture, or performing arts—shaped the iconography of culture-texts that were often repeated in later adaptations. Doré's illustrations to *Don Quixote* and other works, for instance, became the standard by which those works were reimagined and adapted through future visual mediums, including film.[79]

ALTHOUGH MOST of the existing intertextual models for understanding adaptation are grounded in film, television, and the performing arts, they can be reworked for other forms and media. Newell emphasizes the need to understand larger networks of print-based forms of adaptation that include novelization, illustration, literary maps, pop-up books, and ekphrastic literature. This inclusive approach across forms and media shows "what a networked model of adaptation can illuminate—namely, that cultural understandings of literary works originate not exclusively or even necessarily in source texts but in patterns of repetition and reiteration."[80] Most adaptations—and especially those reworking stories with long adaptation and remediation histories—draw on multiple works simultaneously, including illustrations alongside other forms such as text or performance. New adaptations of stories often

---

79. Davidson, *The Drawings of Gustave Doré* (2014).
80. Newell, *Expanding Adaptation Networks* (2017), 197.

include remnants of previous adaptations of the same culture-text (perhaps seen in different forms and media). Painting and illustration have historically informed these approaches, with visual artists guiding literary interpretation and reception, and helping to update texts for new audiences.

Unsurprisingly, Newell's contemporary examples of print-based adaptation networks draw heavily (though not exclusively) from adaptations of nineteenth-century fiction, including *Alice's Adventures in Wonderland* and Robert Louis Stevenson's *The Strange Case of Dr. Jekyll and Mr. Hyde*. These culture-texts are regularly reimagined in multiple forms and media today, and they were also regularly adapted and appropriated in the nineteenth century as well. In looking back to these culture-texts, Newell echoes Kamilla Elliott's repeated arguments for a reconsideration of the dominant novel/film discourse to include a broader range of relationships between words and images and a longer historical trajectory for adaptation studies. Given her training as a nineteenth-century scholar, Elliott's inclusion of illustration and other forms of visual culture comes from seeing the prevalence of adaptation in nineteenth-century "interart," including painting, illustration, theater, and other forms of visual culture that predate film.[81]

The Industrial Revolution made the proliferation of print and visual culture possible through its reproduction and circulation in print and other forms. By the final decades of the Victorian period, as Elliott notes, "prose often took second place to illustration," until the shifting aesthetics of modernist writing asserted the superiority of prose through leading figures like Henry James and Virginia Woolf, all while the popularity of illustrated books gave way to the novelty of film.[82] Resituating all of these forms within the adaptation network of the nineteenth century's arts and culture industries shows us how each form played in a larger tradition of adaptation and transmedia storytelling.

Painting, illustration, and sculpture are among the oldest forms of transmediation. They turn legends and literature into icons and situate adaptation at the center of the history of art, literature, and culture. The examples in this chapter highlight the process of adaptation as an act of original contribution and collaboration between artists and across time, forms, and media. While illustrating the work of writers long past, Blake saw himself working alongside Dante and Milton, not *after* them. Like Boydell and Delacroix earlier in the century, the Pre-Raphaelite artists who adapted Keats and others sought to challenge the authority of academic painting. They sought

---

81. Elliott, *Rethinking the Film/Novel Debate* (2003).
82. Elliott, *Rethinking the Film/Novel Debate* (2003).

to modernize art by returning to older methods that they viewed as unrestricted by convention and updating them. For this reason, they drew heavily from well-known stories, themes, and symbolism, relying on familiar stories in order to experiment with new visual techniques. Although they worked individually, the works of these artists collectively increased the visibility of stories, transporting them across time by adapting them for new audiences through modern visual styles. Comparing the illustrations of one culture-text to another culture-text reveals how these stories served as springboards for new, forward-thinking interpretations instead of merely curational works grounded in reverence or homage. Resituating illustration as a form of adaptation and transmedia storytelling shows us how visual artists became the auteurs of new original works supported by literary texts, but possessing an authority of their own.

The work done by artists of the Romantic period influenced artists in the second half of the century as technological advances drove the period's visual print culture, from expensive books to cheap periodicals. Artists from a range of backgrounds, approaches, and styles began participating in this visual turn, supported by industrialization. Lorraine Kooistra sees this moment as a convergence of historically situated interests:

> As literary painters, decorative artists, and poets committed to experimenting formally with the sister arts, the Pre-Raphaelites brought a theory and a practice to the art of the book that proposed a radical new direction for art and poetry in the modern world. Rather than opposing the fields of restricted and large-scale cultural production, the individual hand of the artist and the machinery of mass production, the Pre-Raphaelites sought to bring them closer together and to acknowledge the social practices and uses of art.[83]

The impact on arts and entertainment industries was remarkable, as illustrated books by the Pre-Raphaelites "challenged the authority of the poet and emphasized the social and collaborative dimensions of art production; they demonstrated the autonomy of readers' imaginations and showed how poems exist in historically specific reading experiences; and they claimed the book as a vehicular form for art in the age of mass production."[84] Despite several artists' fervent embrace of these new forms, the fusion of literary and visual arts had its detractors. Among them was John Ruskin, who worried that trans-

---

83. Kooistra, *Poetry, Pictures, and Popular Publishing* (2011), 42.
84. Kooistra, *Poetry, Pictures, and Popular Publishing* (2011), 43.

forming art into an everyday experience would dilute the experience of more exclusive, grander forms (i.e., original paintings housed in public galleries or private collections). For Kooistra, such anxieties reveal the extent to which "the popularization of symbolic goods brought about by the emerging visual culture in this age of mechanical reproduction thus challenged not only the sway of the verbal but also the social value of national, public art."[85]

Illustrated books epitomized the commercial convergence of the literary, art, and publishing industries. Reading itself began to involve a dynamic awareness of image and text as literary art galleries and museums evolved spatial literacies and print became increasingly visual through mass-produced typography, ornamentation, and—the most memorable visual element—illustration.[86] As one of the period's major multimodal forms, the illustrated book influenced both the immediate and long-term reception of writers across genres, nations, and history. Portraits of authors became more common as frontispieces to books, adding a visual dimension to literary celebrity that made writers recognizable by name and by face. Illustration played a major role in circulation and reception, propelling some writers to international celebrity while sidelining others into relative obscurity.[87] Many nineteenth-century writing careers were sustained through the close ties between text and image, including authors as different as Charles Dickens, Christina Rossetti, and Lewis Carroll.[88] The collaborative nature of these adaptations is also significant, as artists rarely undertook projects without significant input or investment from publishers—and sometimes from the writers too. Production was also a collaborative process; most of the images for illustrated books were designed by one artist and engraved by others, since these two techniques required significantly different skillsets and experience.

Adaptation provides common ground from which to rethink the relationships between text, image, and performance in all of the examples discussed. In text-based adaptations (including but not limited to ekphrastic works and literary rewrites) as well as in visual art, nineteenth-century writers and artists actively wrote themselves into the lineage of literary and artistic history. Surveying the ways these writers and illustrators adapted stories old and new

---

85. Kooistra, *Poetry, Pictures, and Popular Publishing* (2011), 66.

86. Curtis, *Visual Words* (2002).

87. The following studies document the centrality of commercial illustration to nineteenth-century visual culture: Kooistra, *Poetry, Pictures, and Popular Publishing* (2011); Ray, *The Illustrator and the Book in England from 1790–1914* (1976); Goldman, *Victorian Illustration* (2004).

88. Cohen, *Charles Dickens and His Original Illustrators* (1980); Kooistra, *Christina Rossetti and Illustration* (2002); Cohen and Wakeling, *Lewis Carroll and His Illustrators* (2003).

into textual and visual formats shows the pervasiveness of transmediation and extension in the nineteenth century and how it expanded the audience for these works of literature, art, and culture. Without charting adaptation's history across forms and media, we risk failing to see how stories evolve, disperse, and multiply as technology provides new vehicles for storytelling and audience engagement over time.

CHAPTER 4

❧

Culture-Texts and Storyworlds across Nineteenth-Century Media

ADAPTATION REMIXES CONNECTIONS to characters and stories across time, building links between the past and the present, even as narrative media changes. For example, contemporary television features a defining quality of eighteenth- and nineteenth-century storytelling: "round" characters situated in detailed settings that serve as a well-woven backdrop.[1] A similar aesthetic drove the development of the novel in the eighteenth century and its rise as the dominant literary form in the nineteenth century. Characters traveled beyond the borders of source texts in sequels, parodies, or other imitations, transforming new novels like *Gulliver's Travels* (1726), *The Sorrows of Young Werther* (1774), *Ivanhoe* (1819), or *Jane Eyre* (1847) into culture-texts while simultaneously keeping older characters—like Faust or biblical figures—in circulation. In the growing commercial environment of eighteenth- and nineteenth-century cultural production, older works and contemporary fiction could both become cult objects through enough extension.

From Odysseus to Alice to Batman, iconic characters survive independently from source texts, deriving cultural meaning from contexts old and new. They can be repurposed, not only to advance future stories but also to expand complex fictional worlds. Such extensive storyworlds might be carefully coordinated from their initial development, or they might develop over

---

1. Lynch, *The Economy of Character* (1998).

time through unanticipated transmedia extensions that evolve characters' individual stories as well as the larger storyworlds they share. Such characters and stories—especially those in the public domain—all fit the definition of culture-texts. Culture-texts function beyond the scope of an "original" form, which in some cases might get contested, lost, forgotten, or intentionally ignored. Although most iconic characters can be traced back to originating source texts, they owe their widespread recognition and cultural visibility to regular adaptation and extended allusion—to all the storied iterations that collectively make up their respective culture-text.

Paul Davis introduces the term "culture-text" to distinguish between Dickens's novella *A Christmas Carol* (1843) and what he calls the Carol (without italics), the version that exists in the cultural imagination as a popularized concept. Comparing culture-texts to oral traditions, Davis emphasizes the importance of all the parts (individual adaptations) that make up the whole:

> Rather than beginning as an oral story that was later written down, the *Carol* was written to be retold. Dickens was its creator, but it is also the product of its re-creators who have retold, adapted, and revised it over the years. . . . We remember the Carol as a cluster of phrases, images, and ideas. . . . The text of *A Christmas Carol* is fixed in Dickens' words, but the culture-text, the Carol as it has been re-created in the century and a half since it first appeared, changes as the reasons for its retelling change. We are still creating the culture-text of the Carol.[2]

Drawing attention to the story's iconic character, Davis's book places Scrooge at the center of this culture-text, which exists in scattered fragments in literary history and popular culture. Extending the model to the Jekyll and Hyde story, another culture-text with nineteenth-century origins, Brian Rose argues that culture-texts are created "through the processes of consistent readaptation in popular media, and through the reusage and augmentation of motifs first appearing in earlier adaptations, [by which] a body of popular-cultural memories and associations is created."[3] I have been using the term "culture-text" throughout this book because of its equal emphasis on texts and adaptations that exist collectively in the public imagination—the space where they hold the most cultural value. Culture-texts position authors, adapters, and audiences in a dynamic network that reaffirms the dispersed and participatory nature of transmedia storytelling as it has evolved alongside new technologies, economies, and sociopolitical contexts over several centuries.

---

2. Davis, *The Lives and Times of Ebenezer Scrooge* (1990), 3–4.
3. Rose, *Jekyll and Hyde Adapted* (1996), 15.

Seeing culture-texts and storyworlds as the sum of interconnected forms and media helps us discuss storytelling as an ongoing process. The ever-expanding character of culture-texts—what Julie Grossman calls "elasTEXTity"—extends beyond the immediate form of the story and an individual adaptation into a specific medium:

> *Elastextity* is a way of thinking about texts as extended beyond themselves, merging their identities with other works of art that follow and precede them....
>
> The idea of *elastextity* conceives of sources and adaptations as part of a vastly stretched tarp or canvas. As the metaphor implies, the state of being pulled beyond an initial form to encompass other objects, texts, and identities can have monstrous results, as texts appear misshapen or distorted ... at least until we grow accustomed to looking at their new forms.[4]

Using the elasticity of narrative as an anchoring concept, Grossman emphasizes the pliability of texts, fusing conversations from adaptation studies, media theory, and literary history. Drawing from examples as diverse as the Frankenstein culture-text and the expanding storyworld of Fargo, Grossman points to the central role that adaptation plays in creating cultural myths and extending storytelling beyond the form, media, or content of an "original" work. Adaptation and extension are central to these elastic, character-driven storyworlds than can take multiple cultural forms across media and history.

Showtime's recent three-season gothic thriller *Penny Dreadful* (2014–16) highlights the twenty-first-century relevance of character-driven storyworlds with nineteenth-century origins. The series combines the most iconic figures of gothic fiction, stitching together a blended storyworld that includes characters from *Frankenstein, Dracula, The Picture of Dorian Gray,* and others who assemble to battle bigger forces of evil attempting to destroy the world. Conceptually, this mash-up works because a century or more of adaptations have transformed these characters into cult objects—a process that requires fragmentation. Rejecting the notion that nostalgia or preference for an original alone can create iconic status, Umberto Eco insists that the work "must provide a completely furnished world so that its fans can quote characters and episodes as if they were aspects of the fan's private sectarian world.... In order to transform a work into a cult object one must be able to break, dislocate, unhinge it so that one can remember only parts of it irrespective of their original relationship with the whole."[5]

---

4. Grossman, *Literature, Film, and Their Hideous Progenies* (2015), 2.
5. Eco, *Travels in Hyper Reality* (1986), 197–98.

Such twenty-first-century reimaginings mirror many dynamics of storytelling as they developed in the nineteenth century's growing commercial economy. In this chapter, I explore nineteenth-century storyworlds through two examples: the lively characters inhabiting the fictional world that Dickens built to populate modern London, and the modernized legends of Camelot as they were revived for Victorians in various art forms by multiple writers and artists. There are two different models at work in these examples. In the first, culture-texts and storyworlds can be traced back to an origin text or individual author (like *A Christmas Carol* or Dickens). Dickens provides a fascinating example of world-building because most of his works were published in a serial format that anticipates the contemporary television series. Like today's viewers, audiences followed the adventures of their favorite characters, tuning in for the next installment. Through ensembles of memorable characters, Dickens built storyworlds that invited emotional, intellectual, and financial investment from fans who consumed the stories in print, performance, and visual art, as well as commercial products. Conversely, the reinvention of the Camelot culture-text in the nineteenth century exemplifies the second form of fictional world-building. Artists worked in reverse with the Arthurian tradition, taking a single, historical story concept (as shared property) and dispersing new text, art, and performances over multiple sites of authorship and artistry. In both cases, the nineteenth-century preoccupation with the rise of industrialization is mapped onto adaptation. Fictional storyworlds developed alongside their real-world counterparts in the rise of modern cities, one of the primary challenges of which involved navigating the evolving legal landscape and intensification of commercial cultural production.

WRITING (AND COPYRIGHTING) THE WORLD THAT DICKENS BUILT

Adaptations and extensions (in the forms of prequels, sequels, and mash-ups) draw upon and actively build character-driven storyworlds. For example, the BBC series *Dickensian* (2015–16) features a cast of nineteenth-century characters remixed into a single, serialized storytelling experience set in a fictionalized Victorian London. The show combines characters from twelve novels to craft an original "whodunit," neo-Victorian detective story within a world that Dickens built throughout his literary career. Primary characters from a dozen different novels support a single storyline in *Dickensian*, as Inspector Buckett (*Bleak House*) investigates the murder of Jacob Marley (*A Christmas Carol*), with Bill and Nancy Sikes (*Oliver Twist*) considered the leading sus-

FIGURE 4.1. Robert William Buss, *Dickens' Dream* (1875). Unfinished watercolor. Image courtesy of The Dickens Museum, London.

pects. As these characters' individual stories unfold, audiences are dropped into the central plotlines of *Great Expectations* and *The Old Curiosity Shop* while Dickens's best-known story, *A Christmas Carol*, serves as the framing narrative connecting all the character threads. The series draws its inspiration from the many culture-texts that Dickens inspired, fused with the author's own iconic status.

In this twenty-first-century mash-up, author and characters meld into a single storyworld that is equal parts homage and extension. As Sarah Cardwell notes, "The program marks its departures from the specifics of Dickens's works as proudly as it celebrates its allegiances to his imaginative world."[6] The series' opening credits visualize the collapse between the real-world Dickens and the fictional world he built across several novels as individual character silhouettes come together. The technique recalls a Victorian painting by Robert William Buss, whose unfinished *Dickens' Dream* (1875) features Dickens asleep in his study surrounded by an imaginary cloud of his characters as they were illustrated in the nineteenth century (see figure 4.1). The twenty-

6. Cardwell, "A *Dickensian* Feast" (2017), 120.

first-century television series and the nineteenth-century watercolor painting both position Dickens at the center of a fictional, character-driven world and employ the common method of visualizing Dickens's collective works as a unified, imaginary universe.

Produced five years after Dickens's death, Buss's painting depicts Dickens's many characters as fragmented parts of a single, shared dream, suggesting that Dickens will live on in the public imagination through his imaginative characters. More than a century later, *Dickensian* digitally reimagines this theme, using a pixelated technique to suggestively "zoom in" on the many characters that make the author an iconic figure. The new image also integrates the author into the shared universe of his collective works by making him a character within it. Both examples highlight the role of visualization in literary history and textual reception. The figure of the dreaming author was regularly used in nineteenth-century art to symbolize legacies of authorship, and Buss's painting is one of many variations on this theme produced around this time and featuring Dickens.[7]

Dickensian, Dickens fans, and nineteenth-century scholars agree that Dickens is best remembered for his lively characters and vivid descriptions of Victorian London. This process began as a combination of memorable illustrations, successful adaptations, and record-breaking book sales transformed Dickens into a literary celebrity in the nineteenth century, just as they have made him an icon in the present. As Juliet John explains:

> Central to Dickens's cultural survival and pervasiveness has been the evolution of the so-called "Dickens industry," engineered in the Victorian period by Dickens himself. In his lifetime, his reading tours, public speaking engagements, journals, travels, and acting projects made Dickens a celebrity, the most visible author of the nineteenth century. This visibility meant the duplication of his image in newspapers, advertisements, and on commodities, and the ubiquitousness of the idea of Dickens in Victorian mass culture.[8]

Simultaneous success across media, class, and national boundaries makes it difficult to write a straightforward, linear narrative of Dickens's immediate popularity, cultural afterlife, and literary canonization. As we see in figure 4.2, from *Pickwick Papers*, to *Oliver Twist*, to *A Christmas Carol*, many of the culture-texts that originated with Dickens circulated in multiple formats

---

7. Litvack, "Dickens's Dream and the Conception of Character" (2007).
8. John, *Dickens and Mass Culture* (2010), 15.

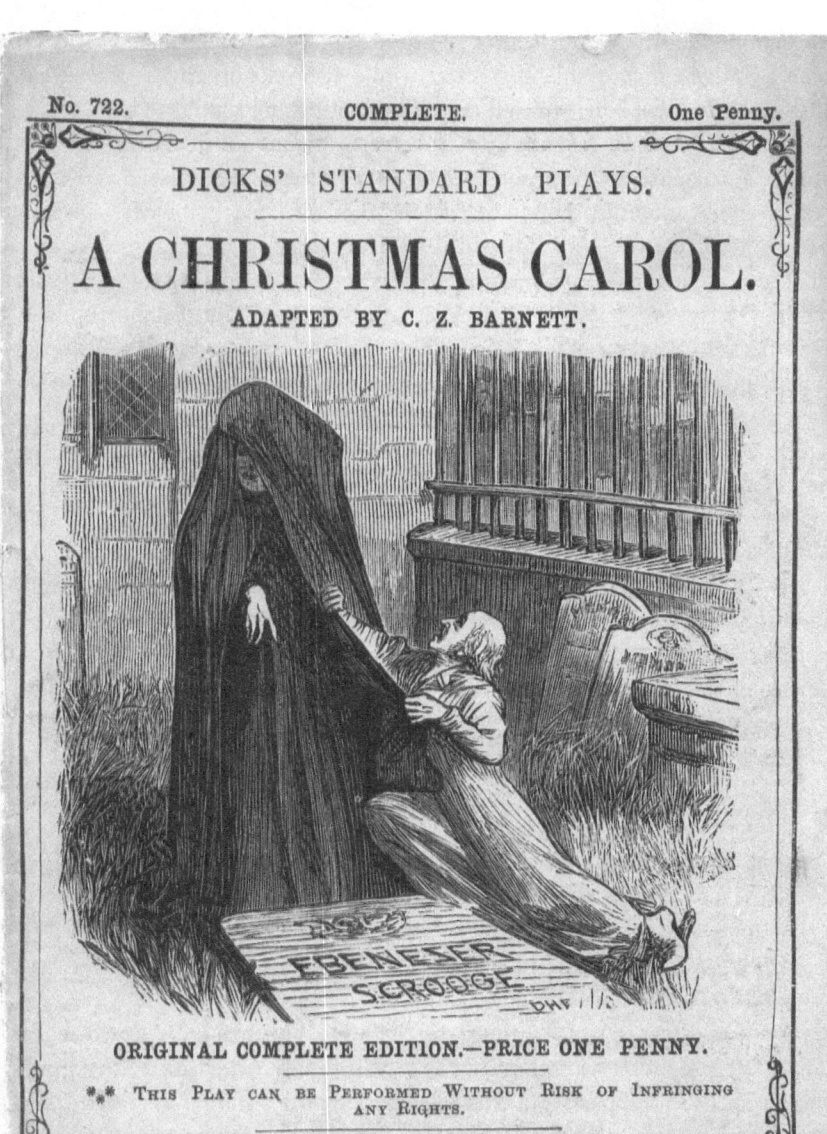

FIGURE 4.2. Title page for stage adaptation of *A Christmas Carol* by C. Z. Barnett, published by Dicks' Standard Plays, no. 722 (1883). Image © The Museum of London.

throughout the nineteenth century without crediting Dickens as author or creator of these memorable characters, while also encouraging repeated circulation and adaptation "without risk of infringing any rights."

The trajectory of Dickens's literary career provides a unique view of multimodal storytelling in the nineteenth century's emerging industrial and commercial environment. Although he was an innovative, modern writer, Dickens had a complicated relationship with the commercial aspects of authorship and creative ownership, simultaneously embracing and resisting industry trends. On the one hand, he was eager to experiment with publication formats. Dickens was the first major author to popularize storytelling in serial format, publishing most works in regular installments and later releasing them as full volumes. The format created a commercial buzz, with readers eagerly awaiting the latest installment to find out the fates of their favorite characters. Serialization also allowed the author to adjust the work according to readers' responses, reviews, and criticism, creating a malleable text that could be altered to accommodate the feedback of audience engagement. The format was particularly well suited for adaptation and transmedia storytelling because, as Carrie Sickmann Han explains, "the serial's reoccurring interruptions and divisions stimulate the reader's desire for continuations," which came to characterize how audiences consumed Dickens's characters.

> Charles Dickens's great art of serial writing aimed to leave his readers repeatedly wishing there was more: more pages, more plot, more world, and above all, more time with their favorite characters. This desire encouraged readers to imagine beyond the novel—to pursue characters outside the pages of *The Pickwick Papers* itself. Their desires were rewarded with a wide range of continuations that included theatrical adaptations, plagiarisms, or unauthorized sequels.[9]

Serialization didn't invent the immersive relationship that audiences bring to adaptation and transmediation, but it certainly intensified its cultural pervasiveness. The emphasis on character and world-building is particularly important here, as Sickmann Han points out, because contemporary reviews indicate that audiences were primarily motivated by extending the experience of characters (as opposed to plot development).

Innovative, serial publishing came with its own set of challenges, as authors had even less control over appropriations of their characters than did their predecessors, whose novels were published only once finished. In Dick-

---

9. Sickmann Han, *"Pickwick's Other Papers"* (2016), 19.

ens's case, plays were produced for his works-in-progress, with adapters creating new storylines and plot twists. Dickens's characters were immediately dispersed into an array of forms and media, with each adaptation or parody paving additional possibilities for audiences to either meet or reencounter Nancy Sikes or Pip. The proliferation of extensions both fascinated and troubled Dickens, and he carried a love-hate relationship with these popular adaptations for the entirety of his career.

While Dickens's objections to unauthorized adaptations might seem obvious or reasonable today, they were misaligned with the commercial aspects of nineteenth-century cultural production. Furthermore, Dickens's desire for control and authority downplayed the collaborative nature of industrial popular culture. As illustrated texts that were published serially, most of Dickens's works featured significant collaboration, despite his adamant insistence that he was the sole author and creator of all his works.

Dickens was the first major author to make full use of the power of mass-produced illustration as a storytelling device, and his first long-form publications were driven by adaptation and transmediation—textual, visual, and performative. From his earliest works, Dickens's fiction participated in the nineteenth-century fascination with spectacle and visual culture, and his novels have been called "proto-cinematic" in their attention to the sights and sounds of London life and its inhabitants. This debt to the visual and performing arts stemmed from his early ambitions to become an actor (which led to a lifelong fascination with, and involvement in, popular theater) as well as his background as a journalist, the profession that launched his writing career.

Comprised of a series of independent character "sketches," Dickens's literary debut "illustrated" daily life in London through the combined use of words and images, as this style became more prominent in English newspapers, periodicals, and the mass-market press. Published as a literary miscellany, *Sketches by Boz Illustrative of Every-day Life and Every-day People* (1833–36) was popular enough to warrant re-publication as a collection, with the famous caricaturist and book illustrator George Cruikshank hired to bring visual cohesiveness to the stories that would appeal to a mass audience.[10] At the time, Cruikshank was more professionally established than Dickens, making him a bigger commercial draw for the collection. Dickens knew as much and was excited to work with the celebrity illustrator.[11] Most importantly, the

---

10. Cruikshank wholly turned his attention to book illustration when he was thirty-one years old, as the demand for illustrated books turned this trade into a respectable, well-compensated profession. Buchanan-Brown, *The Book Illustrations of George Cruikshank* (1980).

11. Kitton, *Charles Dickens and His Illustrators* (1899).

success of *Sketches by Boz* allowed Dickens to permanently transition from journalism to fiction.

The genesis of *The Posthumous Papers of the Pickwick Club* (1836–37) further exposes one of the underlying misconceptions about the relationship between text and image in illustrated works: that text serves as the primary form of storytelling with visuals occupying an inferior place in the work. The history of nineteenth-century illustrated books and periodicals complicates this hierarchy. As Martin Meisel explains, "The nineteenth-century narrative pictorial style depended, not simply on the promiscuous and adulterate habit of the various arts in borrowing from each other . . . but on the conjunction of story and image as a common matrix for signification and effect."[12] The history of textual-visual collaborations across literature, theater, and the visual arts of painting, illustration, and engraving has been obscured in both literary and art history because both fields privilege "originality" (based on individualism and exceptionalism) over collaborative artistic models. However, visuals were central to nineteenth-century print culture in forms ranging from cheap, illustrated periodicals to expensive gift books, with text and image informing each other in the early history of what Patricia Mainardi calls the "globalization of visual media."[13]

In 1836, the publishing house of Chapman & Hall approached Dickens for a new project: a series of vignettes to accompany comical illustrations provided by Robert Seymour, the project's originator and a young, well-known artist who was already working on the images. The job was to write extended captions that would accompany and connect comic scenes of men in various sporting and recreational adventures drawn by Seymour, who like Cruikshank before him, was more established than the twenty-four-year-old Dickens. Dickens quickly negotiated, convincing the publisher that the accompanying text should be longer, making his role more substantial than originally planned and infuriating Seymour in the process. Seymour, who had struggled with mental health issues for years, committed suicide five chapters into the project—leaving Dickens as the creative lead for the serial. After a very short trial run with the artist Robert William Buss for one issue, the young artist Hablot Knight Browne was hired as the new illustrator. Browne adopted the moniker "Phiz" to complement Dickens's nickname "Boz," beginning a collaboration that would go on for years, with Browne illustrating ten of Dickens's novels. For the most part, nineteenth-century authors had little-to-no say in how their writing might be turned into pictures—and they would have no

---

12. Meisel, *Realizations* (1983), 433.
13. Mainardi, *Another World* (2017).

control over how their works might be illustrated and reimagined by later generations.[14] Dickens, by contrast, worked closely with his illustrators, and his early works in particular suggest a more dynamic exchange between author and artist in the creative process, somewhat similar to current trends in book-to-graphic novel production, which often includes author input that's atypical in the film industry.

The production of *Pickwick Papers* illustrates the centrality of caricature and visual culture to Dickens's career as a novelist. What was originally intended as a series of images linked through short, expository fiction evolved into a character-driven novel illuminated by images. In other words, Dickens's first "original" novel was itself a form of adaptation, started as an ekphrastic exercise in narrative extension—a textual expansion of a series of cartoons, a genre best described within today's entertainment industry as novelization.[15] The success of this project revolutionized the aesthetics of the print industry and inspired a host of imitators. It also became central to Dickens's storytelling style.

For his next long project, Dickens returned to Cruikshank. The serial run of *Oliver Twist* (1837–39) was a commercial success, but the collaboration turned sour and marked the end of their professional relationship. The major source of tension was Cruikshank's "interference" in Dickens's creative process, making regular suggestions and drawing illustrations according to his own style and interpretation (which one might point out is the main job of an illustrator). In other words, Dickens saw Cruikshank acting as an adapter as opposed to what he wanted, a visual translator. Cruikshank, on the other hand, saw himself as an equal creator. Years later, Cruikshank publicly claimed coauthorship for *Oliver Twist*'s plot and characters in a letter to the *Times*, expanded into a pamphlet later that year titled *George Cruikshank: The Artist and the Author* (1872). Cruikshank made similar claims about his creative input for the works of two other popular novelists of the day, works that went on to achieve transmedia success through adaptation: Pierce Eagan's *Life in London* (1820) and William Harrison Ainsworth's extremely popular *Jack Sheppard* (1839–40) and *The Miser's Daughter* (1842).[16]

Dramatization complicated the tension between authors and illustrators further, adding yet another layer to the complex network of adaptations and the regular exchange between textual and visual culture in both print and performance. The event that set Cruikshank off, however, was Andrew Halliday's adaptation of Ainsworth's *The Miser's Daughter*, staged at the Adelphi Theatre

---

14. Mole, *What the Victorians Made of Romanticism* (2017)
15. Newell, *Expanding Adaptation Networks* (2017); Baetens, *Novelization* (2018).
16. Buckley, "Sensations of Celebrity" (2002).

in April 1872. Cruikshank was not credited despite the fact that his illustrations had clearly served as the models for the stage scenery, set design, and costuming. When it came to theatrical adaptation, visual artists found themselves even more short-changed than published authors in the nineteenth-century adaptation industry. Set designers used print illustrations as visual cues or models for stage productions; costumes, poses, props, and painted scenery were often copied directly without acknowledgement to visual artists. Cruikshank was livid when he saw Halliday's new adaptation, as it wasn't the first time his visuals had been adapted for the stage without attribution.[17] After nearly four decades, he'd had enough. Cruikshank wanted the equal attribution for the full storytelling experience as it unfolded through a combination of text and image, the collaborative labor of many artists.[18]

For his third novel, *Nicholas Nickleby* (1838–39), Dickens returned to his partnership with Browne (a.k.a. "Phiz"), with whom he worked on most of *The Pickwick Papers* and who would go on to illustrate ten of Dickens's novels published between 1836 and 1852. The long-term collaboration and personal relationship that developed between these two men also ended abruptly when Dickens replaced Browne without warning because he thought Browne's style had become dated. Marcus Stone was hired to update the look of his newest characters in *Great Expectations* (1860–61) and *Our Mutual Friend* (1864–65). Dickens had used other illustrators before; all five of his Christmas books were illustrated by well-known *Punch* cartoonists of the 1840s (notably John Leech), who brought their own professional reputations and celebrity to the projects. Dickens's business-focused shrewdness and behavior toward Browne might seem cutthroat, but it demonstrates that he understood and valued the visual elements of building fictional worlds and was interested in keeping the storytelling experience of his works fashionable for commercial viability.[19]

There's irony in Dickens's endless critique of theatrical hacks and piratical publishers and Cruikshank's parallel interest in receiving credit for his contributions to *Oliver Twist* and other novels popularized through adaptations. *Nicholas Nickleby* details a heated argument between the protagonist and a "literary gentleman who had dramatized in his time two hundred and forty-seven novels" for the popular stage. The "literary gentleman" is a fictionalized caricature of William Thomas Moncrieff and other professional theater "hacks" like Edward Stirling, who at the time competed with Moncrieff to dramatize Dickens faster than the other could.[20] Providing more than a cari-

---

17. Hill, "Cruikshank, Ainsworth, and Tableau Illustration" (1980).
18. Vogler, "Cruikshank and Dickens" (1973–74).
19. Allingham, "'Reading Pictures, Visualizing the Text'" (2012).
20. Bratton, "William Thomas Moncrieff" (2015).

cature of theatrical hacks, the impassioned dialogue advances a rudimentary theory of adaptation and authorship as the latter category evolved during the rise of capitalism and the commercialization of arts and culture. In addition to comparing the literary gentleman to a common pickpocket (see chapter 2 for more discussion), Dickens contrasts theatrical adaptation in the present to its historical counterpart in Shakespeare:

> "Shakespeare dramatised stories which had previously appeared in print, it is true," observed Nicholas.
> "Meaning Bill, sir?" said the literary gentleman. "So he did. Bill was an adapter, certainly, so he was—and very well he adapted too—considering."
> "I was about to say," rejoined Nicholas, "that Shakespeare derived some of his plots from old tales and legends in general circulation; but it seems to me, that some of the gentlemen of your craft, at the present day, have shot very far beyond him—... for, whereas he brought within the magic circle of his genius, traditions peculiarly adapted for his purpose, and turned familiar things into constellations which should enlighten the world for ages, you drag within the magic circle of your dullness, subjects not at all adapted to the purposes of the stage, and debase as he exalted."[21]

Dickens inserts himself into his storyworld, using characters as ventriloquists for his ideas about social issues such as poverty and legal issues like copyright. In this way, the exchange is a metafictional, mimetic moment as it refers to adapters currently dramatizing the novel that Dickens is still writing. The exchange acknowledges the long history and cultural prominence of theatrical adaptation, establishing Shakespeare as one of the most famous adapters of all time. However, as the fictionalized debate makes clear, the nineteenth-century context is different than Shakespeare's. Dickens claims not to have a problem with adaptation, but only if there is no clear author and/or if the adaptation makes the source material better. The scenario is different when adapting the works of living authors, who under the laws of the time were cheated out of income. High/low metaphors abound in this critical exchange, with Shakespeare transforming source materials into "constellations" and "literary gentlemen" stealing from contemporary authors and "debasing" their works. In more ways than one, the publication of *Nicholas Nickleby* marks a turning point in Dickens's career, as Dickens positions himself within the adaptation industry surrounding him. The critical portrayal of the "literary gentleman" takes an explicit stance on adaptation and an implicit position on copyright,

---

21. Dickens, *Nicholas Nickleby* (2003), 598.

which would follow Dickens for the rest of his life, shaping both his fiction and its public reception.

Dickens publicly fought for more control over his works and their adaptations by embedding real-world arguments into his fictional works and also by making speeches on copyright during appearances. During a visit to the United States in 1842, for example, he made impromptu monologues about unethical publishing practices at events and dinner parties, in hopes of curbing pirated editions abroad and unauthorized adaptations at home.[22] It didn't work. Copyright laws were not enforceable internationally. Even within the United Kingdom, which had the most comprehensive laws protecting authors, copyright law only protected a work in its original publication form. In other words, a novel could only be copyrighted *as* a novel, meaning that the form of publication held more legal status than the content of the publication. Laws had to be changed to keep pace with new industrial considerations, and it would take decades for laws to finally address international copyright and derivative works in any substantive way. The Copyright Act of 1842 (controversial but supported by writers such as William Wordsworth) significantly extended an author's rights for a period of forty-two years or seven years after the author's death, but the law only applied nationally.[23] Dickens's trip to the United States coincided with one of these changes in English law, and both the trip and the new law provided source material for *Martin Chuzzlewit* (1842–44).[24] This novel was one of Dickens's least popular works; it was adapted for the stage only twenty-two times by 1850 and approximately forty times by 1900, numbers that paled in comparison to his other works, yet still helps us envision the extent to which Dickens was adapted in the nineteenth century.[25]

By the 1840s, Dickens had begun to realize the impossibility of completely controlling adaptations of his works. In England, through collaborations with illustrators and dramatists, he instead used his celebrity and professional connections to increasingly influence stage adaptations and the immediate reception of his works in London's theaters. In one particularly productive example, Dickens praised Andrew Halliday's stage adaptations, and the two men shared personal and professional connections, having worked together on publication projects. However, industry relationships didn't always go this smoothly, and they could often be contentious. In a letter dated June 24, 1844, Dickens refused a request to write a prologue for an upcoming theatrical adaptation of

---

22. Hoeren, "Charles Dickens and the International Copyright Law" (2016).

23. Zall, "Wordsworth and the Copyright Act of 1842" (1955).

24. Castillo, "Natural Authority in Charles Dickens's *Martin Chuzzlewit* and the Copyright Act of 1842" (2008).

25. Bolton, *Dickens Dramatized* (1987), 222–34.

Chuzzlewit. Instead, writing to the actor-theater manager Robert Keeley (who performed in and produced many dramatizations of Dickens's novels), the novelist offers to attend rehearsals and provide input on the planned production, while adding his (unsolicited) opinion of casting choices:

> I start for Italy on Monday next, but if you have the piece on the stage, and rehearse on Friday, I will gladly come down at any time you may appoint on that morning, and go through it with you all. If you be not in a sufficiently forward state to render this proposal convenient to you, or likely to assist your preparations, do not take the trouble to answer this note.
>
> I presume Mrs. Keeley will do Ruth Pinch. If so, I feel secure about her, and of Mrs. Gamp [played by Robert Keeley] I am certain. But a queer sensation begins in my legs, and comes upward to my forehead, when I think of Tom.
>
> Faithfully yours always.[26]

The play, written by Edward Stirling, premiered two weeks later on July 8, 1844, and was performed 105 times that season at the Lyceum Theatre.[27]

In addition to accepting how others would adapt his characters, Dickens also started experimenting with forms of character extension himself. Capitalizing on previous successes and his rising literary celebrity, Dickens linked earlier projects to new ventures. When he launched *Master Humphrey's Clock* (a literary miscellany published from 1840–41), he used the characters Samuel Pickwick and Sam Weller to connect this project with *The Pickwick Papers*. Making appearances in frame stories, these characters served as narrators and anchors for the serialized issues of Dickens's fourth and fifth novels, *The Old Curiosity Shop* and *Barnaby Rudge*.[28] Through such intertextual experiments, Dickens wrote characters into a larger storyworld operating across his collected works. This technique provided an illusion of both continuity and realism, almost as if Dickens's characters existed in the real world.

As one of the first authors to closely monitor and craft his public persona, Dickens employed various modern-day narrative and marketing techniques, from fashionable illustrations to intentional portraiture to public readings. He would become known for the latter in the last decade of his life. In 1853, Dickens began doing book tours, a format in which he excelled, given his early acting aspirations and lifelong interest in the theater. Indeed, Dickens's public readings were so energetic that people described him as transforming

---

26. Dickens and Hogarth, *The Letters of Charles Dickens* (1880), 105.
27. Bolton, *Dickens Dramatized* (1987), 222.
28. Special thanks to Pamela Gilbert for pointing out this connection to me.

into his characters as he performed them dramatically using different voices and postures. Through public readings and the circulation of his own image in works via print, illustration, and performance, Dickens became a character in his collected storyworld.

Public readings were a new form of publicity, bringing the author into direct contact with the audience for a unique storytelling experience. These in-person appearances helped establish him as the true "owner" and "authority" over his characters.[29] Raymund Fitzsimons notes that the public readings not only provided Dickens with an additional source of income but also kept the aging author active in public once his literary output slowed down after the publication of *Bleak House* (1852–53). The readings were always entertaining and theatrical, as Dickens threw himself into the performances, cutting longer expository prose sections and replacing them with lively character-driven dialogue and gestures—in essence, adapting his prose for the new format. Describing the effect in Dickens's first public reading of *A Christmas Carol*, Fitzsimons summarizes: "The description of the miser . . . was eliminated from the reading. There was no need for it; Scrooge himself was standing on the platform."[30] Like Byron before him, Dickens-the-celebrity was often conflated with his characters. Likenesses of the young Dickens appeared in Cruikshank's illustrations to *Sketches by Boz*. The public readings later in Dickens's career only intensified these connections, as periodicals published illustrations of the aging author, captioning the images to highlight his dramatic performances and the connection between creator and characters.

These images helped Dickens craft his public persona, and they influenced the professional trajectory of modern authorship—artistically, commercially, and legally. Marking the historical moment Dickens went from emerging writer to literary celebrity, Gerard Curtis argues that the author's portrait included in the frontispiece to the final installment of *Nicholas Nickleby* was "central to the subtle change of Dickens from popular writer of caricature sketches to cultural icon and author of dignified novels," and Curtis makes clear that text, image, and performance converged to create Dickens-the-icon:

> Through this passionate interest in copyright, notions of authorship and the business of being a journal publisher, Dickens helped in this process of reconceptualizing the author. In his portraits, he astutely balanced an image of the modern businesslike writer with those traditional and romantic attributes of authorship which kept the "hand" before the public eye. One such

---

29. Adams, "Performing Ownership (2011); Ortiz-Robles, "Dickens Performs Dickens" (2011).

30. Fitzsimons, *The Charles Dickens Show* (1970), 18.

illusion was the anachronistic quill that often appeared as an accessory with cheap mass-produced literature. Certainly he achieved a popular balancing act between the modern commercial nature of authorship, emphasizing copyright and mass production, mass readership, and a business and legal entity, and the competing traditions of "originality" and individualism. In the frontispiece portrait of *Nicholas Nickleby* Dickens managed to unite his self-advertising authorial persona with the disembodied text, creating a legalistic stamp of ownership. By using mass-produced engravings and photographs, he became a mass-marketed, abstract and symbolic image that tied into the promotion of his texts, echoing his lifelong interest not only in changing the status of authorship but also in acting.[31]

Beyond marketing himself as a professional, Dickens paved the way for later authors (most immediately his friend Harrison Ainsworth) to use "their public portraits as trademarks" that might even include the author's signature reproduced as a sign of authenticity.[32] Through a network of adaptations that included text, illustration, theatrical performance, and public readings, Dickens gradually developed into a larger-than-life cultural icon, starting as an "author of the masses," then becoming a literary celebrity, and eventually being canonized in literary history as film, television, and other forms immortalized his characters.[33] As we continue to see in the twentieth- and twenty-first centuries, Dickens-the-icon is undoubtedly and explicitly at the center of the Dickens culture-text, vis-à-vis the "Dickensian" storyworld built by his literary career and the collected extensions of many adapters.

INDUSTRIAL CONVERGENCE AND THE EVOLUTION OF COPYRIGHT

Almost every major writer in the eighteenth and nineteenth centuries found themselves adapted and reprinted without permission, attribution, or royalties, as pirated copies and stage dramatizations appeared everywhere. The lack of international copyright laws hit hard at times, with Harriet Beecher Stowe's *Uncle Tom's Cabin* (1852) among the most egregiously pirated and adapted novels of the nineteenth century in both the United States and England, where

---

31. Curtis, *Visual Words* (2002), 130–31.
32. Curtis, *Visual Words* (2002), 131. For Curtis, advertising and in-text product placement also participated in narrative world-building that collapsed the fictive and real worlds in nineteenth-century fiction.
33. Glavin, *Dickens on Screen* (2003) and *Dickens Adapted* (2012).

the story was reprinted without permission regularly and staged more than a dozen times during London's 1852–53 theatrical season alone. Poets and novelists were often infuriated by these blatant financial abuses on the part of publishers, printers, and the editors of periodicals that fell outside of British copyright law, which itself was undergoing regular change but remained among the most favorable to published authors.[34]

The governing legal rationale explains the prominence of parodies, adaptations, continuations, and other forms of imitation, what David Brewer terms "imaginative expansions," as they produced what he and Franco Moretti call a "social canon" of stories as they existed in the collective popular imagination, complementing if not directly copying printed texts.[35] For Brewer, the term describes "an array of reading practices in eighteenth-century Britain by which the characters in broadly successful texts were treated as if they were both fundamentally incomplete and the common property of all."[36] This position would continue to guide copyright law until the late Victorian period, when Dickens's struggle for more control over his works belonged to a much larger conversation about the business of authorship. Because character-driven stories and detailed, supporting storyworlds were the fabric of eighteenth- and nineteenth-century fiction in an emerging industrialized, commercial economy, mass appeal made well-told stories into marketable commodities, which created competition and the need for new laws to protect their value.[37]

Authors had the best protection of all artists because their works were shielded by the permanence of print. By contrast, theatrical performances had a much more difficult time establishing copyright protection, as each new production was basically a new work. Relatively few plays made it into print, leaving little security for dramatists who were already typically paid obscenely small amounts for their creative output. In the theater, it didn't pay well to be original unless it led to other forms of permanent employment like becoming a house dramatist, and so it made sense to recycle material in order to maintain output levels. For these reasons, copyright was an industry issue more than an individual issue for artists in the theater industry, a dynamic that underwent a major overhaul within the nineteenth-century culture industry as the reading public expanded and writers found themselves at the center of

---

34. Hoeren, "Charles Dickens and the International Copyright Law" (2016).
35. Brewer, *The Afterlife of Character* (2005), 17–18; Moretti, *Distant Reading* (2013).
36. Brewer, *The Afterlife of Character* (2005), 2.
37. Although specifics varied between examples, there are similar processes at work in both England and France. Paraschas, *Reappearing Characters in Nineteenth-Century French Literature* (2018).

a new commodity-driven marketplace where artistic labor increased in value for authors, dramatists, and actors.

Beyond the world of textual extensions, adaptation into another medium existed in a virtually lawless land of free-for-all. The concept of "derivative works" in copyright law was completely new legal territory in the nineteenth century, and it remains a contested area of cultural production today as artists and companies struggle to deal with unlicensed use of their works—which in turn serves to drive interest in those works. Another major consideration in the context of commercial storytelling became the extent to which characters themselves could be considered original works, given that so much of the structure of the novel was founded on the development of "round" characters and their interiority, which Diedre Lynch situates at the center of the development of the novel as both literary form and cultural commodity.[38] Throughout most of the nineteenth century, authors did not need to give permission for their works to be adapted, nor were they entitled to royalties from those adaptations. Adaptations did increase visibility and public interest, and they might lead to greater book sales, new printings, and revised editions; however, writers received direct payment exclusively from initial copyright sales (publication rights sold to publishers). Indirectly, adaptations could produce income by increasing an author's reputation, thus helping them receive new commissioned assignments and publication contracts. Still, authors had no legal right to influence how works were adapted or used for other commercial purposes. To update the laws, an international council was called, which introduced international protections through the Berne Convention of 1886, whose provisions continue to evolve to accommodate industry changes.[39]

The Berne Convention finally acknowledged the variety of copyrightable material, which extended vastly beyond the realm of printed works, including "exclusive control over every mode of copying, adapting, translating or disseminating any original output in the 'literary, scientific, and artistic domain.'"[40] Prior to this international convening, existing laws were inadequate to cover the production, transformation, and recirculation of texts both domestically and internationally. When it came to adaptations and derivative works, the law now protected both types of author: the author of the original work as well as the creator of the adaptation, if the adaptation altered the

---

38. Lynch, *The Economy of Character* (1998).
39. The United Kingdom did not ratify the Berne Convention right away, primarily over disagreement on the adaptation provisions. This changed in the early twentieth century, although English law wasn't brought fully in line with international law until the 1980s. The United States would wait more than one hundred years before joining the agreement in 1989.
40. Atkinson and Fitzgerald, *A Short History of Copyright* (2014), 51.

original content enough to create a new work. When it came to the intellectual property of the originating author, international law now covered "identifiable parts of the form" of the work being adapted.[41] Characters, plots, incidents, and even performances became part of the intellectual property—not only the publication format. This difference remains central to contemporary copyright laws regarding adaptation, derivative works, and multiple distribution formats, where adaptation is now an assumed potential trajectory for all works that fall under the legal protection of intellectual property (literary, artistic, scholarly, scientific, etc.).[42]

Although the specific rights bestowed on original authors remained unclear, the ability to copyright performances in different formats led to new practices. The staging of "copyright performances" was used to establish some legal basis for exclusivity and to market claims to an "authorized" version. For example, Robert Louis Stevenson agreed to Thomas Russell Sullivan's and Richard Mansfield's requests to adapt *Jekyll and Hyde* in 1887, and while other adaptations appeared (as expected), they were dismissed by the press as "unauthorized" or otherwise "inferior" (though not necessarily illegal). Later writers would arrange for immediate public stagings of unfinished pieces or works in progress in order to establish a copyright on performance, to varying degrees of success. In one such case, Bram Stoker staged a lengthy public reading immediately following the publication of *Dracula* (1897), and while it kept *Dracula* off the stage for a while, it did nothing to keep F. W. Murnau from using the story as the basis of his German expressionist film *Nosferatu* (1922), which lifts characters and plot directly from *Dracula* but conceals Stoker's novel as its source by simply changing character names.

Contemporary legal protections for authors and franchise owners are direct legacies of changes to copyright laws spearheaded by major nineteenth-century authors like Dickens, Wilkie Collins, and Hugo, created in direct response to rampant adaptation and publishing piracy in the entertainment industry.[43] Yet even though they differed in the extent to which they claimed rights to their works over time, all of these writers appeared to understand that adaptation and extension (whether authorized or not) made stories circulate more widely. Eventually those stories could become culture-texts through a network of dispersed authorship. Of course, this possibility is obvious only from the perspective provided by long-term reception histories; during their

---

41. Ricketson, *The Berne Convention for the Protection of Literary and Artistic Works: 1886–1986* (1987), 286.

42. Today, standard publishing contracts—even for books with relatively low circulation—include provisions negotiating royalties for derivative works.

43. Bisla, *Wilkie Collins and Copyright* (2013).

own lifetimes, the most popular poets and writers found themselves on the unfortunate end of the deal in their immediate context. One can hardly blame certain nineteenth-century writers for laying the groundwork for today's copyright laws. However, ultimately, Dickens had a rather short-sighted vision of storytelling, focusing on immediate concerns instead of long-term possibilities. Hugo, on the other hand, had a more fluid concept of copyright and adaptations, arguing during his early involvement with the Berne Convention for a balance between the rights of authors and the rights of the public. To be a culture-text that would allow an author to achieve centuries-long fame, adaptation and dispersal were absolutely necessary. Dickens would have seen this process at work in his day through the canonization of major writers like Shakespeare, who was endlessly adapted and reimagined throughout the Romantic and Victorian periods, or through the revival of somewhat-forgotten legends and storyworlds, such as the legends of Camelot as they were adapted and recirculated in the nineteenth century.

CAMELOT; OR, THE ULTIMATE VICTORIAN TRANSMEDIA STORYWORLD AND CULTURE-TEXT

Sometimes the central, unifying point of a culture-text is single authorship (like Shakespeare or Dickens), but culture-texts and their respective storyworlds also develop through systems of multiple authorships and shared universes where characters from different stories appear in crossover adventures.[44] Transmedia narrative strategies like these guide the advancement of works from myths and fairy tales to contemporary superhero and fantasy franchises, as well as other culture-texts with long histories such as Arthurian legends, which have been repeatedly adapted since the fifteenth century. Eventually, culture-texts that start with a single author evolve into storyworlds as new writers take up older works and turn them into transmedia franchises, just as we have seen with *The Lord of the Rings* culture-text; although its storyworld may have originated with J. R. R. Tolkien's novelization, the culture-text nonetheless unfolds and expands in film and video games, each with its own set of new authors or creators.

The most pervasive example of convergence culture and multiauthored, transmedia storytelling across genres, forms, and media in the nineteenth century is the Camelot culture-text. Like Shakespeare in the nineteenth century or Jane Austen today, the legends of Camelot functioned like "public domain"

---

44. Thon, *Transmedial Narratology and Contemporary Media Culture* (2016).

storyworlds, offering endless possibilities for off-shoots, spin-offs, and new directions. By the nineteenth century, the Camelot culture-text was already enough removed from its original medieval contexts that no one could claim its characters as their own, therefore, nearly everyone did. Writers and artists (often at the request of publishers and theater managers) rebooted medieval stories of Camelot for Victorian audiences through a wide-ranging network of adaptations and extensions largely responsible for this storyworld's continued relevance.

The cultural pervasiveness of the legends of King Arthur during the second half of the nineteenth century in England can be partially explained through the period's more conservative political and cultural context, where expansion of the British Empire was central to Queen Victoria's reign, and rampant mechanization and urban expansion ushered in a new wave of interest in a preindustrial past. Although they were typically more tempered than their Romantic counterparts, Victorian textual, dramatic, and visual transmediations of the Camelot storyworld were infused with social commentary aimed at contemporary audiences, leading to anachronistic adaptations notable for historical displacement, reflecting the politics of their new adapters. Ultimately the legends of Camelot functioned as a fictional, idealized setting from which to express the anxieties or possibilities of modern life and reclaim a "history" of Britain's imperial ascendancy that reached mythological status.

The proliferation of Arthuriana in the Victorian period was part of a broader fascination with historicism inherited from earlier artists and writers such as Walter Scott, who pioneered the genre of historical fiction by adapting the literal past for new audiences. Similarly, the Victorians adapted medieval topics for a range of political sensibilities, and their fascination with the middle ages is well-documented in various facets of Victorian society and culture: the elite walls of the nineteenth-century Academy; the artistic principles of the Pre-Raphaelites and their followers; the aesthetic (and gradually socially aware) theories of John Ruskin that critique the rise of capitalism; and the arts and craft movement led by socialist author, artist, and publisher William Morris.[45] The popularity of Arthurian stories was part of this larger interest in recuperating the preindustrial past in a format that could be widely circulated and celebrated, in a new historical moment, via adaptation in textual, dramatic, and visual forms.

Like Byron and Blake before him, Tennyson's canonical status as a poet has obfuscated his role as an adapter himself. Tennyson traded heavily in the art of transmediation, and he almost single-handedly ushered Arthurian revival

---

45. Culler, *The Victorian Mirror of History* (1985); Biddick, *The Shock of Medievalism* (1998).

into the Victorian period through his textual adaptations of many sources. Despite several versions produced between the twelfth and fifteenth centuries (notably Thomas Malory's *Le Morte d'Arthur* [1485], itself a loose adaptation of Geoffrey of Monmoth's *History of the Kings of England* [c. 1136]), the legends of Camelot went dormant in the public imagination until Tennyson started modernizing them for a new generation of Victorian readers.[46] As Laura Conner Lambdin and Robert Thomas Lambdin explain: "The popularization of the Arthurian legends in the nineteenth century can be credited mostly to Alfred Tennyson's versions of them. Malory's vast *Le Morte D'Arthur* with its archaic language and style of narration was too daunting for most readers; far more accessible was Tennyson's abridged and reworked version in *Idylls of the King*."[47] Working as both translator and adapter, Tennyson developed and revised his Camelot-inspired poems over four decades, remixing the legends to interest Victorian readers and inspire a host of other retellings.

Tennyson's first take on the Arthurian storyworld was "The Lady of Shalott" (1832; revised 1842), a subject he returned to twenty years later in "Launcelot and Elaine," the seventh tale in *Idylls of the King*. Although Elaine of Astolat and the Lady of Shalott are technically different characters in the Arthurian tradition, similarities in their stories, especially in the specific iconography of the lady's posthumous arrival at King Arthur's court in Camelot, have led to a conflation of the two stories. Dozens of paintings and book illustrations of Elaine of Astolat and/or the Lady of Shalott were inspired by Tennyson's poems, particularly after *Idylls*.[48] The most popular paintings came from John William Waterhouse, who revisited the poem three times throughout his career, and today his paintings are among the most widely circulated art reproductions of Victorian visual culture. Victorian versions often align in their depiction of the heroine's tragic social entrapment and subsequent mysterious death. Whether depicted at her window, at her loom, on her final boat ride, or at her posthumous arrival in Camelot, Victorian artists found in Arthurian tradition and the character of Elaine/Lady of Shalott specifically an endless source of inspiration for visualizing women's sociopolitical oppression.[49]

For Debra Mancoff, Tennyson's poetic extensions exemplify narrative depth and complex characters, in that "more than a revision of the legend [Tennyson] tested the creed of revivalist chivalry. . . . Through individual experience his characters revealed themselves as human, striving to fulfill

---

46. Moll, *Before Malory* (2003).
47. Lambdin and Lambdin, *Camelot in the Nineteenth Century* (2000), 14.
48. Landow, *Ladies of Shalott* (1985).
49. Szwydky, "Forms and Media: Adapting Tragedy" (2019).

their aspirations."⁵⁰ Mancoff places Tennyson at the center of the Victorian revival of Camelot; however, she also notes that the revival was a transmedia phenomenon where meaning was dispersed among creators and consumers for a range of different sensibilities:

> As the legend reached a wider audience, it took on a more human scale and a more subtle dimension. . . . Editions of Malory in modernized language appeared and poets and painters drew upon the full canon, expanding the vista established by revivalist chivalry and heroic personifications. As Arthurian characters were returned to their narrative context, they developed in complexity. . . . [Tennyson's] readers, as well as the painters who employed his work as the new Arthurian canon, embraced this more poignant vision of the men and women of Camelot.⁵¹

The tone of each adaptation or extension could vary from idealistic to pessimistic, depending on the voice or vision of the adapter.

Many visual artists adapted Tennyson's poems, including William Holman Hunt, Dante Gabriel Rossetti, and John Everett Millais—the three original members of the Pre-Raphaelite Brotherhood (all of whom were featured in the 1857 "Moxon Edition" of Tennyson's *Poems*).⁵² Writing in the late Victorian period, George Somes Layard notes that, among the illustrators belonging to the Pre-Raphaelite Brotherhood, "Millais has realized, Holman Hunt has idealized, and Rossetti has sublimated, or transcendentalized, the subjects which they have respectively illustrated" with Rossetti "contradict[ing] the text" at times.⁵³ Similar to Blake's relationship to Dante and Milton, Tennyson's illustrators functioned as visual interpreters and critics, sometimes shining light to illuminate Tennyson's text, and at other times refracting it to encompass a range of new interpretations and themes from both textual and visual sources. Unlike Dickens, whose original illustrators were reproduced in later editions, establishing the visual continuity of Dickens's collective storyworld over decades, Tennyson's poems kept getting reillustrated by new artists. The number and variety of print illustrations—not only of Tennyson's versions of the Camelot legends but also of other artist's visual adaptations—created more

---

50. Mancoff, *The Arthurian Revival in Victorian Art* (1990), 210.
51. Mancoff, *The Arthurian Revival in Victorian Art* (1990), 210.
52. Millais was the only original member of the Pre-Raphaelite Brotherhood who remained interested in illustration throughout his career, leaving behind more than three hundred designs produced between 1852 and 1883, significantly more than all of the other members combined. Goldman, *John Everett Millais* (2004).
53. Layard, *Tennyson and His Pre-Raphaelite Illustrators* (1894), 9.

and more fragmentation. The Camelot culture-text was strengthened through this dispersal, as its popular reach increased through printed visuals that held more permanence (as opposed to stage performances or original paintings in galleries).

Sometimes adaptations crossed linguistic and literacy barriers. Among Gustave Doré's most celebrated projects were his illustrations to Tennyson's *Idylls*. In the 1860s—following up successful illustrated editions of Tennyson's poetry, including the 1857 "Moxon Tennyson" and the 1859 edition of *Idylls*— English publisher Edward Moxon commissioned Doré. Doré's illustrated editions of Tennyson's poems proved especially profitable, going through several printings beginning in 1867 and inspiring single volumes dedicated to some of the Camelot storyworld's major female characters, including Elaine, Guinevere, Vivien, and Enid. These illustrated editions of Tennyson prompted translations in France, Spain, Germany, the Netherlands, and the United States between the 1860s and 1890s, gaining the English Poet Laureate an international readership.[54] In most cases, Doré's illustrated editions were the first translation of *Idylls* into European languages.[55] As seen in *Vivien and Merlin Repose* (1868, see figure 4.3), Doré visualized Tennyson's Camelot through his own characteristic style, broadening the potential market to include the artist's own following.

Doré was one in a long line of successful translators and adapters to capitalize on the Camelot craze introduced to a new generation.[56] Illustrated gift books were regularly produced by different publishers featuring new illustrations displaying a range of aesthetics and techniques. Tennyson himself even commissioned the celebrated Victorian photographer Julia Margaret Cameron to illustrate an 1874 edition of *Idylls* in this new, popular medium. She produced more than two hundred images for this project, which failed commercially because of the expense of printing photographs; today the book exists only in a limited format, and most of the photos have been lost.[57] Cameron's photographic illustrations are a unique addition to the Camelot culture-text, not only for their significance as a notable accomplishment in the history of photography, especially women's art, but also because they have a critically mixed reception. On the one hand, they are generally considered "failed" illustrations because they are heavily influenced by Tennyson's earlier illustrators (i.e., not "original" enough) and because some felt the new technology of photography produced "a realistic effect which can only be termed incon-

---

54. Ormond, *The Reception of Alfred Tennyson in Europe* (2017), 367–68.
55. Soubigou, "Gustave Doré: Interpreter of Tennyson's *Idylls of the King*" (2017).
56. Hogg, *King Arthur through the Ages* (1990).
57. Olsen, "Idylls of Real Life" (1995).

FIGURE 4.3. Gustave Doré, *Vivien and Merlin Repose* (1868). Digital image courtesy of Alamy Stock Photo.

gruous" with the fantastical nature of the subject.[58] In her representations of gender, Cameron significantly departs from most of her male contemporaries. Cameron's photograph depicting *Vivien and Merlin* (1874), for instance, clearly displays striking differences from Doré's engravings. Where Doré focuses on setting to determine mood and fantasy, Cameron captures her subjects up close, creating a uniquely modern style that favors realism and appears detached from any particular historical moment (see figures 4.4 through 4.6). The women often appear near or at eye level with male characters, subverting traditional gendered power dynamics, and Vivien appears more dominant in Cameron's photographs. As Helmut Gernsheim notes, Cameron's place in the history of photography is undisputed, as is the place of this nineteenth-century technology in the cultural history of the medieval legends of Camelot and its role in bridging the illustrative technologies of book engraving and photographic reproduction.

Far too vast to detail in full, the extent of the Arthurian transmedia storyworld includes paintings, operas, and sculptures, later migrating into radio, television, and film.[59] Unlike culture-texts that can be easily traced to a source text, Tennyson popularized Victorian Arthuriana, but the Camelot culture-text thrived because it was unhindered by any single, authoritative textual version. While its adaptation history may differ from those of other culture-texts more closely tied with an originating source-text, like *Frankenstein,* the return of Camelot in the nineteenth century echoes the features of the oldest culture-texts, those dispersed (sometimes orally) so many times that adaptations and offshoots start new culture-texts of their own. In its array of texts by different writers, the Camelot revival challenged the primacy of single authorship, relying instead on a collective form of storytelling attached to a storyworld.

New, "authoritative" texts added to this cross-media storyworld by now-canonical nineteenth-century artists included several literary and theatrical forms. Matthew Arnold's "Tristram and Iseult" (1852) was "the first English retelling of the story of these specific characters in nearly 400 years" and was followed by Wagner's opera *Tristan und Isolde* (1865), Tennyson's "The Last Tournament" (1871), and the epic poem *Tristram of Lyonesse* (1882) by Algernon Charles Swinburne. William Morris included in *The Defence of Guenevere and Other Poems* (1858) eight poems that either expanded or alluded to Arthurian characters, and he planned an epic-length work, but only completed a fragment titled "The Maying of Guenevere."[60] Mark Twain would satirize the

---

58. Gernsheim, *Julia Margaret Cameron* (1975).

59. Fulton, *A Companion to Arthurian Literature* (2009); Mancoff, *The Arthurian Revival in Victorian Art* (1990); Simpson, *Radio Camelot* (2008).

60. Lambdin and Lambdin, *Camelot in the Nineteenth Century* (2000), 51–52 and 71–72.

FIGURE 4.4. Julia Margaret Cameron, *Vivien and Merlin* (1874). Albumen photograph. Public Domain. Digital image courtesy of the J. Paul Getty Museum Open Content Program, Los Angeles.

Victorians' obsession with the Arthurian tradition and their romanticization of chivalry and all things British in his novel *A Connecticut Yankee in King Arthur's Court* (1889), as the American author emphasized a displaced, critical distance from Camelot's cultural history.

The range of Camelot adaptations produced during the nineteenth century highlights new social and political contexts for the culture-text that, according to Mancoff, must always be historically situated:

> In reviving the Arthurian legend, Victorian artists and writers ... [and audiences] sought a window on the past in a desire to learn from the heroic and noble ancestors. What they forged, however, was a mirror of the present, projecting their own ideals and ambitions, dreams and fears, onto legendary characters and events. In a romanticized portrait they captured a vivid reflection of themselves. Through the poetry and painting of the Arthurian Revival, we can see how a society interpreted its own identity and informed its present view by remaking the cultural legacy of its past.[61]

Old characters were also revisited through modern eyes to forge new futures. In this collective transmedia storyworld rebuilt in the nineteenth century,

---

61. Mancoff, *The Return of King Arthur* (1995), 8.

FIGURE 4.5. Julia Margaret Cameron, *Vivien and Merlin* (1874). Albumen photograph. Public Domain. Image courtesy of The Metropolitan Museum of Art, New York.

FIGURE 4.6. Julia Margaret Cameron, *The Parting of Launcelot and Guinevere* (1874). Albumen photograph. Public Domain. Digital image courtesy of the J. Paul Getty Museum Open Content Program, Los Angeles.

Camelot serves as a medieval stand-in for Victorian London, an idealized cityscape where modern possibilities were read against the past.[62]

These adaptations fit a range of social and political ideologies. Known for his moderate-conservative political leanings, Tennyson's adaptations often recast morally ambiguous characters in a new light, such that Guinevere, for example, "emerges not as one participant in a complex tale of sin and betrayal, as in Malory, but as almost [the] sole cause of what has instead become a simple (not to say simplistic) tragedy."[63] On the other hand, William Morris's Guinevere is a sympathetic character and active agent in her own rescue, a characterization aligning with his progressive, socialist views. In Morris's dramatic monologue, the Queen adapts the techniques of Scheherazade, deploying rhetorical mastery to skillfully stall her execution for adultery. Both poems reimagine Guinevere against modern backdrops and Victorian sensibilities, with artists using the iconic figure to either reinforce or challenge restrictive Victorian gender roles. Through adaptation, these characters became cultural icons, symbols of virtue or temptation. (Useful to note here is how Enid, the least known of the four women central to Tennyson's *Idylls,* is also the least adapted over time.)

Camelot also supported subversive or critical interpretations as its expanding transmedia storyworld came with many female characters ready to be redeployed across a range of print and visual forms. The Lady of Shalott—the character who launched Tennyson's own written travels into Camelot—made cameos through various degrees of allusion in several nineteenth-century novels known for highlighting the oppressive social and political restraints of gender and poverty, including Charlotte Bronte's *Villette* (1853), Charles Dickens's *Little Dorrit* (1855-57), George Eliot's *Middlemarch* (1871), and Thomas Hardy's *Jude the Obscure* (1895).[64] "Besides being an archetypal 'subject in crisis,'" Lynne Pearse points out that the character is

> a bountiful symbol of material oppression; she is the imprisoned woman, the condemned woman, the murdered woman of many centuries. And she is also, more specifically, the middle-class, genteel and educated woman of too many Victorian novels and too many social statistics. Propertyless and hence powerless, she is the domestic angel condemned forever to a drawing room existence.[65]

---

62. Bryden, "Arthur in Victorian Poetry" (2009).
63. Fries, "What Tennyson Really Did to Malory's Women" (1991), 53.
64. Gribble, *The Lady of Shalott in the Victorian Novel* (1983).
65. Pearce, *Woman / Image / Text* (1991), 74.

Similar symbolism was tied to some of Camelot's more controversial women. A stark contrast to the Victorian ideal of the "angel in the house," at the hand of women poets and illustrators, Guinevere could be rewritten to represent an array of nineteenth-century conceptualizations of womanhood: as a bold version of the New Woman, as an allegory chastising adultery, or radically revised to embody conservative Victorian ideologies.[66] Working through versions by both Tennyson and Morris (but siding more closely with the politics of the latter), Mary Elizabeth Braddon adopts the fallen woman's perspective in her little-known dramatic monologue "Queen Guinevere" (1861), in which the speaker expresses herself through a mixture of tragic and melodramatic modes that make her "the prisoner of my griefs remaining, / My own dark doom do seal" (lines 7–8).[67] Writers and readers might draw parallels and contrasts between the medieval queen and her contemporary real-life counterpart in Queen Victoria—the two figures not only bookending British history but also symbolizing polar opposite models of English womanhood as it highlighted tensions between private and public spheres. Clare Saunders develops this connection as follows: "In the nineteenth-century obsession with queenly women, ideas of queenship are used to illustrate a wider issue of the expectations of all women in a society that still codifies gender behavior along chivalric lines: with this agenda the legendary queen of Camelot is the archetypal repentant adulteress."[68]

These tensions and binary representations of womanhood informed the work of women illustrators into the early twentieth century. Comparing images by four women who illustrated Tennyson's *Idylls* in different styles—Julia Margaret Cameron (1874), Jessie M. King (1903), Eleanor Fortescue Brickdale (1911), and Florence Harrison (1923)—Saunders sees the pervasiveness of Victorian and Edwardian medievalism not only as an effort "to uphold patriotism, nationalism and the building of the empire" but more importantly as a space from which "at the same time, from within the same discourse, women writers overturned such political gender ideologies, and exposed them as sterile for both sexes" by visualizing "iconic, passive femininity to have an articulate voice, expressed by women rereading, and rewriting medieval legend."[69] Cameron and King take a sympathetic view of Guinevere, portraying her as passionate and strong instead of focusing on her transgressions or penitence. Yet despite this sympathetic view, their respective visuals convey different power dynamics. Cameron, adapting Tennyson's conservative vision,

---

66. Saunders, *Women Writers and Nineteenth-Century Medievalism* (2009).
67. Braddon, *Garibaldi and Other Poems*. (1861), 269–71.
68. Saunders, *Women Writers and Nineteenth-Century Medievalism* (2009), 150.
69. Saunders, *Women Writers and Nineteenth-Century Medievalism* (2009), 182–83.

portrays the lovers in a more traditional, paternalistic pose (see figure 4.6). In contrast, King echoes Morris's more progressive vision as Guinevere looks down at Lancelot, providing comfort while portraying strength (see figure 4.7). Harrison's illustrations take a different approach altogether, highlighting religious imagery and focusing more on sin and shame. In these modernizations, historical accuracy or textual fidelity to originating sources hardly factor as criteria for evaluating these works—though each artist made their decisions in conversations with textual versions of the story.

By engaging the Camelot culture-text, these artists built on previous adaptations and ensured their respective places within its history, attaching their names to the established storyworld through various forms of character expansion. The Camelot culture-text thus not only includes references to previous versions of the Arthurian tradition but also situates these techniques within a visual tradition through what Julia Thomas calls "interpictoriality," or intertextuality between visual forms—yet another form of adaptation and recycling through a shared visual language.[70] Illustrated texts extend the immediate words on the page into a visual mode. The visuals draw on a shared understanding of previous illustrations and printed forms to create a temporal connection between past and present. There's an archival quality to this practice, as Victorian illustrated books are easily identifiable by their aesthetic look and feel. They draw on the longer tradition of illuminated manuscripts, but no matter how much they invoked medievalism in their subjects or styles, most illustrated books were, by virtue of their use of engraved frontispieces, mechanical typesetting, paper type, and book binding, distinctly modern technologies. Illustrated books were the new media of the nineteenth century: portable storytelling devices that could be brought home, increasingly found in the homes of professionals and merchant-class families as status symbols.

The many textual adapters and visual illustrators of Arthurian poems produced in the Victorian period carried Camelot-inspired stories into the twentieth century by providing modernized language and visual iconography to transport these medieval legends into the modern age, with its new social codes, mores, anxieties, and possibilities. Similar trends continue to characterize the Camelot culture-text's presence in the twenty-first century, whether as a narrative framework to feature contemporary heartthrob Charlie Hunnam in the action film *King Arthur: Legend of the Sword* (2017) or as a pseudo-historical backdrop to the expanding, futuristic storyworld of the Transformers franchise in *Transformers: The Last Knight* (2017).

---

70. Thomas, "Reflections on Illustration" (2007).

FIGURE. 4.7. Jessie M. King. Illustration to William Morris, *The Defense of Queen Guinevere* (1904). Image courtesy of Alamy Stock Photo.

WHETHER SITUATED in the past or in the present, characters and places were at the center of nineteenth-century storyworlds. Through character-based fictional worlds, writers and artists expressed a mix of cultural fascination and anxieties about the rise of the modern city amidst rapid industrialization, an intensifying marketplace, and progressive social movements. Dickens's London comes to life as a narrative playground for memorable characters, within which readers follow them on adventures through the sights and sounds of the modern city. The revamped legends of Camelot cast Victorian London through a filter of medievalism, as it was constructed/construed in the nineteenth century.

We see parallel trends continue in the adaptation industry, especially in contemporary recreations of the past through present-day filters. Diane Sadoff ascribes a similar function to the rise of costume-heavy period dramas produced for film and television since the 1980s, which she calls "heritage films" for their equal interest in preserving a literary or cultural past using the technology and sociopolitical sensibilities of the present. Like the many adaptations of the Camelot culture-text in the nineteenth century, contemporary adaptations of Jane Austen, or the Brontë sisters, or Dickens reimagine the nineteenth-century past through a twenty-first-century lens. We see this trend most clearly in adaptations of fiction by women authors or stories otherwise targeting a female audience, as nineteenth-century heroines are radically transformed into more legible feminist (or postfeminist) icons, usually at the expense of historical accuracy.[71]

Far from a passing trend, heritage films and related forms have become culturally enmeshed enough to develop a neo-Victorian aesthetic, a phenomenon with commercial, cultural, and educational functions, outlined by Marie-Luise Kohlke as follows:

> Neo-Victorianism does more than simply adapt the period's canonical works, iconic figures, its cataclysmic as well as disregarded events, and its aesthetic, cultural and ideological discourses. It irrevocably alters their very character, substance, form, function and condition, while retaining aspects of the superficial features, going well beyond redeploying nineteenth-century traces in new contexts so as to produce new narratives for audiences' combined entertainment and instruction (or 'edutainment'). . . . Rather than any attempted recovery of the nineteenth-century world as such, neo-Victorianism involves a potentially (but not essentially) self-conscious *conversion*—both the transformation of our own time into historical guise

---

71. Sadoff, *Victorian Vogue* (2010).

and of the earlier period into something Other than what it was, namely into what we *want* "the Victorian" to signify here and now.[72]

Today's period dramas, such as *Dickensian* and *Penny Dreadful,* are the newest iterations of a twenty-first-century neo-Romantic or neo-Victorian aesthetic spearheaded in the 1990s by films and television aimed at introducing modern audiences to literary classics through adaptation. These adaptations take well-known characters from the public domain and turn them into new commercial products, while simultaneously functioning as a form of cultural preservation. In many ways, neo-Victorianism can be described as an extension or reboot of Victorian medievalism; both historical trends use the past as a way of confronting and processing the present. These historically distanced (or displaced) adaptations ask audiences to compare and contrast the social, political, and cultural differences between their own moment and the historical contexts portrayed.

These nearly identical aesthetic trends in two distinct historical periods shed light on how adaptations determine the ongoing life of established culture-texts through various forms of character extension and world-building. In the case of Camelot in the nineteenth century, the Arthurian revival invigorated a storyworld that risked being entirely forgotten. In the case of *Dickensian* in the twenty-first century, we see how a literary mash-up (no matter how short-lived) participates in keeping an author in the public eye. Both examples show us that continued adaptation and remixing influence the reception histories of canonical works and their ever-expanding culture-texts.

Although distinct ideas, culture-texts and transmedia storyworlds should be considered relationally in both past and present cultural production. Both narrative techniques approach storytelling as a dispersed, elastic, evolving practice. Both include central points (or people) of creation, while also acknowledging the power of collaborative storytelling. Both provide opportunities (whether intentionally or not) for audiences to become active participants and depend wholly on adapters and audiences for circulation. The major difference between the two lies in the extent to which the stories are controlled or dispersed, or the extent to which new creators and fans push the boundaries of that control by adapting, remixing, and adding their own story to a popular culture-text. Unlike today's carefully planned transmedia franchises, which do involve storyworlds, culture-texts cannot be created instantaneously, nor can they be completely controlled by central, administrative structures like corporations and copyrights. Instead, many different creators weave archetypes into

---

72. Kohlke, "Adaptive/Appropriative Reuse in Neo-Victorian Fiction" (2017), 175–76.

culture-texts through diverse dispersals over time. Despite this difference, the emphasis on recurring character and place that we see in both culture-texts and transmedia storyworlds suggests interconnected cultural meanings and commercial importance as these narrative phenomena move stories into new forms or contexts in an ever-expanding network of adaptations.

CHAPTER 5

∽

Nineteenth-Century Tie-Ins, Commercial Extensions, and Participatory Culture

THE PRECEDING CHAPTERS have outlined industrial and artistic convergences that shaped transmedia storytelling through various types of adaptation since the rise of consumer culture in the eighteenth century. Most of the examples pull from now-canonical literature, showing how popular culture worked to disperse these stories across forms and media, thereby making them accessible to a wide range of audiences, particularly those who would not otherwise purchase expensive books. Chapters 1 and 2 emphasized industrial contexts and the emergence of arts-based professions as they shaped storytelling practices in a new, commercial economy. Chapters 3 and 4 stressed the importance of visual culture in the making of culture-texts, showing how painting and illustration extended literary characters and landscapes to create a popular canon, a figurative space where literature and fine arts meet commercial mass culture. The following chapter focuses more closely on mass culture, specifically through two of the most commercialized forms of adaptation—genre fiction and merchandizing. Specifically, I look at how gothic fiction and toy theaters functioned as early forms of participatory culture, allowing fans of all ages to extend their experiences of their favorite characters and genre conventions by creating their own versions of their favorite works.

In the late eighteenth century, the gothic mode emerged as a dispersed aesthetic with broad-based appeal that could be used in any form, medium, or genre. Crossing socioeconomic classes, the gothic aesthetic dominated mass culture and could be found in cheap serialized fiction, melodrama, magic lantern shows, and songs. Philosophers, poets, novelists, and painters also adopted the gothic mode, further fusing it into literature and art. The result was a simultaneous cultural "elevation" of a popular form that increased the commercial and influential reach of literary culture outside of its immediate, exclusive circles. Similarly, toy theaters were commercial crossovers that bridged the fine arts and popular culture, adapting the storyworlds of adults for children. Toy theaters encouraged children to create their own plays at home, extending the theatrical experience into the domestic sphere and introducing children to literary and popular stories through active, creative play. The goal of bringing these two forms of nineteenth-century mass culture together in the following chapter is to show how mass-produced, print-based forms of adaptation and transmedia extension influenced cultural production through audience engagement and participation. While they are typically overlooked as cheap forms of low-brow entertainment, nineteenth-century gothic fiction and toy theaters produced a mass reading public and supported a growing popular literacy. Aimed primarily at women, younger audiences, and the working classes, pulp fiction and toy theaters expanded the number of creators and consumers making and experiencing stories across forms, media, class, and ages.

Popular genres and commercial tie-ins connect the practices of twenty-first-century transmedia storytelling and nineteenth-century popular culture. Today's transmedia franchises are dominated by genre-based storytelling from science fiction to superhero stories. Because of their respective generic conventions and formulas, speculative genres are easily adapted and expanded into larger storyworlds through crossovers, prequels, and sequels. Most forms of character-based story extensions include an array of commercial products like action figures, video games, children's books, and detailed guidebooks that provide multiple points of entry and engagement for audiences. Based on tried-and-true models, these commercial iterations support the growth of new culture-texts by adapting and extending the storytelling experience through various world-building practices.

In contemporary media studies, this chaotic world of endless sequels, spin-offs, off-shoots, and merchandise epitomize convergence culture, bringing together the "technological, industrial, cultural, and social" dimensions of transmedia storytelling that value industry-produced adaptations alongside fan-produced content. Henry Jenkins describes fan-produced content as "participatory culture," and he convincingly eschews passive models of consumption by reframing fan culture and transmedia products as forms of active, audience-driven engagement sometimes offering opportunities for alternative or subversive interpretations and experiences. In this way, "participatory culture contrasts with older notions of passive media spectatorship. Rather than talking about media producers and consumers as occupying separate roles, we might now see them as participants who interact with each other."[1] Though he cautions against oversimplifying this dynamic as utopian or democratic (corporations still retain a lot of power, and socioeconomic disparities mean that not all audiences have equal access or opportunities to become media producers), Jenkins uses his self-described position as an "aca-fan" (an academic and a fan) to explore fan-driven products as active forms of audience engagement, media literacy, and even political participation. Whether writing fan fiction, blogging as characters, joining role-playing leagues, participating in cosplay, or developing add-ons for existing digital media to customize video gaming experiences, Jenkins positions these users as influencers of cultural production, not just consumers of centrally produced content. Jenkins theorizes convergence culture as both a top-down and bottom-up process that combine corporate franchises and user-generated content for an integrated-yet-dispersed story experience with endless possibilities that can also support a thriving social network of communal engagement and active creation.

Commercialization, merchandizing, and audience-produced content like action figures and fan fiction might cast doubt on the "seriousness" or artistic value of transmedia franchises and the fan-led productions and activities they inspire. However, their cultural and historical impact is undeniable, and they link today's transmedia storytelling franchises to commercialized forms of storytelling in the past. Deidre Lynch highlights the communal consumption of eighteenth-century literature and culture:

> In Britain more than in other national cultures, characters have belonged not only to literary history but also to a transmedia context—the public's experience of the characters in their novels has been experience garnered not only in the seclusion of solitary reading but also at print-shop windows, at waxwork displays, and in shops that sell china figures. One aspect of the intimate relation between Britain's commercial economy and British characters is that from the early eighteenth century on there have often been so many ways to buy and to collect them.... It helped ... to create new sorts of relays between character and the norms of sociable commerce and circulation.[2]

---

1. Jenkins, *Convergence Culture* (2006), 3; see also *Textual Poachers* (1992); *Fans, Bloggers, and Gamers* (2006); *Reading in a Participatory Culture* (2013).
2. Lynch, *The Economy of Character* (1998), 11.

In the eighteenth and nineteenth centuries, literary characters were dispersed across forms of elite and mass culture and were turned into commercial commodities. The storyworlds of Crusoe, Gulliver, Pamela, Clarissa—characters originated by Daniel Defoe, Jonathan Swift, and Samuel Richardson, and extended and developed by others—continued their adventures in literary sequels and sophisticated parodies, and they were also turned into waxwork tableaus, bawdy ballads, abridged chapbooks, and adaptations for children including books, pantomimes, and toys. Such a wide array of adaptations and commercial extensions helped various entertainment industries cut across class divisions and age groups. Families could experience a story together by watching a pantomime at the theater or back at home through individual products aimed at their particular reading levels or entertainment preferences. All of these forms of adaptation and extension popularized stories and were instrumental in the development of a popular cultural literacy.

From the late eighteenth century onward, commercial storytelling was dominated by the gothic mode that, like today's transmedia superhero franchises, expanded and evolved through adaptations and extensions across mediums and generational markets. Both gothic and superhero genres have their origins in mass culture, specifically forms of cheap publication, from nineteenth-century chapbooks to twentieth-century comic books. Adaptation, world-building, and character extension drive the production of these print-based forms, providing opportunities for employment and enjoyment through an array of commercial tie-ins and extensions while also straddling the worlds of adult and children's media. Nineteenth-century gothic fiction and toy theaters help us see several aspects of convergence culture and participatory culture as they emerged in earlier forms of commercial entertainment and media industries.

GOTHIC ADAPTATIONS: MASS CULTURE AND THE EVOLUTION OF A GENERIC MODE

Just as they were adapted in their own time, nineteenth-century characters from gothic fiction regularly show up in modern and contemporary transmedia franchises. During the Classical Hollywood era, Universal Studios' film adaptations of nineteenth-century fiction solidified the company's finances and made it an industry giant. Classic monster movies launched Universal's emerging brand in the 1930s, with *Frankenstein, Dracula,* and *The Invisible Man* each producing individual franchises of their own, generating multiple sequels and various tie-in products and memorabilia. Eventually, the sequels spawned franchised mash-ups, as the Universal monsters regularly made cinematic appearances in each other's storyworlds during the 1940s. The entertainment and media giant is currently rebooting these now-classic film characters as the "Dark Universe" franchise to reestablish their combined storyworlds in the twenty-first century. Other fictional takes on these public domain characters with nineteenth-century origins include "The League of Extraordinary Gentlemen," a mash-up by Alan Moore and Kevin O'Neill, whose 1999 comic book series was soon expanded through a 2003 film adaptation. In both cases, now-classic (and mostly gothic) nineteenth-century characters are recast as superheroes, infusing literary classics with action-packed adventures and epic supernatural battles.

Showtime's recent gothic thriller *Penny Dreadful* (2014–16) follows a similar formula, as characters from *Frankenstein, Dracula, The Picture of Dorian Gray,* and *Jekyll and Hyde* join classic film monsters like werewolves to fight even bigger forces of evil trying to destroy the world. The "Penny Dreadful" universe not only combines an array of literary characters but also resituates them in new adventures following the basic structures of other successful transmedia storyworlds and universes. Created by John Logan for Showtime, this transmedia franchise includes board games, action figures, comic books, and highly stylized behind-the-scenes guidebooks. There are even new printings of the public-domain, nineteenth-century novels by Mary Shelley, Oscar Wilde, and Bram Stoker sold as tie-in merchandise, brandishing coordinating book covers identifying them as part of the officially licensed "Penny Dreadful Collection." The television series ended in 2016, but the storyworld continues to expand in an ongoing series published by Titan Comics, with its lead artists acknowledging the parallels between nineteenth-century penny publications and contemporary comic books.

Conceptually, mash-ups and crossovers like Universal's "Dark Universe" and "Penny Dreadful" work because their core characters are cult icons, thriving on fragmentation through repeated adaptation, appropriation, and extension. Iconic characters and the storyworlds they inhabit are always attached to a broader network of associations (historical or authorial), as well as to fictional worlds that are genre-specific or mythological. They straddle old worlds and new ones, blending fantasy and reality through metafictional techniques that acknowledge classic characters and source texts while intentionally creating new, stand-alone stories that spur additional adaptations. Transmedia franchises like "Penny Dreadful" and "The League of Extraordinary Gentlemen" also capitalize on the twenty-first-century popularity of Neo-Victorianism; present-day repurposing of the past parallels the nineteenth century's historical fascination with medieval settings and ruined castles, an aesthetic that characterized the rise of the gothic as a storytelling mode. The gothic engenders a series of confrontations: real world versus speculative universe, old world versus modernity, conservatism versus subversion, mass culture fused with fine art.[3] Literature, art, and popular culture collide and combine in these contemporary mash-ups, much as they did in nineteenth-century gothic fiction, which in its print-based forms comprised multiple formats, including triple-decker novels, novellas, chapbooks, abridgements, and serialized penny dreadfuls (also referred to as "penny bloods" and "shilling shockers" at different periods, depending on their print quality and prices).

The most popular transmedia genres of the twentieth and twenty-first centuries take their cultural cues from the gothic as a commercially viable transmedia genre from the nineteenth century, when adaptation and appropriation popularized the gothic. One of the ironies underscoring today's "Penny Dreadful" universe is that it invokes the form of nineteenth-century mass culture to retell the stories of the period's most literary monsters. Frankenstein and his Creature, Dorian Gray, Dracula, Dr. Jekyll—each made their debut appearances in novels now considered the "literary gothic," canonical works of literary fiction that extend the gothic mode popularized through mass culture into the world of high culture, though many were quickly adapted into penny publications marketed primarily to working class readers. All of the characters in the "Penny Dreadful" universe have literary origins in nineteenth-century texts that were invented *after* the "heyday" of the first wave of gothic fiction (1760 through the 1820s), which later dispersed and guided the evolution of new genres including sensation fiction, detective fiction, true crime, science fiction, and epic fantasy, all of which emerged and developed using similar mass-culture, transmedia storytelling strategies.

From its origins, the gothic was a transmedia phenomenon creating classification challenges, and contemporary scholars variously refer to it as a genre, an aesthetic, or an artistic mode. Diane Long Hoeveler likens the "repetitive quality" of gothic to a musical riff, specifically calling attention to the role of adaptation within the gothic's evolution as it moved through the "collateral genres" of less culturally valued forms like chapbooks, ballads, and melodramas.[4] Situating the rise of the gothic in the technological and commercial milieu of the Industrial Revolution and the rise of capitalism, David Jones likens the gothic to a machine that "exists . . . in the recurrent interaction between signs and genre, between repetition and deviation . . . this dynamic set of relations . . . create a technology of extremely complex

---

3. Hoeveler, *Gothic Feminism* (1998) and *Gothic Riffs* (2010).
4. Hoeveler, *Gothic Riffs* (2010).

adaptation."⁵ All definitions and models embrace the gothic mode's propensity for adapting, recycling, and transmediation. The gothic, for Jones, is a "vista of trans-medial entertainment comprising a vast and complex panoply of disparate cultural milieus, all the way from penny broadsides to large publishing houses, from itinerant peep shows to extravagant theatrical spectacles" driven by eighteenth- and nineteenth-century technology such as the printing press or the magic lantern or new methods of energy and lighting effects, alongside other social and political factors. The gothic "stretched the bounds of any sense of a pre-established literary genre" through patterns of "adaptation, mutation and hybridity."⁶ The gothic never dies; it just morphs and evolves through adaptation as it is redeployed in print, visual, and theatrical cultures. Much of its long-term appeal lies precisely in these shapeshifting abilities, allowing the gothic mode to adapt to any cultural or historical context.

Literary scholars have traditionally divided the gothic tradition through a high/low binary, with "literary gothic" in one category and the other category comprising the "trade gothic" of mass-produced chapbooks, bluebooks, penny dreadfuls, and other inexpensive works marketed primarily to women, the working classes, and adolescents.⁷ However, critics like Hoeveler and Potter have critiqued these boundaries as artificial, showing that the literary gothic and even high Romanticism borrowed heavily from mass culture in general and the popularity of the gothic in particular. In its textual incarnations, the gothic includes long-form novels dating back to Horace Walpole's *Castle of Otranto* (1764) and the sprawling fictions of Ann Radcliffe published in the 1790s, up to the aestheticized Victorian gothic of Oscar Wilde's *The Picture of Dorian Gray* (1890). In its pulp fiction formats, the gothic includes mass produced volumes published by the Minerva Press (1790–1820), which grabbed the attention of concerned critics and avid consumers alike.⁸ For these reasons, I look at these two categories relationally because they intersected consistently and directly through adaptation and formulaic or generic repetition.

Through their repetitive nature, gothic narratives traded in a communal language of shareable storyworlds populated by an array of ruined castles, guilt-ridden hermits, damsels in distress, and monstrous villains. The laundry list of gothic conventions consisted of imaginative props and intertextual references that demanded a reader not only be engaged but also be a regular visitor into gothic storyworlds, as they were popularized through the pulp productions. These texts were produced quickly and in large numbers. Many

---

5. Jones, *Gothic Machine* (2011), 11.
6. Jones, *Gothic Machine* (2011), 9, 15.
7. Potter, *The Monster Made by Man* (2004), 6.
8. Haining, *The Shilling Shockers* (1978).

titles were published anonymously or by authors otherwise dismissed as hack writers, few of whom are remembered today despite filling their publishers' catalogs with sensational, attention-grabbing titles. Overall, their output was nothing short of impressive. The Minerva Press produced roughly one third of all new novels published in England between 1790 and 1820, a remarkable representation in the market, especially for a low-brow, commercial publishing house in the early nineteenth century. It's no wonder that six of the seven "horrid novels" listed in Jane Austen's gothic parody *Northanger Abbey* (1817) were titles published by the Minerva Press.[9]

The gothic's formulas—its established conventions—consist of shared, recycled material that Elizabeth Neiman describes as "a network of intertextual exchange that connects women's national tales . . . with Walter Scott's historical novels" through "adaptive reuse" of genre conventions, including plot, character, and settings. For Neiman, repetition—and specifically repetition with variation—is a way that Minerva novelists

> forge connections among each other, creating a collective (or "generic") model of authorship that is not simply derivative. These novelists are connecting with each other over space and time via a market-driven system of exchange, the circulating-library novel. . . . Minerva authors communicate with each other by way of constant and often subtle modifications on and infractions to popular formulas. These modifications come into view when the novels are read collectively and with a definition of intertextuality that is flexible enough to include literary formula.[10]

Neiman points to shared languages and conventions as part of a larger project of Romantic authorship, seen in writers with styles and politics as diverse as Percy Bysshe Shelley and Jane Austen, both in their immediate literary circles as well as in the broader public community of writers and readers. This type of exchange is not uniquely gothic, but it was intensified in the gothic's reach across elite and mass culture, giving it a large readership that few if any other genres could claim.

Just as these shared systems connected authors and readers, they also created imagined communities of fans. For example, as a parody in the literary gothic tradition, *Northanger Abbey* functions within the shared storyworld of gothic narratives, a system dominated by intertextual references and allusions that can only be fully experienced by a built-in audience of repeat read-

---

9. Neiman, *Minerva's Gothics* (2019); Thomson, Voller, and Frank, *Gothic Writers* (2002).
10. Neiman, "A New Perspective on the Minerva Press's 'Derivative' Novels" (2015), 634–35.

ers. *Northanger Abbey*'s extensive intertextual allusions to other gothic novels underscore the importance of the gothic's "shared language" and fan networks, the latter of which are embodied in the friendship between Catherine Morland and Isabella Thorpe and their mutual love of reading gothic novels. *Northanger Abbey*'s success as a parody depends heavily on readers' familiarity with popular gothic novels—a point very easily lost on today's readers who are unfamiliar with the titles and plots that Austen critiques in her novel. One might say that Catherine Morland belongs more to the shared narrative universe of gothic heroines than to the fictional worlds in which Austen's characters usually reside. Without a detailed familiarity with this shared circuit of adapted genre conventions, Austen's novel falls flat as the sophisticated intentionality of the parody goes unrecognized. Like fans now, the gothic's target audiences not only expected but reveled in these repetitions and intertextual references—today called "easter eggs" in the movie industry—as they formed and affirmed communities of readers and forged links between their favorite stories.

Though Minerva titles primarily circulated through lending libraries, they shared common readers with gothic chapbooks and periodicals, all of which borrowed from page and stage alike, blending structures and content. Trade publishers regularly drew directly from stories that were popular in print or in performance. Like the nineteenth-century dramatists who spent most of their time adapting novels for the stage, the professional writers of the trade gothic circuit adapted existing works into new forms sold as inexpensive chapbooks or in periodicals that would later be collected into single volumes or anthologies. Publishers specialized in gothic abridgements, novelizations, and other textual forms of adaptation.

For example, the weekly stories in the *Endless Entertainment* series are representative of the content, plots, and characters shared by circuits of writers who made a living writing for the trade gothic commercial markets.[11] Like the "literary gentlemen" of the theater, the (mostly women) writers of trade gothic borrowed from various sources, mixing multiple versions of a story while retaining some of the core plot, characters, or situations of stories from textual and theatrical sources. The material came from both literary and popular culture, as we see in issues no. 6 and no. 7 of the 1825 series with prose adaptations of stories from Lord Byron and Mary Shelley that borrow even more substantially from respective stage adaptations. The gothic story of "The Dwarf; or, The Deformed Transformed," is a textual mash-up of Joshua Pickersgill's novel *The Three Brothers: A Romance* (1803), which along with

---

11. Neiman, *Minerva's Gothics* (2019).

Goethe's *Faust* (1808) was the source of inspiration for Byron's dramatic fragment *The Deformed Transformed* (1824).[12] *The Three Brothers* was also adapted by Matthew Gregory Lewis into the drama *One O'Clock: or, The Knight and The Wood Demon* (1811), which along with Byron's published fragment also served as a source for Mary Shelley's "The Transformation" in 1830. The version published in *Endless Entertainment* in 1825, according to Potter, capitalizes on Byron's recent publication, simplifying the plot of the longer gothic novel and highlighting moments that "overwhelm the reader with waves of depravity and revenge."[13]

Similarly, the anonymously published short story "The Monster Made by Man; or, The Punishment of Presumption" (1825) combined elements of both Shelley's *Frankenstein* (the novel) and Peake's *Presumption* (the play) to tell its monstrous creation story (see figure 5.2). The Creature in this textual adaptation speaks, as he does in Shelley's novel, but the title of the story, the presence of a lab assistant, and the final death by avalanche are imported directly from Peake's play. "The Monster Made by Man" also appears to have influenced stage adaptations that came immediately after its publication in 1825. The French play *Le Monstre et le Magicien* (1826), by Jean-Toussaint Merle and Antony Béraud, and Henry Milner's English melodrama *Frankenstein; or the Man and the Monster* (1826) both echo the title of the anonymously published pulp gothic print adaptation. Some of the textual adaptation's imagery may have also been incorporated into later stage adaptations. Milner introduced the first staged creation scene to *Frankenstein*'s dramatic history, possibly riffing on the illustrated frontispiece to the *Endless Entertainment* textual adaptation, which generated if not anticipated audience interest in the monster's creation scene (which gets scant attention in Shelley's novel and takes place just outside of audience view in the original stage directions for Peake's play).

Stories like these made up a considerable market of literary entertainment, affordability being a main draw. As the title pages to the *Endless Entertainment* advertise (see figures 5.1 and 5.2), stories sold for twopence individually, or they could be collected in a single-bound anthology of eighteen stories for a higher cost of 3s, 6d, a version that would appeal to collectors or other committed fans. (This model is exactly how comic books are published today.) A cursory look at the titles of representative cheap literature published between the 1830s and the 1860s suggests the reading public's extensive consumption of adaptations—as well as adaptations of adaptations—in textual forms. Indeed, adaptations make up almost the entirety of titles produced midcentury, with

---

12. Robinson, "The Devil as Doppelgänger" (1997).
13. Potter, *The Monster Made by Man* (2004), 144. For analysis of Byron's play and the 1825 textual adaptation, see Pitcher, "Byron's 'The Deformed Transformed' Transformed" (1984).

ENDLESS ENTERTAINMENT.

A SERIES OF ORIGINAL
COMIC, TERRIFIC, AND LEGENDARY
TALES.

No. 6. FRIDAY, JUNE 10, 1825. Price 2d.

CONTENTS.—*The Dwarf; or the Deformed Transformed.*

See page 85.

THE DWARF;
OR THE DEFORMED TRANSFORMED.

ARNULF, from an accident in his infancy, was at his approach to manhood a dwarf in height, and deformed in person; the passions of envy, hatred, and cruelty, made his mind as detestable as his body was mis-shapen, while his face was a true index of their crookedness.

VOL. I.   G

FIGURE 5.1. Illustrated front page of "The Dwarf; or, The Deformed Transformed" from *Endless Entertainment* (1825). Public Domain, Google Digital Collections.

ENDLESS ENTERTAINMENT.

A SERIES OF ORIGINAL

COMIC, TERRIFIC, AND LEGENDARY

TALES.

| No. 7. | FRIDAY, JUNE 17, 1825. | Price 2d. |

Contents.—THE MONSTER.

See page 101.

THE MONSTER MADE BY MAN;
OR, THE PUNISHMENT OF PRESUMPTION.

IN every age of the world woman's curiosity has been equalled by man's presumption, and one of the most astonishing events produced by the latter quality is related in Germany, that native country of every thing non-natural.

In one of the most romantic parts of it resided Wallberg, a

H 2

FIGURE 5.2. Illustrated front page of "The Monster Made by Man; or, The Punishment of Presumption" from *Endless Entertainment* (1825). Public Domain, Google Digital Collections.

many writers such as James Malcolm Rymer and Thomas Prest churning out adaptations as fast as their colleagues who wrote for the stage.[14]

The *Endless Entertainment* series shows us how the adaptation phenomenon intentionally fused the page and stage, drawing from print, performance, and illustration in its storytelling processes. Each form held equal weight, and questions of authority or originality played little to no part in the popularity or success of these adaptations.

At times, originality and authority were blurred to the point of confusion. One example comes from the famous penny dreadful turned hit drama *The String of Pearls: A Romance* (1846–47), published anonymously in eighteen parts, featuring the sensationalized character of the murderous barber Sweeney Todd. Before the serial's final installments, the piece was performed at the Britannia Saloon. The successful melodrama by George Dibdin Pitt, *The String of Pearls; or, The Fiend of Fleet Street* (1847), quickly became the standard version, with many crediting Dibdin Pitt as the original author, as documented by Sharon Aronofsky Weltman's study of its early adaptation history:

> One reason for this confusion is that when Dibdin Pitt's [retitled] melodrama *Sweeney Todd* was finally published in Dick's Standard Plays, the wrong year of 1842 was listed for its initial performance, when in fact it was not performed until 1847. For years, people assumed erroneously that the serial story in the *People's Periodical and Family Library* was a novelization of Dibdin Pitt's play.[15]

To date, the author of the penny dreadful publication remains unclear; nonetheless, the story emerged as a culture-text when it might have easily fallen into obscurity, with most subsequent adaptations following Dibdin Pitt's stage adaptation of the penny publication. Adaptation transported Sweeney Todd from anonymity to infamy. The case illustrates Linda Hutcheon's argument that "an adaptation is not vampiric, it does not draw the life-blood from its source . . . nor is it paler than the adapted work. It may, on the contrary, keep that prior work alive, giving it an afterlife it would never have had otherwise."[16] This recuperative model solidifies adaptation's originating role as a catalyst for widespread recognition. There's no way that *The String of Pearls* could have made it out of the pages of the inexpensive periodical on its own—most of its peer publications have been effectively forgotten. The early adaptation essentially became the "original" text, with later adaptations following the first stage

---

14. Léger-St-Jean, *Price One Penny: A Database* (2018).
15. Weltman, "1847: Sweeney Todd and Abolition" (2013).
16. Hutcheon, *A Theory of Adaptation* (2006), 176.

version more closely than its print predecessor, as was also the case with the adaptation histories of other literary gothic examples like *Frankenstein* and *The Strange Case of Dr. Jekyll and Mr. Hyde*. Even in its most inexpensive, mass-produced forms, the gothic brought together the worlds of literature, fine arts, and mass culture. Readers of pulp fiction were encountering versions of Byron, Shelley, Faust, and other literary culture whether they could recognize the sources or not. The worlds of literary and mass culture came together to reach a growing segment of working-class audiences as literacy rates increased, due in part to the widespread availability of reading material.

The gothic also had its counterparts on stage and in painting and illustration as the gothic aesthetic permeated all areas of nineteenth-century cultural production. From the mid-1790s through the 1820s, London's major and minor theaters alike were staging gothic-inspired plays based on the novels of Anne Radcliffe, Matthew Lewis, and others.[17] In one example, portions of Lewis's *The Monk* were staged throughout the nineteenth century across the genres of melodrama, opera, and dance. The most famous adaptation of the shocking novel was the ballet *Raymond and Agnes* (1797), which was reimagined by H. W. Grosette as a melodrama for the Haymarket in 1811 and as an opera in 1855 by Edward Loder (with Edward Fitzball penning the English libretto). Of these forms, melodrama was the most prevalent in the nineteenth century, and its subgenres offered the possibility of politically or socially subversive subtexts, especially in its most "illegitimate" forms. Invented and popularized in France during the Revolution, melodrama was imported to England via a gothic narrative in Thomas Holcroft's successful *A Tale of Mystery* (1802), an unacknowledged translation of René Charles Guilbert de Pixérécourt's *Coelina ou l'Enfant du Mystère* (1800), itself an adaptation of a popular French novel by François Guillame Ducray-Duminil published in 1798 (see chapter 2).

Melodrama took off in part because it combined well with the gothic mode and the period's emerging democratic aesthetics.[18] As Diego Saglia explains:

> The Gothic stage . . . both endorsed canonical forms such as tragedy and subverted hierarchies by dissolving and reconfiguring existing models, usually by mixing high and low forms or adapting from other genres. Instigating hybridity through its characteristic cross-fertilisation of modes and types, stage Gothic undermined conventions—both literary and theatrical—and

---

17. Saggini, *The Gothic Novel and the Stage* (2015).
18. Hoeveler, "Thomas Holcroft and the Swerve of Melodrama" (2003) and "Illustrating Thomas Holcroft's *A Tale of Mystery*" (2012).

forced their redefinition, as well as . . . the epistemological principles and ideological frameworks they encapsuled.[19]

Gothic drama was not alone in these formal, artistic, and political experimentations; melodrama was also a sophisticated discursive mode that emerged, according to Elaine Hadley, "as a polemical response to the social, economic, and epistemological changes that characterized the consolidation of market society in the nineteenth century," as melodrama's reach extended well beyond the stage to include speeches, physical gestures, clothing, and political actions.[20] The gothic and melodrama both borrowed from the tragic mode through their focus on human suffering, while redeploying its tropes for new readers and audiences. Tragic art, in turn, adapted textual and dramatic techniques from these popular forms. The picture that emerges is what David Duff calls a "genre-system," where competing genres and media adapt and transform one another.[21] In a testament to their interconnectedness, gothic adaptations appeared as melodramas perhaps more frequently than any other theatrical genre in the 1820s and 1830s, even as the gothic mode dispersed across available nineteenth-century media and formats, including fiction, poetry, drama, song, ballet, and technological phenomena such as magic lantern shows.[22]

Major writers and artists of the period infused gothic elements into their works if not fully embraced them as a central aesthetic.[23] Painters including Henry Fuseli, Francisco de Goya, and Gustave Doré all worked within gothic conventions in their visual art. Unable to deny its hold on the popular imagination, mainstream writers also found ways to adapt the conventions of the gothic into literary forms associated with high art. In the British tradition, we find the gothic mode infused into the works of Romantic poets and Victorian novelists, as well as in the work of their contemporaries across Europe and the United States, connecting Radcliffe and Lewis to Samuel Taylor Coleridge and John Keats, as well as Dickens and the Brontës to Edgar Allan Poe and Nathaniel Hawthorne. The gothic's popularity persisted as it was transformed by the rise of realism in literature and art during the latter part of the nineteenth century. We see this transition in Victor Hugo's *Notre-dame de Paris,*

---

19. Saglia, "The Gothic Stage" (2016), 78; Fraistat and Reiman, *Shelley's Poetry and Prose* (2002).
20. Hadley, *Melodramatic Tactics* (1995), 3–4.
21. Duff, *Romanticism and the Uses of Genre* (2009), 20.
22. Hoeveler, *Gothic Riffs* (2010).
23. Gothic is often considered a subgenre of Romanticism, but there isn't a clearly identifiable chronological order to their cultural emergence. Hoeveler, *Gothic Riffs* (2010).

as it was translated into English as *The Hunchback of Notre-Dame* and turned into plays that blended gothic and domestic melodrama with happy endings, produced in London in 1834, 1836, and again in 1871.[24] At midcentury, Charlotte Brontë's *Jane Eyre* was dominated by realism, using gothic elements sparingly to heighten sensation at key moments, and this blending of gothic romance and domestic realism would follow *Jane Eyre* to the stage.[25] As realism became a dominant aesthetic driving the novel, adaptation supported the evolution of the gothic into the various branches of detective, sensation, and science fiction invented during the Victorian period. Popularized by writers like Wilkie Collins, Mary Elizabeth Braddon, and Robert Louis Stevenson, these styles and their most famous examples were dramatized, adapted, and appropriated throughout the second half of the nineteenth century and into the next.

Gothic forms crossed gender, class, and generational divides. Men and women contributed to the production and consumption of gothic stories; however, gothic fiction was largely associated with women writers and readers through the 1820s, a critical time in the expansion of the reading public and the commercial growth of publishing as an industry of mass entertainment. In its print-based forms, the gothic expanded professional opportunities for women writers in both literary and mass-market fiction, and young women made up a substantial market of avid readers. It also had commercial, aesthetic, and ideological potential, as women writers and readers used the fictional form to explore the conditions of living within—and the potential of escaping from—real-life oppressive structures.[26] At least one third of Minerva's titles were published anonymously, largely because women made up a majority of their writers.[27] While there were prolific professional women writers associated with the press, like Sarah Wilkinson, many of the Minerva novels are suspected to have been written by newcomers to authorship, placing these amateur authors as the literary ancestors of fan fiction writers today, some of whom go on to establish themselves as professional authors.[28]

While women made up a large share of the Minerva Press readership through the 1820s, that dynamic would soon reverse as Victorian penny

---

24. Szwydky, "Victor Hugo's *Notre-Dame de Paris* on the Nineteenth-Century London Stage" (2010).

25. Stoneman, *Jane Eyre on Stage* (2007).

26. Gilbert and Gubar, *The Madwoman in the Attic* (1979); Hoeveler, *Gothic Feminism* (1998).

27. Blakey, *The Minerva Press* (1939).

28. One recent example is E. L. James's *Fifty Shades of Grey* series, which began as *Twilight* fan fiction before it was developed into its own independent storyworld with sequels and film adaptations.

dreadfuls increasingly targeted male audiences, from preteens to adults. By the mid-nineteenth century, the trade gothic was dominated by male authors writing for a (presumed) male reader. Despite this gendered audience shift, the working and middle classes still comprised much of the market for these works. Through their deletions, amplifications, and distortions, "these chapbooks shed light on how the laboring classes interacted with the dominant cultural and ideological formations of the period."[29] Neiman's understanding of the circuits of shared literary material among Minerva authors points in this direction too, as the titles regularly champion humble protagonists, especially as they provide narratives of accessible—albeit not always realistic—models of social mobility. Gothic chapbooks and other popular forms offered a way for the working class or the newly emerging middle classes to turn the cultural gaze back on to high society, in order to reaffirm their own values.

TOY THEATERS AND THE CONVERGENCE OF INDUSTRIES

After 1820, the Minerva Press stamp no longer appeared on new books that filled popular circulating libraries. The press remained in operation, however; it simply shifted its target market and audience, and under the new imprint A. K. Newman & Co., the publishing house specialized in books for young readers until 1859.[30] The shift from popular fiction for adults to a focus on children follows contemporaneous economic shifts, market trends, and social changes. As Andrew O'Malley explains, popular fictions in the form of mass-produced novels and chapbooks

> participate in a popular culture wherein common readers "poach" from the grounds of an elite or dominant culture, adapting, for example, literary materials "to their own interests and their own rules." . . . The case can be made that children's culture and reading operate in similar ways, as children, like plebeian readers, reorganize fragments of an adult culture, whose production does not usually involve them, into unauthorized forms that suits their needs and interests.[31]

One of the markers of the burgeoning economy that developed around the nineteenth-century culture industry was the diversification and expansion of

---

29. O'Malley, *Children's Literature, Popular Culture, and Robinson Crusoe* (2012), 77–78.
30. Blakey, *The Minerva Press* (1939), 29.
31. O'Malley, *Children's Literature, Popular Culture, and Robinson Crusoe* (2012).

audiences interested in purchasing engaging content in various formats who were key to the period's emerging media industries.

This period also marked the emergence of a commercial market for entertainment designed for children and adolescents. Indeed, much of the period's cheap adventure literature was produced for and marketed to children.[32] Fairy tales and nursery rhymes were regularly adapted into pantomimes and illustrated books. Several of the works produced for children also received critical praise, eventually becoming canonical through regular adaptations and extensions. By the 1860s, Christina Rossetti was publishing child-friendly verses in appealing illustrated editions.[33] In 1865, Lewis Carroll unveiled *Alice's Adventures in Wonderland,* a storyworld that through its combination of textual nonsense and whimsical illustrations would immediately become a transmedia phenomenon—one of the first culture-texts specifically intended and produced for children's amusement.[34] As Carolyn Sigler explains, the nearly two hundred parodies, imitations, and revisions of Carroll's Alice books produced between 1869 and 1930 form a diverse matrix of "extraordinarily coherent, creative, and often critical responses" to the Wonderland storyworld.[35] The rise of children's media throughout the nineteenth century wasn't centrally coordinated; it was, however, a site of industrial and ideological convergences.[36] Historically, the post-Enlightenment revolutionary period brought a major shift in the conceptualization of childhood, with children now seen as individuals who needed nurturing and education.[37] The late eighteenth century brought children's readers, anthologies of age-appropriate verses and texts meant to teach reading and introduce literary heritage—new skills for an industrial era. By the early nineteenth century, popular theater had the interest of young viewers, and toy theaters emerged as a popular form of interactive storytelling and functioned as an early form of tie-in merchandise.

Like today's action figures and accessories, toy theaters replicated real theaters, the actors who performed on their stages, and the plays they produced.[38] Great attention was paid to imitating the look and feel of theatrical spaces, cos-

---

32. James and Smith, *Penny Dreadfuls and Boys' Adventures* (1998).

33. Kooistra, *Christina Rossetti and Illustration* (2002).

34. For comprehensive overviews of *Alice*'s adaptation history in print, performance, and visual culture, see: Cohen and Wakeling, *Lewis Carroll and His Illustrators* (2003); Foulkes, *Lewis Carroll and the Victorian Stage* (2005); Kérchy, *Alice in Transmedia Wonderland* (2016).

35. For a compilation of twenty adaptations produced between 1860 and 1928, see Sigler, *Alternative Alices* (1997), xi.

36. Drotner, *English Children and Their Magazines* (1988).

37. McGavran, *Literature and the Child* (1999); Rowland, *Romanticism and Childhood* (2015); Fleming, *The Legacy of the Moral Tale* (2016).

38. Jenkins, "Adaptation, Extension, Transmedia" (2017).

tumes, and the likenesses of actors. Toy theater collector and historian George Speaight confirms that "the Juvenile Drama grew out of the adult drama, and the Toy Theatre was just exactly the big theater in miniature; actors, costumes, scenery, were all faithfully copied from actual productions on the London Stage, and reproduced for their miniature performance."[39] These nineteenth-century toys have a remarkably long, popular, and well-documented life, due to their simultaneous roles as open and extended amusement for adolescents, nostalgic theatrical memorabilia for adults, and archival artifacts of theater history.

Toy theaters quickly became one of the most popular toys across Europe in the nineteenth century due to a dynamic relationship between printers, theatergoers, and other consumers of popular culture—exemplifying the confluence of technological, industrial, cultural, and social practices of convergence culture. Speaight describes the emergence of toy theaters as a series of "logical developments" driven by commercial interests to capitalize on the popularity of theatrical culture. Around the turn of the nineteenth century, single-sheet, full-length portraits of actors in costume were sold by local printers specializing in visual print culture. Around 1810, the images became smaller to fit two to four costumed actors per sheet, and they were presented as characters from the same play for a sense of cohesiveness. Within a few years, the portraits became smaller to include a full set of characters on a single sheet. Although not initially intended as toys, the miniature prints began to interest children. As sales increased, minor characters were added, then characters in different poses. Finally, at the request of parents, scenes were added, then other pieces of theatrical images—a proscenium, a stage, an orchestra.[40]

An important point to underscore for both cultural historians and contemporary media scholars is that toy theaters were not created as a top-down corporate practice meant to target a new group of exploitable customers. Instead, they developed due to customer demand through "a sort of dialogue between [the first toy theater publisher in England, William] West and his young customers."[41] As the illustrated sheets (one penny for plain, two pennies for color) caught on, children and parents requested backgrounds, props, theater wings, and stage directions. Intricate sets developed because children imagined the possibilities of adaptation in this format and requested new accessories to complement their existing designs and setups. Today, prize specimens are housed in museums and purchased by collectors, with an *Oli-*

---

39. Speaight, *Juvenile Drama* (1946), 22–23.
40. Speaight, *Juvenile Drama* (1946), 19.
41. Powell, *William West and the Regency Toy Theatre* (2004), 13.

ver Twist-themed set of character sheets fetching over $1,600 in 2008 (two to three times its then-estimated value).[42]

The attention that artists, engravers, and publishers paid to the visual elements of toy theaters did not carry over to the textual elements sometimes included in those sets. When preprinted scripts were included (they were often sold separately or otherwise not available), they weren't full printings of plays but instead abridged versions adapted from the stage and simplified as needed for younger users. An advertisement by the toy theater publisher William Cole, published in several English newspapers in 1825, promised that his collection of Juvenile Drama was "written to the Scenes and Characters, containing no sentiment or expression improper for the tender minds of youth."[43] For sets based on characters from William Shakespeare and Walter Scott, the toys served as literary-theatrical primers for children of all ages, resembling today's animated films and illustrated children books—what Thomas Leitch calls "entry-level classics."[44] Toy theaters supported the growth of an emerging cultural literacy that was literary, historical, and a source of national pride, as children became familiar with the nation's culture-texts and literary icons. Given that the nineteenth century is largely considered the period that created modern notions of "childhood" as a distinct developmental stage, toy theaters show us how cultural production was (literally) invested in emerging concepts of human development in relation to literacy and imagination—ideologies supported by industrialization and commercialism.

Toy theaters developed through collaborative business practices that brought together various skilled laborers and their supporting textile industries (paper, copper, and other materials used to make props and accessories). This makes them a site of convergence for multiple industries. Despite the fact that most character sheets and scenes were stamped with the name of their publishers, the practice was by no means a solitary effort, requiring a variety of workers to create a sellable final product (see figure 5.3).

Toy theater publishers also employed artists, engravers, and carpenters as part of their enterprise. Artists provided the illustrations of characters and scenes, the latter often drawn by set designers who worked for local theaters. Copper plates were made for each new set and sometimes the plates for the most popular sets had to be replaced once they had worn out. Toy theater publisher William West reportedly paid his coppersmith between "£70 and £80 a year for plates only" (roughly the annual salary for the average skilled laborer at the time). Further services were added as the popularity of the sets

---

42. Christie's "Sale 1981 Record, Lot 55" (2008).
43. "Advertisement," *Bristol Mirror* (1825).
44. Leitch, *Film Adaptation and Its Discontents* (2007).

FIGURE 5.3. Sample wooden toy theater featuring pasted paper scenery and characters from Redington's *The Corsican Brothers* (1857). Image © The Museum of London.

grew and additional accessories increased in demand. In an interview with Henry Mayhew in 1850, West recalls the evolution of the toy and its growth in demand as follows:

> We was asked by the customers for theayters [sic] to put the characters in, so I got up the print of a stage front, thinking that the customers would get the woodwork done themselves. But after the stage front they wanted the theayters [sic] themselves of me more than ever, so I got some made, and then the demand got so great that I was obliged to keep three carpenters to make em for me. One was a horgan [sic] builder and could make anything

in machinery. I turned out the first toy theayter [sic] for children as ever was got up for sale, and that was in the year 1813.⁴⁵

When business was good, West was making approximately fifty toy theaters per week (not counting the character and scenery sets for individual plays). These numbers were higher during the holiday season. He estimates he sold approximately 2,500 theaters per year of different sizes, varied levels of technical sophistication, and a range of overall embellishment—all of which together determined their respective prices. (This figure represents only the box theaters, not the plays, characters, and props.)

A new commercial practice was born that incorporated a range of textile industries, artistic practices, skilled labor, technological innovation, and transnational exchange. As toy theaters became mass-produced, the wooden frames were replaced by cardboard, eventually featuring perforated characters and props that required less skill in cutting. Yet their function remained the same, and they continued to be modeled on older plays, with the occasional new play added to publishers' catalogs. The toys were common throughout Europe, with publishers in France, Spain, Demark, and Austria, as well as in the United States. In England and Germany, where the toys were post popular, each country had approximately fifty known publishers and toy theater makers.⁴⁶ Personal accounts in the existing scholarship show that the juvenile drama sets were sometimes purchased as souvenirs by well-to-do parents who traveled, suggesting at least some mobility across nations, even if the sets were primarily seen as a domestic pastime more patriotic than cosmopolitan.

Sold in different sizes and with different degrees of embellishment, toy theaters facilitated fan-driven transmedia storytelling through adaptation. Sets were based on fairy tales (*Cinderella* and *The Sleeping Beauty*), adventure and action stories (*Robinson Crusoe* and *Blackbeard the Pirate*), and narrative poems (Sir Walter Scott's *The Lady of the Lake* and Lord Byron's *Mazeppa*).⁴⁷ Notable novels that were frequently reproduced by several publishers included *Don Quixote, Oliver Twist, The Corsican Brothers,* and *Uncle Tom's Cabin*. Several gothic titles were also available for purchase: *Blue Beard, The Vampire* (based on a stage adaptation of John Polidori's novella), and *Raymond and Agnes* (based on Lewis's *The Monk*). Some titles were published in multiple genres, including *The Castle of Otranto,* reimagined as both *Harlequin and*

---

45. Mayhew, "Letter XXXVIII: Monday, February 25, 1850."
46. "A Child's View: 19th-Century Paper Theatres" (2010).
47. The National Museum of Australia has digitized more than two hundred full-color images of nineteenth-century toy theaters as part of the "Everitt and George Family Collection of Toy Theatres."

FIGURE 5.4. Title sheet for Redington's *Characters and Scenes in Oliver Twist* (c. 1870). Image © The Museum of London.

the Giant Helmet and a melodramatic version titled *Manfredi*. Two literary authors were favorites: at least thirteen Shakespearean plays were represented in the regularly available catalog, and at least ten known theatrical sets were based on adaptations of Scott's works.[48] The primary source texts for these sets were not the "original" novels or narrative poems but instead dramatic adaptations of the texts as melodramas, pantomimes, and harlequinades, based on popular stage adaptations of the stories.

Authorship does not appear to have been a major motivator in the production, sale, or use of toy theaters, making them hard to classify within existing cultural and reception histories. Someone purchasing Redington's *Oliver Twist,* for example, may not have known the toy characters were taken from a novel by Charles Dickens, as there was no mention of Dickens on the character sheets (see figure 5.4). Unlike the insider-ness of gothic participatory culture, the younger the customer, the less likely they would make the association on their own. However, through play sets, children could begin to develop a cultural lexicon. Toy theaters facilitated the popularization of

---

48. Speaight, *Juvenile Drama* (1946), 236.

literary-theatrical characters, creating additional sites where they could exist in the cultural imagination independent from their source texts. Familiarity rested primarily on titles; the names of novelists or playwrights rarely if ever appear on the title sheets for toy theater play sets. Ideas of "authorship" were also largely abandoned as publishers bought plates and simply reproduced the images under the names of their own publishing houses, reiterating how much toy theaters were primarily commercial extensions of the theater industry and not primarily motivated by fidelity interests in specific works of literature.

For the next four decades, toy theaters held on to that market, producing new titles but largely maintaining the same model by replacing printers who sold their businesses and inventory. But as children grew up and the media industry evolved, so did the production, marketing, and distribution of toy theaters. As the market for cheap, serialized fiction grew, new journals aimed at younger readership emerged and flourished, especially in England and the United States, where between the 1840s and the 1920s there were dozens of catalogued periodicals exclusively for children and adolescents.[49] In the 1860s many of these periodicals began to include toy theater sheets in the printed issues as free giveaways in order to increase sales.[50] Some of these plays were reprints of the older, classic titles of the 1820s and 1830s, such as a toy theater set for *The Red Rover* that was distributed in 1865, interspersed throughout issues of a journal called *Black Eyed Susan*, which took its title from a famous nautical comedy written by Douglas Jerrold and first performed in 1829 with T. P. Cooke in the lead role. The children's journal connected the generation growing up in the 1860s with an older generation of parents or grandparents who would have grown up watching these plays.

In addition to reissuing older plays, at least a few new toy theater play sets were produced in association with these children's periodicals, with one title, *Alone in the Pirate's Lair*, turned into a toy theater directly from a story serialized in the inaugural issue of *The Boys of England* (published in England and the United States from 1866 through 1900). A few months later in September 1867, *Alone in the Pirate's Lair* was adapted from its periodical and toy theater versions by the professional dramatist Colin Henry Hazlewood and staged at the Britannia Theatre.[51]

One fascinating detail that emerges when studying nineteenth-century toy theaters is the way sets were used as product placement, branding, and self-promotion for publishers. Title sheets, which featured all of the play's principal characters, were stamped with the names of publishers, not authors,

---

49. Drotner, *English Children and Their Magazines, 1751–1945* (1988).
50. Speaight, *Juvenile Drama* (1946), 141.
51. Speaight, *Juvenile Drama* (1946), 141; Norwood, "The Britannia Theatre" (2009), 137.

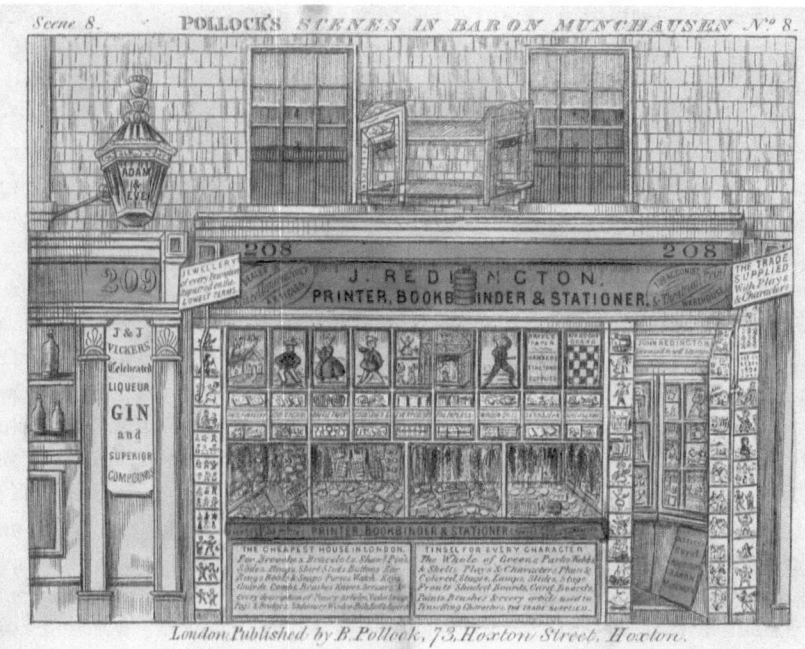

FIGURE 5.5. Pollock's scenes in *Baron Münchausen*, featuring the façade of John Redington, Printer, Bookbinder & Stationer storefront in London (c. 1857). © Look and Learn / Peter Jackson Collection.

dramatists, actors, or artists. Toy theater publishers embedded themselves into the visual landscape of stock street scenes, creating an intertextual and metadiscursive presence in the toy theater sets they published and sold. In background scenes meant to represent a generic shot of street life, one finds the façades of actual sites where additional play sets could be purchased. At least four storefronts appear as generic background scenes, including those of the most prominent toy theater publishers, such as West, Skelt, Webb, and Redington, with later publishers sometimes republishing the storefronts under their own names.[52] As we see in the scene from a *Baron Munchausen* toy theater adaptation, the plates could include additional forms of advertisements, as the reproduced storefront announces not only the sale of toy theater sheets, but also "Tinsel for Every Character" and other supplies needed to complete sets and produce plays at home (see figure 5.5).

---

52. Baldwin, *Toy Theatres of the World* (1992).

From a twenty-first-century perspective, with rampant branding and the product placement of toys, action figures, and other commercial tie-ins saturating today's commercial landscape, it's difficult to view the nineteenth-century children's media market without a degree of skepticism. However, these early industrial forms of commodified, interactive, transmedia storytelling bridged the otherwise separate worlds of adults and children. Dennis Denisoff situates nineteenth-century childhood firmly in the realm of British consumer culture, "a large-scale phenomenon that relied for its development on small-scale acts of identity formation. . . . Just as actual youngsters fulfilled key roles in events such as the Industrial Revolution, the solidification of capitalism, and the formation of an economy driven by a consumerist ethos, new notions of the child and childhood."[53] Agreeing, but pushing back against any image of passive consumption or spectatorship, Farr notes "testaments [from nineteenth-century psychologists Herbert Spencer and Grant Allen, as well as Robert Louis Stevenson] speak to the powerful effect of juvenile drama on youthful imaginations," however these toys "were not simply streamlined vehicles for conveying ideological messages to a passive audience," but were instead "sites of cultural ambivalence, a means to test reality against its representations."[54] The appeal of these toys created avid fans who added to their collections regularly by buying or making more sheets of their own. Yet they also played key roles in the imaginative life and formative years of many children who would go on to become prominent authors and consumers, connecting them to the broader landscape of cultural production meant for sophisticated audiences.

TOY THEATERS, FAN FICTION, AND NINETEENTH-CENTURY PARTICIPATORY CULTURE

Robert Louis Stevenson, who played with toy theaters as a child, writes fondly about them in a frequently reprinted essay "Penny Plain, Twopence Coloured" (1884), published in *Memories and Portraits* (1887):

> I have, at different times, possessed *Aladdin, The Red Rover, The Blind Boy, The Old Oak Chest, The Wood Dæmon, Jack Sheppard, The Miller and his Men, Der Freischutz, The Smuggler, The Forest of Bondy, Robin Hood, The Waterman, Richard I., My Poll and my Partner Joe, The Inchcape Bell* (imper-

---

53. Denisoff, "Introduction. Small Change" (2008), 1–25.
54. Farr, "Paper Dreams and Romantic Projections" (2008), 53.

fect), and *Three-Fingered Jack, the Terror of Jamaica*; and I have assisted others in the illumination of *The Maid of the Inn* and *The Battle of Waterloo*. In this roll-call of names you read the evidences of a happy childhood; and though not half of them are still to be procured of any living stationer, in the mind of their once happy owner all survive, kaleidoscopes of changing pictures, echoes of the past.[55]

Stevenson's tone ranges from nostalgic fun to the scrutinizing voice of a collector calling out the "imperfection" of his copy of Edward Fitzball's 1828 melodrama, staged at the Surrey Theatre and loosely based on the Scottish legend retold in Robert Southey's poem "The Inchcape Rock" (1802).[56] Stevenson describes these stories as if they were the books and plays of his own youth, as if he's seen them live on stage or experienced them as their immediate intended audience, despite the fact that he was born in 1850, more than twenty years after the premiere of Fitzball's play and with even more time separating him from the other titles listed here. Stevenson's essay reads as an exercise in transmedia fandom—with the young child playing with toy replicas before growing up to become a published "expert" on their history and legacy—showing that the interactive, imaginative toy played a major role in his development as a writer.

The essay also points out how the toys were sites of community among users. Stevenson recalls not only owning at least sixteen different titles himself but also assisting others in the illumination of additional plays. Much of the appeal of these toys came from the range of activities and processes that went into launching a production, which encouraged collaboration and social interaction. Children would come together to color, embellish, and tinsel their penny-plain pieces. Performances required group work, and some sets included directions and suggestions for how to manage the extra "hands," divide the labor among the actors, and make the most enjoyable experience for the audience. Different ages could participate in the production of the plays, with older children staging the piece while younger siblings, parents, and other adults enjoyed the performance. Images from the nineteenth century point to toy theaters as a social activity, as they were often portrayed as a form of family or group entertainment.

Instead of producing passive consumers, toy theaters encouraged imaginative role-playing activities as actors, playwrights, and producers. Detailed instructions for "How to perform the Play" were sometimes included. Writ-

---

55. Stevenson, "A Penny Plain and Twopence Coloured" (1907), 198–99.
56. Burwick, *British Drama of the Industrial Revolution* (2015), 224.

ten directly to the juvenile consumer, the instructions provide suggestions for managing all aspects of a public performance: invite siblings and friends to voice characters, but "you do not need more than two people actually pushing the characters on the stage, or they will get in each other's way." Users were encouraged to create "theatrical atmosphere" through music, lighting, and stage effects, and there are guides for creating theatrical illusions both on the toy stage and behind the scenes, where "it will greatly help the effect if you can screen the stage with curtains, or a large piece of cardboard, so that the audience do not see you at work behind the scenes while the play is in progress." The instructions challenged children to "maximize the experience of your guests (once you've practiced enough to put on a public performance)" by providing "tickets and programmes" and ushering "patrons" into "comfortable seats" in communal family areas of the home.[57]

The paper toys also encouraged remixing and other intertextual practices. As children bought individual sheets, adding to their collections in pieces, sets were likely mixed at home. Indeed, selling practices suggest that remixing was the norm as scenes were repurposed from other play sets. Publishers also put out sheets of generic scenes, props, and characters that could be used with different plays, such as fairies, clowns, and other "extras" to fill out backgrounds for city settings, dance numbers, or battle scenes. If a child was missing characters, they could turn to other sets or sheets to complete their miniature productions.

Like LEGO and contemporary engineering toys, nineteenth-century toy theaters promoted forms of open-ended, creative play that were tailored to different interests and incorporated a range of activities.[58] Mechanically inclined children might spend more time on the technical aspects of theatrical production, including setting up footlights and other effects to heighten the spectacle. Anecdotes recorded in journals even describe children using gunpowder to add explosions to climactic moments (anticipating the need for the "Do not try this at home" warnings ubiquitous in today's media culture). For introspective children who preferred to spend their time drawing, painting, and crafting, toy theaters also appealed to creative sensibilities.

Most of all, these transmedia extensions produced a consumer-driven network of storytelling that fused literacy and entertainment, a commercial practice that continued to grow steadily through the present day. Stevenson recalls that the most exciting part of getting a play set was both the initial purchase (in and of itself a testament to the commercial pleasures of toy theaters as

---

57. Jackson, *A Pollock's Toy Theatre* (1976), 10.
58. Lee, "The Plastic Art of LEGO" (2014).

objects of desire and consumerism) and the coloring, cutting, pasting, and assembling of pieces. He expresses less interest in actually staging the play. For Stevenson, the least satisfactory part of the toys were the accompanying "Book of Words," consisting mostly of stage directions and basic dialogue suited for young audiences. As Stevenson writes in the personal essay, "Indeed, as literature, these dramas did not much appeal to me. I forget the very outline of the plots."[59]

In response to the shoddy scripts that came with these sets, children often created original plays using the scenes and characters from existing sets to craft new stories—much like fan fiction today. Most anecdotes that document the experience of toy theaters point toward children writing their own plays instead of simply following instructions. The diary of a twelve-year-old Benjamin Musser, written in 1901, provides a snapshot of how toy theaters engaged the imagination:

> Nov. 19 . . . I found in Fred's closet a little theatre which he and I made a year ago and which I loved. He said it could be his and mine together, and we will often have plays in it for Julia and her friends. Gee but we'll have fun! Today I've been writing a play to be acted in it. The play is woven around the French revolution, dealing with Louis XVI, Marie Antoinette, Cardinal Roan, etc. It is very tragic, especially the last act. The theatre is about 2 ft. each way, the stage I mean, and has arrangements for the curtains and is slick. . . . Norris also has a theatre, not a big homemade one like ours but one of those flimsy ones you buy at Swartzes, still it isn't bad. He is writing a play for his, and he wants me to draw the actors for in it[.] I said I would.[60]

Two days later, Musser mentions the progress of his original historical drama, which he has now titled *The Guillotine*. The twelve-year-old dramatist-actor-producer is eager to make his sister Julia "be fearfully moved and cry maybe," making the play "very tragic" for this reason. In response to his collaborator Fred, who chides him for being a Royalist in his overly sympathetic portrayal of Marie Antoinette and her children and for being too emotionally expressive in his writing, young Musser asserts his authorial right to reveal his beliefs in his play because "feelings ought to show, that's what writers are for." By writing their own plays, creating their own characters, and immersing themselves in extended communal storytelling, children developed an engaged form of media consumption that gave them opportunities to rehearse their learning,

---

59. Stevenson, "A Penny Plain and Twopence Coloured" (1907), 198–99.
60. Musser, *Diary of a Twelve-Year-Old* (1932), 48–49. All quotes are from this page.

ideas, and interpretations of literature, history, and the role of writers as social agents and producers of meaning.[61] Young Ben doesn't just write for his own amusement but instead to participate in a communal, affective, transmedia storytelling experience that could be used to negotiate the intersections of politics, history, literature, and entertainment through interactive forms of adaptation.

Farr underscores the multiplicity of meanings and the long-lasting impact this type of play had on the intellectual, social, and cultural development of nineteenth-century children, especially the boys who made up the target market for these toys. She writes:

> Through its adaptability, the toy theater was a vehicle for a particular cultural education. It extended beyond stylistic and formal features by introducing versions of an eclectic range of literary texts, [plays, folk tales, cultural stories] . . . historical battles and crimes. This array of seemingly disparate materials was funneled through a product aimed at juvenile consumption, and came to occupy the shared imagination of roughly two generations of grown men.[62]

The impressions left on the imagination followed many into adulthood, where collectors of vintage prints transformed the trade from a site of play to a site of theatrical memorabilia and cultural history. Much of the late Victorian market was driven by reprints of the same titles that dominated the 1820s and 1830s.[63] The intricacy of some theaters and character sets suggests that adults made up a distinct target audience of collectors. In his study of *Robinson Crusoe* and popular children's culture (which had at least two different versions of character sheets for toy theaters), O'Malley writes, "Indeed, the larger sized theatres came at a cost that suggests adult consumers from more privileged classes and were sufficiently complex that they imply a quite sophisticated user."[64] Driven by a mixture of nostalgia and commercialism, collectors became immersed in these activities, through which they not only reignited the market for old prints but also became content experts and financial investors.

Beyond their transformation into nostalgic objects, toy theaters eventually became vintage artifacts for theater historians and collectors of theatri-

---

61. McPharlin, *The Puppet Theatre in America* (1949).
62. Farr, "Paper Dreams and Romantic Projections" (2008), 51.
63. Some Victorian titles were added along the way—most notably *Oliver Twist*, but as toy theater historian George Speight explains, this is the reason why we have ten titles by Scott in the catalog of existing plays published in England but only one title adapted from Dickens.
64. O'Malley, *Children's Literature, Popular Culture, and Robinson Crusoe* (2012), 132.

cal memorabilia. To date, character and scenery prints from toy theaters are among the most useful archival materials for recovering the look and feel of the nineteenth-century popular stage. The prints were themselves adaptations of multiple sources: performance venues, celebrity actors, dramatic genres, and popular literature. Like today's action figures, they were designed as replicas—striving for accuracy and, one might even say, "fidelity."[65] They anticipate contemporary practices of world-building and character extensions through lowbrow merchandise and collectible items. While there are some notable differences between now and then, the toy theater industry of the nineteenth century reveals that today's corporate-driven media environment did not invent transmedia storytelling and tie-in merchandise but instead adapted and expanded it from nineteenth-century business and cultural models. For collectors and historians, the history of toy theaters is inextricably tied to the history of the nineteenth-century stage, but the reverse relationship is also important. The stage, of course, existed without its miniature replica; however, toy theaters eventually became among the most readily available items in the visual archive of the nineteenth-century popular stage, continuing to provide access to the theatrical past in the present.

MANY OF the major nineteenth-century writers grew up playing with toy theaters and reading popular fiction like gothic chapbooks. The Shelleys notably describe childhoods filled with fantastic stories, with Percy publishing two gothic novellas, *Zastrozzi: A Romance* (1810) and *St. Irvyne; or, The Rosicrucian: A Romance* (1811), while an undergraduate at Oxford. A deep shared fascination with reading and writing gothic fiction placed these writers at the center of the most famous ghost story competition ever held, resulting in the birth of two now-iconic monsters and with four of its five participants holding prominent places in literary history. The competition itself was an exercise in extension and adaptation—the challenge to write a new story that reimagines the generic conventions of the emerging popular form. It was inspired by an amateur 1812 French translation of a collection of German ghost stories, *Fantasmagoriana* (published 1811), written by several writers who are now mostly forgotten. Early nineteenth-century pulp gothic, that is to say, created the cultural conditions from which a literary gothic developed. The latter would not be possible without the former. How different, might we ask, is the ghost story competition that created *Frankenstein* at Villa Diodati in the summer of 1816

---

65. Jenkins, "Adaptation, Extension, Transmedia" (2017).

when compared to groups of young adults gathering in 2018 to read their favorite stories and write their own fan fiction?

Victorian writers would also benefit from early forays of participatory storytelling like toy theaters. Dickens, Stevenson, Carroll and Wilde point to the importance of these toys in their intellectual and creative development, with Stevenson explaining that the inadequacy of the writing in the Juvenile Drama scripts prompted him to write the stories himself. In all of these cases, some of the biggest names in nineteenth-century literary history got their start as avid consumers of mass culture and became active influencers of literary and cultural history. The formative influence of mass culture in the form of gothic pulp fiction, toy theaters, and other children's media didn't represent a watered-down or less sophisticated form of literary culture; instead it helped produce a more literate society and nurtured early forms of imagination into more developed literary creations. Through toy theaters and similarly marketed transmedia merchandise, children negotiated adult worlds and found spaces to become active consumers and creators of art and culture in an industrial economy.

These historical examples ask us to rethink similar transmedia storytelling practices in the present, especially given the popularity of genre fiction and merchandizing. Today's multi-billion-dollar superhero franchises show us how genres can function as extended narrative worlds unto themselves, and they fuse multiple culture-texts into an even larger universe of ever-expanding adaptations and commercial products. Single-character storyworlds (such as Spider-Man or Batman) can be combined to create larger universes as we see with Marvel's *Avengers* or DC Comics' *Justice League*.[66] These transmedia universes travel across all cross-sections of contemporary cultural production, from fine art forms like painting to tie-in merchandise like toys. In addition to an array of toys, games, kitsch, and other popular merchandise, the Batman culture-text includes critically acclaimed and culturally important film and television like the installments that make up *The Dark Knight* trilogy (2005–12), written and directed by Christopher Nolan (notably some of this culture-text's most gothic-infused adaptations), and more recently the 2019 launch of a television series that stars a queer Batwoman who (in addition to Gotham villains) fights for gender equality and LGBTQIA+ visibility (both within the show and in the media landscape that produces it). The mobility from pulp fiction to higher art is possible only through repeated adaptation across forms and media—from comic books and action figures to film and television, and

---

66. Scolari, Bertetti, and Freeman, *Transmedia Archaeology* (2014); Meikle, *Adaptations in the Franchise Era* (2019).

back again. As the most recent culture-texts to emerge, the cultural visibility of superhero and science fiction transmedia franchises ranges from "authorized" or "licensed" stories in print or film that are considered "canonical" to unauthorized, user-created content like fan fiction, published through inexpensive, internet-based media platforms. Games and toys add still more layers of transmedia storytelling and sites of engagement as users invent their own stories through role-playing and other activities.

The ubiquity of multi-billion-dollar superhero storyworlds today is impressive given the genre's humble origins in American comic books of the 1940s through the 1960s. This form of pulp fiction, targeted primarily at younger readers, was regularly criticized for having a negative influence on youth—the exact same critique made of the novel in the mid-eighteenth century, and of gothic fictions across forms and media in the nineteenth century. Gothic novels and comics have come a long way since their first appearances; both forms now have mass culture and high culture equivalents in literary fiction and graphic novels, respectively. But more importantly, they share similar origin stories, as both started as commercial print culture intended for mass consumption.

Yet, as we've seen, the nineteenth century's "Gothic machine" was similarly powered by a fusion of forms, mediums, and new technologies, all converging through the commercialization of cultural production, showing us that today's transmedia storytelling practices and fan-based content have clear roots in the nineteenth-century culture industry. The major differences between then and now are shaped by technological changes, but the practices behind these transmedia adaptations are very similar. Many of the newer forms themselves are adaptations of the older ones: podcasts are updated forms of radio plays; graphic novels are part of the developing trajectory of older, pulp comic book forms and illustrated penny dreadfuls. The new narrative media are natural extensions of older forms, and they resemble older models of commercial storytelling except for the specific technologies used to create and disperse them.

CONCLUSION

A New (Popular) Literary History

Adaptation and Canon Formation

HOW MANY WAYS can we experience Jane Austen today? We can read the six completed novels she wrote two hundred years ago, but we can also encounter her heroines reimagined in a range of contemporary fiction for children, teenagers, and adults. Austen's screen debut came with a fifty-five-minute made-for-television drama adaptation of *Pride and Prejudice,* written by Michael Barry and airing on BBC TV in May 1938, and was soon adapted for the big screen in *Pride and Prejudice* (1940).[1] Since then dozens of adaptations have appeared on both big and small screens. These screen versions were preceded by several stage plays, as well as shorter, dramatized scenes published in Victorian anthologies. A collective history of transmedia adaptations has launched Austen's mass appeal in the present, which today includes not only film and television but also official spin-offs told across Twitter feeds and YouTube videos. There are also card games (*Marrying Mr. Darcy* and *Jane Austen's Matchmaker*), board games, graphic novels, print books, dolls, abridged and illustrated books for children, and more.

In the twenty-first century, Austen is both a source for countless individual cottage industries and also a draw for big businesses, including tourism. Shannon Hale's novel *Austenland* (2007) and its 2013 film adaptation satirize the world of immersive Austen-themed tours in the context of a multi-

---

1. Bolton, *Women Writers Dramatized* (2000), 8–22.

million-dollar travel industry. Tens of thousands of people each year visit landmarks, museums, and Regency-themed reenactments related to Austen's life and works. Austen and the characters she created inhabit multiple mediated worlds grounded in real, virtual, or other representational cultural forms. There is much to celebrate and to critique in these endless extensions, which straddle the seemingly disparate worlds of consumer-driven commercialism and immersive educational experience. However, the biggest revelation in this sea of Austen commodities is how centrally adaptation and transmedia storytelling drive cultural memory, literacy, and canonicity. As Devoney Looser makes clear, authors are made not born, and Austen's transformation from anonymous writer to cultural icon has been created by a long history of adaptation that includes the usual arenas of theater, film, and television, but also book illustrations, private clubs, public demonstrations, and even academic scholarship.[2]

Throughout this book, my model of historical adaptation has been defined broadly to show how adaptation drives popular culture and artistic production alike. I have avoided close readings of specific adaptations, instead choosing to approach adaptation and transmediation as a polydirectional and dispersed practice where multiple pieces are needed to create the whole picture. Gordon Slethaug articulates the need for a poststructuralist model of adaptation studies that is "open, dialogically negotiated, and distributed across the system . . . so that adaptation, derivation, translation, and copy have the same cultural currency as the original."[3] The best way to break down existing hierarchies in adaptation and media studies is through a historical view. Gregory Semenza has recently called for adaptation scholars to take a "collective turn to diachronic historiography and the *longue durée*" seeing the need for "an even broader and more ambitious approach to adaptation studies, one systematically tuned into the importance of the past as a way into the future."[4] The examples discussed in the previous chapters show how dialogical relationships inform the history of commercialized literary adaptation through various historical, political, social, industrial, and artistic contexts. The culture-text approach I've adopted throughout this book breaks down hierarchies, acknowledging the cultural value of multiple versions of a story and their role in cultural and reception histories.

Because adaptation doesn't simply follow a text, it can also shape the writing process as well as authorial identity. The early reception history of Charles Dickens's *Nicholas Nickleby*, for instance, demonstrates a dynamic structure of

---

2. Looser, *The Making of Jane Austen* (2017).
3. Slethaug, *Adaptation Theory and Criticism* (2014), 25–26.
4. Semenza, "Towards a Historical Turn?" (2018), 65.

author-audience exchange (see chapters 2 and 4), where adaptations actively influence the production of a source novel or other original artwork, sometimes contributing to a cycle of feedback and engagement between writers, readers, adapters, and audiences. Describing adaptation's productive relationship to the literary canon, Julie Sanders argues that "adaptation both appears to require and perpetuate the existence of a canon, although it may in turn contribute to its ongoing reformulation and expansion."[5] This rationale has grounded my book, as I have expanded this claim to position adaptation earlier in and at the center of literary history. The fact that new texts get adapted on a constant basis proves that adaptation doesn't require a canon; instead, adaptation creates both popular and literary canons by trying and extending the immediate cultural reach of texts or authors.

Instead of approaching adaptations as popular forms of canon *extension* or canon *preservation*, adaptation should be understood as a central, driving factor of literary production, reception, and canon *formation*. A historical approach to adaptation studies clearly shows that adaptation predates the emergence of any literary canon. Stories have always been adapted, and not all works that are adapted become popular or canonical. Yet the most adapted stories are the ones that have survived long enough to create literary canons. These texts, in turn, remain culturally relevant through repeated adaptations across genres, forms, and media. To become a "classic," a text or author usually must be accepted not only within the academy but also in the popular imagination. In order to remain canonical or culturally relevant, regular and continuous adaptation is thus required.

In addition to contesting a traditional canon of so-called great books determined by vague notions of universality and timelessness, the historical examples I have covered in this book ask us to rethink how culture-texts, authorial celebrity, and literary canons get established democratically and commercially, disrupting a top-down model of canonicity as wholly determined by aesthetic criteria, cultural elitism, and academic institutions. The stakes are important to both literary studies and adaptation studies. In the case of the former, the criteria traditionally used to evaluate artistic production are revealed as incomplete or ineffective tools for measuring the cultural importance of specific texts and authors. The questions I receive most often about my research (from scholars who do not identify as adaptation scholars) are variations on the same evaluative theme: "Are the nineteenth-century stage adaptations any good?" or "Which adaptation most closely follows the 'original' work?" Such questions position authors or texts in relation

---

5. Sanders, *Adaptation and Appropriation* (2006), 8.

to vague notions of originality and diminish the dynamic, dialectical relationship between literary works and their adaptations, a problem worsened by a general failure to acknowledge that "original" works are often adaptations themselves. Literary discourse often focuses too much on critiquing the fidelity of film adaptations of Shakespeare but give comparatively minimal (if any) attention to how much Shakespeare followed his own sources. As the literary gentleman of Dickens's *Nicholas Nickleby* reminds us, Shakespeare traded in adaptation too. Most of his plays adapt historical sources, folk tales, or contemporary texts with less cultural visibility than his works enjoyed, even in their time. After his death, it was only through continuous stage revivals, illustrations, and other extensions that Shakespeare became a canonical author. Repositioning adaptation at the heart of canon formation (both as process and product) provides a new perspective that more accurately reflects how stories are produced and transformed into culture-texts as well as how literary authors become cultural icons.

Adaptation studies also stands to benefit from a view of adaptation as a more material and transhistorical cultural practice that has undergone significant change over the centuries, evolving to fit the needs and demands of new historical contexts, economic conditions, political changes, and social movements, yet it still has much in common with contemporary models. Adaptation and transmedia storytelling occur in every age; the differences are driven by each period's cultural moment and available mediums for storytelling. This longer view offers adaptation studies a way to move questions of canonicity in new directions, as we are able to see how adaptation works in the early lives of texts, not just as an "afterlife" or afterthought. These models appear throughout adaptation history. The Romantics borrowed from their predecessors, not to copy them directly but to use them as a form of cultural legitimation by which they could establish their own places in literary history. We see similar patterns of appropriation in every historical age and aesthetic movement, forming the basic structure of storytelling itself. Focusing too much on more contemporary adaptations of the existing literary canon incorrectly places canonical literature at the center of a much more diverse and dispersed cultural practice. For this reason, the study of popular adaptations should be seen as interconnected with the study of literature's history. Together, the examples in this book uncover a need for more overlap between literary, theater, and media studies—especially in their respective points of artistic and commercial convergence. Because of its inherent interdisciplinary emphasis on forms and media, adaptation studies is uniquely positioned to bridge these areas through an ongoing cultural practice that links past to present and will continue to drive future storytelling.

Ironically, Hollywood has embraced its relationship to adaptation more openly than academics in both literary and film studies. From the medium's earliest years, filmmakers and producers used literature to bolster film's credibility as an emerging art form, and that relationship paid off commercially. As Dudley Andrew argues, "Study of adaptation is logically tantamount to the study of cinema as a whole."[6] Universal Studios built its 105-year-old brand largely by adapting and appropriating from a range of sources, when Carl Laemmle Jr. made the prescient decision to invest in a horror lineup of nineteenth-century gothic adaptations. *Dracula* (1930), *Frankenstein* (1931), *The Invisible Man* (1933), and their respective sequels built the cultural capital needed to solidify Universal as an industry giant, and the decision to adapt these works was based on their commercial potential, not on any desire to pay homage to Bram Stoker, Mary Shelley, H. G. Wells, or any other writers of a bygone era. Similarly, *All Quiet on the Western Front* (1930), an immediate adaptation of Erich Maria Remarque's 1928–29 novel, clearly wasn't motivated by a sense of canonicity or desire to preserve a cultural or literary past as much as by an interest in exploring a contemporary story's possibility in a new medium. In both cases, literary adaptation helped establish the film industry as a viable, commercial industry.

Hollywood's long-term, open embrace of adaptation proved more than just financially profitable. To date, adaptations make up a large proportion of the greatest artistic achievements in cinema history. The Academy Awards have included a version of the "Best Adapted Screenplay" category since the inaugural Oscars ceremony in 1929. *All Quiet on the Western Front* brought Universal its first "Best Film" Oscar. Indeed, through 2014, fifty-five adaptations have won the Academy's most coveted "Best Film" award, a winning rate of 64 percent.[7] In 2014, the winner was *12 Years a Slave*, notable for the multiplicity of issues and questions it poses: as a direct adaptation of a published slave narrative, as an adaptation of history more broadly, as biopic, and as representation of the past through a present-day lens.[8] And although the 2015 winner *Birdman or (The Unexpected Virtue of Ignorance)* was based on an original screenplay, a stage adaptation of Raymond Carver's "What We Talk About When We Talk About Love" is central to the film's plot. The range of this brief survey of celebrated cinema positions adaptation at the crux of conversations about the most award-winning films of all time.

---

6. Andrew, "Adaptation" (1984), 103.

7. Adapted from Fernandez, "Oscars 2014: How Adaptations Continue to Shape the Conversation" (2014). Fernandez's figures are based on films derived from novels, nonfiction books, newspaper articles, or staged plays.

8. Stevenson, "*12 Years a Slave*" (2014); Raw and Tutan, *The Adaptation of History* (2013).

Given this history, it's no wonder that more than 50 percent of films produced each year are adaptations of novels, short stories, comic books, or other genres.[9] Presently, as the most popular form of narrative storytelling in the early twenty-first century, television is following a similar model of embracing adaptation. At least seventy television series announced or in development in 2014 were adaptations, appropriations, remakes, or reboots, not counting mash-up shows like Showtime's *Penny Dreadful* (2014–17) or ABC's *Once Upon a Time* (2011–18).[10] Several of the most critically acclaimed television series currently in production stray significantly from the works on which they are based, but that's not stopping Hulu's *The Handmaid's Tale* (2017–) or Netflix's *The Haunting of Hill House* (2018–) from drawing positive reviews from critics, audiences, and even at times from the novelists who originated these stories. Web series are following the same trends. Pemberley Digital describes itself as "an innovative web video production company that specializes in the adaptation of classic works [into] the new media format."[11] Between 2012 and 2015, the company released several critically acclaimed web series based on nineteenth-century fiction, including *The March Family Letters*, *Emma Approved*, and *Frankenstein, M. D.*, as well as the Emmy-award-winning transmedia series *The Lizzie Bennet Diaries*. In partnership with PBS Digital Studios, Pemberley Digital's use of social media, web videos, and traditional print formats draws on a longer tradition of transmedia adaptation reimagined for an audience of digital natives more likely to watch YouTube than network or cable television.

As this book has shown, the adaptation-based franchise system dominating film and television is an intensified commercial model inherited from the past. Far from an anachronistic flattening, clear links exist between the culture industries of the past and today's media and entertainment industries, with Karen Laird and Timothy Corrigan making strong cases for further historical ties between adaptation in the nineteenth century and later media and art forms. Laird shows how silent films were almost entirely based on popular plays of Victorian novels staged during the nineteenth century. Her meticulous case studies of the early stage and screen histories of *Jane Eyre*, *David Copperfield*, and *The Woman in White* establish a direct lineage between nineteenth-century playscripts and silent films, which in turn influenced films of the sound era.[12] Corrigan also makes connections between the nineteenth-

---

9. MacCabe, Murray, and Warner, *True to the Spirit* (2011).
10. Thomas, "Everything's an Adaptation" (2014).
11. Pemberley Digital Studios (http://www.pemberleydigital.com).
12. Laird, *The Art of Adapting Victorian Literature* (2015).

and twentieth-century media industries with broader cultural relevance: "Between the high cultural ground being articulated in universities and museums and the low cultural fairgrounds from which the movies would spring, the nineteenth century predicted a long line of anxieties and claims about the relationship of the movies to the other arts."[13] These anxieties included the blurring of class distinctions and shifting cultural attitudes about a range of social issues including race, gender, and sexuality. Transmedia adaptation continues to bring together the literary arts and popular culture, forcing critically engaged interactions, as opposed to passive consumerism.

As both an industrial and an artistic practice, as well as a form of reading and interpretation, adaptation functions as an "invisible genre" that Thomas Leitch suggests "has a serious claim to be not only a genre [itself], but the master Hollywood genre that sets the pattern for all the others."[14] Beyond passive or derivative, adaptation influences reception, guides interpretation, and creates meaningful connections between a diversity of stories and cultural forms. Leitch asks us to consider reading and adapting as parallel practices

> since reading any book, attending any play, looking at any painting, or watching any film allows an audience to test assumptions formed by earlier experiences of books or plays or paintings or films against a new set of norms and values. The distinctiveness of adaptation as a genre is that it foregrounds this possibility and makes it more active, more exigent, more indispensable. Comparisons that are discretionary in all texts, because they are all intertexts, become foundational to the extent that any audience experiences an adaptation as an adaptation.[15]

Useful is Leitch's characterization of adaptation as an active process that asks audiences to make connections between texts, visual art, and cultural artifacts. No matter the form or medium, storytelling practices are linked through allusion, intertextuality, archetypes, and other patterns of repetition, all of which function under the larger umbrella of adaptation practices. Adaptation's invisibility affords it ubiquity, allowing it to shape popular literacy and drive cultural production.

Bringing these modes into closer proximity with one another may help build stronger bridges between adaptation studies, scholarship on transme-

---

13. Corrigan, "Literature on Screen" (2007), 38.
14. Leitch, "Adaptation, the Genre" (2008), 106.
15. Leitch, "Adaptation, the Genre" (2008), 117.

dia storytelling, and historically focused literary and cultural studies.[16] As I've argued in this book, adaptations show us how the nineteenth-century theater and print industries evolved in similar ways to twentieth-century film and contemporary media industries. Adaptation's impact was both immediate and long-term, not just commercially, but also aesthetically. For example, the illustrated book played up the relationship between text and visuals without privileging one form over the other. This fusion of text and image made illustrated books desirable commodities and drove related markets, from low-priced periodicals to expensive gift books. Through new illustrated editions, texts received regular facelifts as updated designs reintroduced familiar characters by resituating them in modern contexts that would resonate with new audiences and eventually inspire the next generation of artists, writers, and readers in ongoing cycles of adaptation.[17]

Within the emerging industrial and commercial context, adaptation supported the rise of celebrity authors and professional artists, especially with regard to the increasing prominence of arts-based professions and their permanent influence on art and culture (see chapters 2, 3, and 4). As artistic production and mass culture converged through the period's various arts and entertainment industries, repetition through adaptation turned authors, artists, actors, and even characters into cultural icons, making them recognizable like never before and turning them into major figures in literary and cultural history. As I've stressed in chapters 1, 4, and 5, adaptation and various forms of character extension are important to literary, visual, and cultural histories because they help to accurately gauge circulation and cultural influence as they provide markers by which to measure impact beyond an immediate target audience or sphere of influence.

Canonicity requires availability, and adaptations increase books sales and the demand for new editions. When *Frankenstein* was published anonymously in 1818, only five hundred copies of the text were printed. No other printings occurred until the stage premiere of *Presumption,* at which time William God-

---

16. Leitch, Hutcheon, and others frequently make brief historical connections, but these are decidedly outside of the focus of their scholarship. Notably, in "Adaptation, the Genre," Leitch discusses the works of Alexandre Dumas (both father and son) and mentions an early nineteenth-century stage adaptation penned by Dumas himself. However, the example is given to support Leitch's argument about genre, not to historicize adaptation studies as a field. Hutcheon quickly acknowledges the proliferation of adaptations in the Victorian period, but the connection isn't explored at length.

17. Lynch, *The Economy of Character* (1998); Mole, *What the Victorians Made of Romanticism* (2017). Lynch and Mole describe how new editions regularly introduce new contexts, intertextual elements, and other critical interventions without explicitly referring to them as adaptations.

win (Mary Shelley's father) arranged for a new printing of 1,500 copies, this time with the author's name revealed. A new edition of the novel was published in 1831 as part of the *Bentley's Standard Novels* series. Between 1823 and 1831, only two thousand copies of the novel existed in print, nearly the number of seats in many of the main theatrical venues in London and Paris. William St. Clair puts these numbers into perspective:

> The English Opera House, where *Presumption* opened in 1823, was able to hold about 1,500 persons. The Coburg Theatre, where *Frankenstein; or, The Demon of Switzerland* opened shortly afterwards, held over 3,800. . . . Every single night when one of the *Frankenstein* plays was performed brought a version of the story of the manmade monster to more men and women that the book did in ten or twenty years.[18]

The Paris production of *Le Monstre et le Magicien* (1826) ran for more than eighty nights at the Théatre de La Porte Saint-Martin in its first season, popular enough for the play to be issued in print—and to inspire its own set of parodies. No matter the venue, on the night of any given performance in London, Paris, or elsewhere, more people could encounter the monster on stage than they could in print. This was the cultural environment that convinced Bentley in 1831 to include *Frankenstein* in its lineup of important contemporary novels. Without Peake's *Presumption* and other early *Frankenstein* adaptations that immediately followed in its footsteps, the now-iconic monster may have been overlooked or forgotten due to the limited print availability of the novel.

Later *Frankenstein*-inspired works often took direct cues from early adaptations rather than from the novel. The dramatists of the 1820s remixed each other's unique additions while contributing original flourishes, with some even adapting their own earlier adaptations.[19] New textual abridgements and variations in nineteenth-century pulp fiction mixed elements from both the novel and its stage adaptations (see chapter 5). Victorian versions riffed on the plays of the 1820s, and the earliest films also more closely resemble their nineteenth-century stage brethren than Shelley's vision.[20] Such wide dispersal through a multimedia network of adaptations is what makes *Frankenstein* such an exemplary model of a culture-text. As Francesca Saggini, Anna Soccio, and others have recently argued, adaptations, parodies, and other forms of imita-

---

18. St. Clair, *The Reading Nation in the Romantic Period* (2004), 369.
19. Milner also wrote the now-lost drama *Frankenstein; or, The Demon of Switzerland* (1823), which turned out to be a financial flop (see Forry, *Hideous Progenies* [1990]).
20. Szwydky, "*Frankenstein*'s Spectacular Nineteenth-Century Stage History and Legacy" (2018).

tion beyond the novel kept the Frankenstein story alive in the nineteenth-century popular imagination, just as theater, film, television, radio, comics, web series, novelizations, and video games continue to do through the present.[21] Two hundred years after the publication of Shelley's novel, Frankenstein and his Creature are global icons, as are an array of characters inhabiting the fictional universes of the nineteenth-century gothic and their cultural legacies.

If for no other reason than adaptation's wide-ranging impact, literary studies needs to make a space, as Julie Grossman proposes, where "instead of imagining the trajectory of textual children as 'hideous' because of their appropriation by the forces of cultural consumption, we might instead embrace the potential for shifts in perspectives and changes in orientation on source texts and the authors and cultures that produce them."[22] Be it through live performance, book illustration, textual abridgements, novelizations, or screen-based storytelling, adaptations contribute to the survival and cultural relevance of stories in their own day and for future generations. We should recognize these "hideous" versions beyond their immediate ability to reflect or materialize the "originals" on which they are based. Grossman finds obvious yet productive monstrous metaphors for adaptation in the Frankenstein culture-text, specifically in the way the Creature embodies the power of fragmentation and its relationship to an unruly, distorted-yet-fully-formed whole. But the Frankenstein culture-text also helps us see the cultural power of adaptation from a historical perspective that includes the novel's publication history.

In a similar way, a steady stream of adaptations—including stage dramatizations, parodies, textual sequels, character extensions, and visual illustrations—similarly supported the literary celebrity and professional careers of nineteenth-century writers (see chapters 2 and 4). Byron insisted his works weren't meant for the stage, yet they all found their way onto it. Scott, on the other hand, directly pursued adaptation of his works, collaborating closely with actor-manager Daniel Terry to produce his novels for the stage as quickly as possible, partly in hopes of outshining competing stage versions of his stories. Dickens struggled with the speed of adaptation of his works and only embraced the process after fighting it throughout the 1830s and 1840s, while also refusing to actively endorse any stage versions of his novels. Hugo embraced *Notre-Dame*'s theatrical possibilities almost immediately, even penning his own adaptation, which radically rewrote his tragic plot to include a happier ending for Esmeralda after staged melodramas written by English dra-

---

21. Cutchins and Perry, *Adapting Frankenstein* (2018); Saggini and Soccio, *Transmedia Creatures* (2018).

22. Grossman, *Literature, Film, and Their Hideous Progeny* (2015), 20.

matists consistently saved her from the gallows.[23] Despite their different takes on adaptation, nineteenth-century poets and novelists nevertheless acknowledged adaptation's impact in widening the reach of the literary works, making them accessible to audiences who would not otherwise have access. In all of these examples, early and frequent adaptation is the common denominator of texts that go on to become culture-texts while also establishing themselves in literary history. A similar dynamic continues to drive contemporary cultural production, in that a new story's likelihood of becoming a canonical work or culture-text rests primarily on its continuous adaptability across media, as well as on audience interest in extending its characters and storyworld(s) across generations.

Adaptation's place in canon formation and literary history is further underscored by examples that occupy less privileged, though no less important, places in literary history. "Great works" by "great authors" are certainly among the most regularly represented texts/stories in adaptation studies, but they don't make up the majority of works that find themselves adapted in any given historical moment. Many stories adapted across forms and media have become culture-texts even if they haven't been canonized in the traditional sense, including stories that were incredibly popular in the nineteenth century but hold a different place in today's cultural imagination—for example, the popular history of Three-Fingered Jack. During the first half of the nineteenth century, the eighteenth-century Jamaican rebel bandit was a popular icon, with at least five textual and stage versions circulating in England between 1799 and 1830 (he even had his own toy theater set). Although he faded from cultural memory after the mid-nineteenth century, Three-Fingered Jack has more recently been recovered by Romanticists, particularly those working on cultural representations in the context of British imperialism. This recovery would not have been possible without the historical record of numerous adaptations and appropriations of Three-Fingered Jack in nineteenth-century literary and popular culture. Cases like this one suggest a symbiotic relationship between popular adaptation and literary canonization, making adaptation central (not tangential or marginal) to content discussed in classrooms and published in academic circles. Today, Three-Fingered Jack is better known among Romanticists than he was half a century ago, and he could become better known still through successive adaptations.

Instead of confirming academic institutions as the primary arbiters of aesthetic taste and cultural value, the cultural history of commercial adaptations

---

23. Szwydky, "Victor Hugo's *Notre-Dame* on the Nineteenth-Century London Stage" (2010).

suggests that popular appropriations play an equally important (and perhaps even stronger) role in determining which texts survive, both in mass culture and in curricula. Sarah Cardwell notes the prominent overlap between the entertainment industries and educational institutions:

> The authors who are most favored by the makers of [television] adaptations—Austen, the Brontes, Dickens, Eliot, Hardy, and so on—tend also to dominate the academic construction and study of English literature . . . and likewise predominate in the catalogue lists of publishers of classic novels. . . . The reasons for this convergence are multiple and complex. Books that are adapted for television will sell more copies; books on school syllabuses and those that are most widely read are more likely to be adapted; and so on. There is a circular affirmation of a certain range of books commonly perceived as classics. Consistency across various areas of the public sphere means that certain texts (or . . . certain authors) are held by the reading and viewing public, programme-makers and educationalists to be classics; in this way the identity of some novels as 'classic novels' is accepted and perpetuated in common parlance.[24]

Cardwell sketches an ongoing cycle connecting the production of adaptations, the printing of novels, and the teaching of particular texts. Artistic creativity and academic inquiry work alongside commercial entertainment and popular culture; they are not mutually exclusive. Together, they determine which narratives get transformed into culture-texts and, as a result, which narratives appear in the critical conversation.

Adaptation also provides opportunities to speak back to the canon, offering open and continuous critique of its existence as well as direct challenges to its interpretations. According to Yvonne Griggs:

> Re-visionist adaptations become part of the ongoing debate surrounding the canonical texts that engender their creation but they can also attain their own place within that canon: they are neither consumed by nor solely defined by it but rather present us with other manifestations of the cultural anxieties that circulate around the initiating canonical text *and* its various adaptations. The canonization of texts is, like adaptation itself, an ongoing process that reacts to and interacts with the cultural and critical preoccupations of its time of production.[25]

---

24. Cardwell, *Adaptation Revisited* (2002), 2–3.
25. Griggs, *The Bloomsbury Introduction to Adaptation Studies* (2016), 8.

Griggs's view of adaptation and canonization as parallel, ongoing processes complements Cardwell's understanding of the cyclical relationship between adaptation and the literary canon, showing how adaptation provides ways to rethink existing canons and establish new ones. In other words, the best way to diversify both the canon and how we think of canonicity is to continuously adapt it.

As I've argued throughout this book, a text's or author's ability to maintain a place in cultural consciousness depends on new, successful adaptations, suggesting a need for longer reception histories of canonical works that fully embrace adaptation as a critical component of both their creation and their survival. Just as a historical approach reveals the ways adaptation builds and scaffolds the critical canons of literary, theater, and film histories, the more recent trajectories of transmedia storytelling help us forecast the influence adaptation and extension will continue to exert on twenty-first-century television, video games, and new media. Only with this understanding can we fully comprehend how adaptation has worked throughout history and, more importantly, how it will continue to shape transmedia storytelling and canon formation in the future.

BIBLIOGRAPHY

100 Great Paintings in The Victoria & Albert Museum. V&A, 1985.

Adams, Amanda. "Performing Ownership: Dickens, Twain, and Copyright on the Transatlantic Stage." *American Literary Realism* 43, no. 3 (Spring 2011): 223–41.

"Adelphi Theatre," *Times,* November 19, 1834: 3. The Times Digital Archive, 1785–2013. Gale Cengage. https://www.gale.com/c/the-times-digital-archive.

"Adelphi Theatre," *Times,* April 11, 1871: 9. The Times Digital Archive, 1785–2013. Gale Cengage. https://www.gale.com/c/the-times-digital-archive.

Adorno, Theodor W. "Culture Industry Reconsidered." *New German Critique* 6 (1975): 12–19.

———. *The Culture Industry: Selected Essays on Mass Culture,* edited by J. M. Bernstein. Routledge, 1991.

Adorno, Theodor, and Max Horkheimer. *Dialectic of Enlightenment.* Verso, 1995. Originally published 1944.

"Advertisement." *Bristol Mirror,* September 10, 1825. British Newspaper Archive. https://www.britishnewspaperarchive.co.uk/viewer/bl/0001044/18250924/010/0001.

Alexander, Isabella. *Copyright Law and the Public Interest in the Nineteenth Century.* Hart Publishing, 2010.

Alff, David. "Swift's World of *Gulliver's Travels.*" *The Routledge Companion to Imaginary Worlds,* edited by Mark J. Wolf, 332–38. Routledge, 2018.

Alighieri, Dante. *The Divine Comedy,* edited by John Ciardi. New American Library, 2003.

Allingham, Philip V. "'Reading Pictures, Visualizing the Text': Illustrations in Dickens from *Pickwick* to the *Household Edition,* 1836 to 1870, Phiz to Fred Barnhard." In *Reading Victorian Illustration, 1855–1875: Spoils of the Lumber Room,* edited by Paul Goldman and Simon Cooke, 159–78. Ashgate, 2012.

Andres, Malcolm. *Charles Dickens and His Performing Selves: Dickens and the Public Readings.* Oxford University Press, 2006.

Andrew, Dudley. "Adaptation." In *Concepts in Film Theory*, 96–106. Oxford University Press, 1984.

Appleton, William, ed. *Recollections of O. Smith: Comedian, During a Period of Fifty Years in the Profession. Performing Arts Resource* 5. Theatre Library Association, 1979.

Aragay, Mireia, and Gemma Lopez. "Inf(l)ecting *Pride and Prejudice*: Dialogism, Intertextuality, and Adaptation." In *Books in Motion: Adaptation, Intertextuality, Authorship*, edited by Mireia Aragay, 201–19. Rodopi, 2005.

Ashton, Geoffrey. *Shakespeare's Heroines in the Nineteenth Century.* Buxton Museum and Art Gallery, 1980.

Asleson, Robyn, ed. *A Passion for Performance: Sarah Siddons and Her Portraitists.* The Paul Getty Museum, 1999.

Atkinson, Benedict A. C., and Brian Fitzgerald. *A Short History of Copyright: The Genie of Information.* Springer, 2014.

Auerbach, Nina. *Ellen Terry: Player in Her Time.* University of Pennsylvania Press, 1997.

Austen, Jane. *Jane Austen: Complete Novels.* Anthem, 2013.

Baetens, Jan. *Novelization: From Film to Novel.* Ohio State University Press, 2018.

Baker, Michael. *The Rise of the Victorian Actor.* Rowman and Littlefield, 1978.

Baldwin, Peter. *Toy Theatres of the World.* Zwemmer, 1992.

Barnett, Jane. "How To Do Things with Birds: The Janus Effect in Theatrical Adaptation." *Journal of Adaptation in Film & Performance* 9, no. 2 (July 2016): 131–34.

Behn, Aphra. *Oroonoko*, edited by J. Lipking. Norton, 1997.

Behrendt, Stephen C. *The Moment of Explosion: Blake and the Illustration of Milton.* University of Nebraska Press, 1983.

———, ed. *Presumption; or, The Fate of Frankenstein* by Richard Brinsley Peake. Romantic Circles Praxis Editions. Romantic Circles. https://romantic-circles.org/editions/peake/index.html.

Bennett, Betty T., ed. "Letter to Leigh Hunt, 1823." In *The Letters of Mary Wollstonecraft Shelley.* 3 vols. Johns Hopkins University Press, 1988.

Béraud, Antony, and Jean-Toussaint Merle. *Le Monstre et le Magicien, Mélodrame Féerie en Trois Actes, A Grand Spectacle.* Musique de M. Alexandre, Ballet de M. Coraly, Décors de Mrs Lefebvre et Tomskin. Paris: Chez Bezo Libraire, 1826.

Berenson, Edward, and Eva Giloi, eds. *Constructing Charisma: Celebrity, Fame, and Power in Nineteenth-Century Europe.* Berghahn Books, 2010.

Bermingham, Ann, and John Brewer, eds. *The Consumption of Culture, 1600–1800: Image, Object, Text.* Routledge, 1995.

Biddick, Kathleen. *The Shock of Medievalism.* Duke University Press, 1998.

Bindman, David. *Blake as an Artist.* Phaidon and Dutton, 1977.

Bisla, Sundeep. *Wilkie Collins and Copyright.* Ohio State University Press, 2013.

Blaim, Artur. *Robinson Crusoe and His Doubles: The English Robinsonade of the Eighteenth Century.* Peter Lang, 2016.

Blake, William. *The Complete Graphic Works of William Blake,* edited by David Bindman and Deirdre Toomey. Putnam, 1978.

———. *The Complete Poetry and Prose of William Blake*, edited by David V. Erdman and Harold Bloom. University of California Press, 2008.

Blakey, Dorothy. *The Minerva Press: 1790–1820*. Bibliographic Society at the University Press, Oxford, 1939.

Bland, David. *A History of Book Illustration: The Illuminated Manuscript and the Printed Book*. Faber and Faber, 1958.

Boase, T. S. R. "Macklin and Bowyer." *Journal of the Warburg and Courtauld Institutes* 26, no. 1–2 (1963): 148–77.

Bolton, H. Philip. *Dickens Dramatized*. G. K. Hall, 1987.

———. *Scott Dramatized*. Mansell, 1992.

———. *Women Writers Dramatized: A Calendar of Performances from Narrative Works Published in English to 1900*. Mansell, 2000.

Boni, Marta, ed. *World Building: Transmedia, Fans, Industries*. Amsterdam University Press/University of Chicago Press, 2017.

Booth, Michael R., *English Melodrama*. Herbert Jenkins, 1965.

———, ed. *English Plays of the Nineteenth Century*. 6 vols. Clarendon, 1969–76.

———. *Victorian Spectacular Theatre 1850–1910*. Routledge, 1981.

Bortolotti, Gary, and Linda Hutcheon, "On the Origins of Adaptation: Rethinking 'Success'—Biologically." *New Literary History* (2007): 443–58.

Braddon, Mary Elizabeth. *Garibaldi and Other Poems*. Bosworth and Harrison, 1861.

———. *Lady Audley's Secret*. Penguin, 2010.

Bratton, Jackie. "William Thomas Moncrieff." *Nineteenth-Century Theatre and Film* 42, no.1 (May 2015): 9–21.

Brewer, David. *The Afterlife of Character 1726–1825*. University of Pennsylvania Press, 2005.

Brontë, Charlotte. *Jane Eyre*, edited by M. Mason. Penguin Group, 1996. Originally published 1847.

Brooks, Peter. *The Melodramatic Imagination: Balzac, Henry James, Melodrama, and the Mode of Excess*. Yale University Press, 1976. Reprint 1995.

Brough, Richard, and Barnabus Brough. *Frankenstein; or, The Model Man*. 1849. Reprinted in Steven Forry, *Hideous Progenies: Dramatizations of* Frankenstein *from Mary Shelley to the Present*, 227–50. University of Pennsylvania Press, 1990.

Bruccoli, Matthew J., ed. *The Profession of Authorship in America, 1800–1870*. Ohio State University Press, 1968.

Bruhn, Jorgen. "Dialogizing Adaptation Studies: From One-Way Transport to a Dialogic Two-Way Process." In *Adaptation Studies: New Challenges, New Directions*, edited by Jorgen Bruhn, Anne Gjelsvik, and Eirik Frisvold Hanssen, 69–88. Bloomsbury, 2013.

Bruntjen, Sven H. A. *John Boydell, 1719–1804: A Study of Art Patronage and Publishing in Georgian London*. Garland, 1985.

Bryden, Inga. "Arthur in Victorian Poetry." In *A Companion to Arthurian Literature*, edited by Helen Fulton, 368–80. Blackwell, 2009.

Brylowe, Thora. *Romantic Art in Practice: Cultural Work and The Sister Arts, 1760–1820*. Cambridge University Press, 2019.

Buchanan-Brown, John. *The Book Illustrations of George Cruikshank*. Charles E. Tuttle Company, 1980.

Buckley, Matthew. "Sensations of Celebrity: 'Jack Sheppard' and the Mass Audience." *Victorian Studies* 44, no. 3 (Spring 2002): 423–63.

———. *Tragedy Walks the Streets: The French Revolution and the Making of Modern Drama.* Johns Hopkins University Press, 2006.

Bueler, Lois E. *Clarissa: The Eighteenth-Century Response, 1747–1804.* 2 vols. AMS Press, 2010.

Burgess, Miranda. *British Fiction and the Production of Social Order, 1740–1830.* Cambridge University Press, 2000.

Burwick, Frederick. *British Drama of the Industrial Revolution.* Cambridge University Press, 2015.

———. "Introduction." In *The Boydell Shakespeare Gallery,* edited by Walter Pape and Frederick Burwick, 1–15. Peter Pomp, 1996a.

———. *Romantic Drama: Acting and Reacting.* Cambridge University Press, 2009.

———. "The Romantic Reception of the Boydell Shakespeare Gallery." In *The Boydell Shakespeare Gallery,* edited by Walter Pape and Frederick Burwick, 143–57. Peter Pomp, 1996b.

———. "Staging the Byronic Hero." *European Romantic Review* 29, no. 1 (2018): 3–11.

Burwick, Frederick, and Paul Douglass, eds. *Dante and Italy in British Romanticism.* Palgrave Macmillan, 2011.

Burwick, Frederick, and Manushag N. Powell, *British Pirates in Print and Performance.* Palgrave Macmillan, 2015.

Byron, George Gordon. *Byron: Complete Poetical Works,* edited by Jerome McGann et al. Oxford University Press, 1970.

Calè, Luisa. *Fuseli's Milton Gallery: 'Turning Readers into Spectators.'* Clarendon, 2006.

Cardwell, Richard A., ed. *The Reception of Byron in Europe.* 2 vols. Continuum, 2004.

Cardwell, Sarah. *Adaptation Revisited: Television and the Classic Novel.* Manchester University Press, 2002.

———. "A *Dickensian* Feast: Visual Culture and Television Aesthetics." In *Adaptation in Visual Culture: Images, Texts, and Their Multiple Worlds,* edited by R. Barton Palmer and Julie Grossman, 119–37. Palgrave MacMillan, 2017.

Carroll, Rachel, ed. *Adaptation in Contemporary Culture: Textual Infidelities.* Continuum, 2009.

Cartmell, Debra, and Imelda Whelehan, eds. *Adaptations: From Text to Screen, Screen to Text.* Routledge, 2013.

Castillo, Larisa T. "Natural Authority in Charles Dickens's *Martin Chuzzlewit* and the Copyright Act of 1842." *Nineteenth-Century Literature* 62, no. 4 (2008): 435–64.

Cervantes, Miguel de. *Don Quixote,* translated by John Ormsby, edited by Joseph Ramon Jones and Kenneth Douglas. W. W. Norton, 1981.

Cheney, Liana De Girlami, ed. *Pre-Raphaelitism and Medievalism in the Arts.* Edwin Mellen Press, 1992.

"A Child's View: 19th-Century Paper Theatres." Bruce Museum, from the Private Collection of Eric. G. Bernard, 2010. https://brucemuseum.org/site/exhibitions_detail/a_childs_view_19th-century_paper_theaters.

Christ, Carol T., and John O. Jordan, eds. *Victorian Literature and the Victorian Visual Imagination.* University of California Press, 1995.

Christensen, Jerome. *Byron's Strength: Romantic Writing and Commercial Society.* Johns Hopkins University Press, 1993.

Christie's. "Sale 1981 Record, Lot 55" (2008). Accessed June 1, 2019. https://www.christies.com/lot-finder/Lot/oliver-twist-pollock-benjamin-publisher-pollocks-5048581-details.aspx.

Clarke, M. J. *Transmedia Television: New Trends in Network Serial Production*. Bloomsbury, 2013.

Clayton, Jay. *Charles Dickens in Cyberspace: The Afterlife of the Nineteenth Century in Postmodern Culture*. Oxford University Press, 2003.

Clifton, Larry Stephen. *The Terrible Fitzball: Melodramatist of the Macabre*. Bowling Green State University Popular Press, 1993.

Clinton, Catherine. *Fanny Kemble's Civil Wars*. Simon & Schuster, 2000.

Clubbe, John. *Byron, Sully, and the Power of Portraiture*. Ashgate, 2005.

Cohen, Jane R. *Charles Dickens and His Original Illustrators*. Ohio State University Press, 1980.

Cohen, Morton N., and Edward Wakeling. *Lewis Carroll and His Illustrators: Collaborations, Correspondence, 1865–1898*. Cornell University Press, 2003.

Cohen, Ralph. *The Art of Discrimination: Thomson's* The Seasons *and the Language of Criticism*. University of California Press, 1964.

Collins, Wilkie. *The Works of Wilkie Collins*. 30 vols. Collier/Scholarly Press, 1972.

Colman, George (the younger). *The Iron Chest: A Play in Three Acts*. W. Woodfall, 1796.

Cook, Daniel, and Nicholas Seager, eds. *The Afterlives of Eighteenth-Century Fiction*. Cambridge University Press, 2015.

Cooper, James Fenimore. *The Novels of James Fenimore Cooper*. 25 vols. The Co-operative Publication Society, 1900.

Corbeau-Parsons, Caroline. *Prometheus in the Nineteenth Century: From Myth to Symbol*. Routledge, 2013.

Corrigan, Timothy. "Emerging from Converging Cultures: Circulation, Adaptation, and Value." In *The Politics of Adaptation: Media Convergence and Ideology*, edited by Dan Hassler-Forest and Pascal Nicklas, 53–65. Palgrave Macmillan, 2015.

———. "Literature on Screen, a History: In the Gap." In *The Cambridge Companion to Literature on Screen*, edited by Deborah Cartmell and Imelda Whelehan, 29–43. Cambridge University Press, 2007.

"Covent-Garden Theatre," *Times*, February 3, 1836: 5. The Times Digital Archive, 1785–2013. Gale Cengage. https://www.gale.com/c/the-times-digital-archive.

Cowen, Frederic H. *The Corsair. Dramatic cantata, adapted from Lord Byron's poem adapted by R. E. Francillon. The Music Composed expressly for the Birmingham Triennial Festival*. Boosey & Co, 1876.

Cox, Jeffrey N. "Romantic Tragic Drama and its Eighteenth-Century Precursors." In *A Companion to Tragedy*, edited by Rebecca Bushnell, 411–34. Blackwell, 2005.

———. "Theatrical Forms, Ideological Conflicts, and the Staging of *Obi*." In *Obi: A Romantic Circles Praxis Volume*, edited by Charles Rzepka. Romantic Circles, 2002. https://romantic-circles.org/praxis/obi/cox/cox.html.

Cox, Philip. *Reading Adaptations: Novels and Verse Narratives on Stage, 1790–1840*. Manchester University Press, 2000.

Crone, Rosalind. *Violent Victorians: Popular Entertainment in Nineteenth-Century London*. Manchester University Press, 2012.

Cross, Nigel. *The Common Writer: Life in Nineteenth-Century Grub Street.* Cambridge University Press, 1985.

Cruz, Gabriela. "The Flying Dutchman, English Spectacle and the Remediation of Grand Opera," *Cambridge Opera Journal* 29, no. 1: (March 2017): 5–32.

Culler, A. Dwight. *The Victorian Mirror of History.* Yale University Press, 1985.

Curtis, Gerard. *Visual Words: Art and the Material Book in Victorian England.* Ashgate, 2002.

Cutchins, Dennis. "Bakhtin, Intertextuality, and Adaptation." In *The Oxford Handbook of Adaptation Studies,* edited by Thomas Leitch, 71–86. Oxford University Press, 2017.

Cutchins, Dennis R., and Dennis R. Perry, eds. *Adapting Frankenstein: The Monster's Eternal Lives in Popular Culture.* Manchester University Press, 2018.

Cutchins, Dennis, Laurence Raw, and James M. Welsh, eds. *Redefining Adaptation Studies.* Scarecrow Press, 2010.

Danahay, Martin A., and Alexander Chisholm, eds. *Jekyll and Hyde Dramatized: The 1887 Richard Mansfield Script and the Evolution of the Story on Stage.* McFarland, 2004.

D'Arcy, Geraint. "The Corsican Trap: Its Mechanism and Reception," *Theatre Notebook* 65, no. 1 (February 2011): 12–22.

David, Deirdre. *Fanny Kemble: A Performed Life.* University of Pennsylvania Press, 2007.

Davidson, George. *The Drawings of Gustave Dorè: Illustrations to the Great Classics.* Arcturus, 2014.

Davis, Paul. *The Lives and Times of Ebenezer Scrooge.* Yale University Press, 1990.

Davis, Tracy C. *The Economics of the British Stage 1800–1914.* Cambridge University Press, 2000.

Davis, Tracy C., and Peter Holland, eds. *The Performing Century: Nineteenth-Century Theatre's History.* Palgrave Macmillan, 2007.

Deazley, Ronan, Martin Kretschmer, and Lionel Bently, eds. *Privilege and Property: Essays on the History of Copyright.* OpenBook, 2010.

Defoe, Daniel. *Robinson Crusoe,* edited by Michael Shinagel. W. W. Norton, 1994.

Denisoff, Dennis. "Introduction. Small Change: The Consumerist Designs of the Nineteenth-Century Child." In *The Nineteenth-Century Child and Consumer Culture,* edited by Dennis Denisoff, 1–25. Ashgate, 2008.

Dentith, Simon. *Parody.* Routledge, 2000.

Dibdin, Thomas. *The Reminiscences of Thomas Dibdin.* 2 vols. Henry Colburn, 1837.

Dickens, Charles. *Nicholas Nickleby.* Penguin, 2003. Originally published 1837.

———. *The Works of Charles Dickens.* 20 vols. Humphrey Milford/Oxford University Press, 1930.

Dickens, Mamie, and Georgina Hogarth, eds. *The Letters of Charles Dickens: Edited by his sister-in-law and his eldest daughter.* Vol. 1 (1833–56). Chapman and Hall, 1880.

Disher, Maurice Willson. *Blood and Thunder: Mid-Victorian Melodrama and Its Origins.* Frederick Muller, 1949.

Dobson, Michael. *The Making of a National Poet: Shakespeare, Adaptation, and Authorship, 1660–1769.* Clarendon Press, 1992.

Douglas-Fairhurst, Robert. *Becoming Dickens: The Invention of a Novelist.* Harvard University Press, 2011.

Dowden, Stephen D., and Thomas P. Quinn, eds. *Tragedy and the Tragic in German Literature, Art, and Thought.* Camden House, 2014.

Drotner, Kirsten. *English Children and Their Magazines, 1751–1945*. Yale University Press, 1988.

Duff, David D. *Romanticism and the Uses of Genre*. Oxford University Press, 2009.

Dunbar, Pamela. *William Blake's Illustrations to the Poetry of Milton*. Clarendon, 1980.

Dyson, Anthony. *Pictures to Print: The Nineteenth-Century Engraving Trade*. Farrand, 1984.

Easley, Alexis. *Literary Celebrity, Gender, and Victorian Authorship, 1850–1914*. University of Delaware Press, 2011.

Eco, Umberto. *Travels in Hyper Reality: Essays*. Translated by William Weaver. Harvest/Harcourt, 1986. Originally published 1967.

Elliott, Kamilla. "Adaptation Theory and Adaptation Scholarship." In *The Oxford Handbook of Adaptation Studies*, edited by Thomas Leitch, 679–97. Oxford University Press, 2017.

———. *Portraiture and British Gothic Fiction: The Rise of Picture Identification, 1764–1835*. Johns Hopkins University Press, 2013.

———. *Rethinking the Novel/Film Debate*. Cambridge University Press, 2003.

———. "Theorizing Adaptations/Adapting Theories." In *Adaptation Studies: New Challenges, New Directions*, edited by J. Bruhn, A. Gjelsvik, and E. Frisvold Hanssen, 19–45. Bloomsbury, 2013.

———. "What Can Victorian Studies Learn from Adaptation Studies?" *Streaky Bacon: A Guide to Victorian Adaptations*. January 27, 2017. http://www.streakybacon.net/forums/kamilla-elliott-what-can-victorian-studies-learn-from-adaptation-studies/.

Emboden, William. *Sarah Bernhardt*. Macmillan, 1975.

Emeljanow, Victor. *Victorian Popular Dramatists*. Twayne, 1987.

Engel, Laura. *Fashioning Celebrity: Eighteenth-Century British Actresses and Strategies for Image Making*. Ohio State University Press, 2011.

"English and American Plays of the Nineteenth Century," edited by George Freedley and Allardyce Nicoll. Readex Microprint, 1965.

Essick, Robert N. *The Separate Plates of William Blake*. Princeton University Press, 1983.

———. *William Blake's Commercial Book Illustrations*. Clarendon, 1991.

"Everitt and George Family Collection of Toy Theatres." The National Museum of Australia http://collectionsearch.nma.gov.au/.

Farr, Liz. "Paper Dreams and Romantic Projections: The Nineteenth-Century Toy Theater, Boyhood, and Aesthetic Play." In *The Nineteenth-Century Child and Consumer Culture*, edited by Dennis Denisoff, 43–61. Ashgate, 2008.

Fernandez, Jay A. "Oscars 2014: How Adaptations Continue to Shape the Conversation." *Signature*, February 24, 2014. http://www.signature-reads.com/2014/02/oscars-2014-how-adaptations-continue-to-shape-the-conversation/.

Fielding, Henry. *Complete Works*, edited by William Earnest Henley. 16 vols. Barnes and Noble, 1967.

Fisch, Audrey A. *Frankenstein: Icon of Modern Culture*. Helm Information, 2009.

Fitzball, Edward. *Thirty-Five Years of a Dramatic Author's Life*. 2 vols. Newby, 1859.

Fitzsimons, Raymund. *The Charles Dickens Show: An Account of His Public Readings, 1858–70*. Geoffrey Bles, 1970.

Flanagan, Martin. *The Marvel Studios Phenomenon: Inside a Transmedia Universe*. Bloomsbury, 2016.

Fleming, Patrick C. *The Legacy of the Moral Tale: Children's Literature and the English Novel, 1744–1859*. University of Tennessee Press, 2016.

Forry, Steven. *Hideous Progenies: Dramatizations of* Frankenstein *from Mary Shelley to the Present*. University of Pennsylvania Press, 1990.

Fosca, François. *French Painting: Nineteenth Century Painters, 1800–1870*. Translated by Peter Simmons. Universe Books, Inc. and Pierre Tisné Éditeur, 1960.

Foulkes, Richard. *Lewis Carroll and the Victorian Stage: Theatricals in a Quiet Life*. Ashgate, 2005.

Frank, Frederic S. *The First Gothics: A Critical Guide to the English Gothic Novel*. Garland, 1987.

Franssen, Gaston, and Rick Honings, eds. *Idolizing Authorship: Literary Celebrity and the Construction of Identity, 1800 to the Present*. University of Chicago Press, 2017.

Freeman, Matthew. *Historicising Transmedia Storytelling: Early Twentieth-Century Transmedia Storyworlds*. Routledge, 2017.

Frick, John W. *Uncle Tom's Cabin on the American Stage and Screen*. Palgrave Macmillan, 2015.

Fries, Maureen. "What Tennyson Really Did to Malory's Women." *Quondam et Futurus* 1, no. 1 (Spring 1991): 44–55.

Fulford, Robert. "What We Talk About When We Talk About *Birdman*," *National Post* (Arts Section), February 23, 2015. http://news.nationalpost.com/arts/what-we-talk-about-when-we-talk-about-birdman.

Fuller, Matthew. *Media Ecologies*. MIT Press, 2005.

Fulton, Helen, ed. *A Companion to Arthurian Literature*. Blackwell, 2009.

Gage, John. "Boydell's Shakespeare and the Redemption of British Engraving." In *The Boydell Shakespeare Gallery*, edited by Walter Pape and Frederick Burwick, 27–32. Peter Pomp, 1996.

Gallant, Christine. "Blake's Coded Designs of Slave Revolts." *Wordsworth Circle* 42, no. 3 (Summer 2011): 211–17.

Gamer, Michael. *Romanticism and the Gothic: Genre, Reception, and Canon Formation*. Cambridge University Press, 2000.

Garrett, Peter K. *Gothic Reflections: Narrative Force in Nineteenth-Century Fiction*. Cornell University Press, 2003.

Geduld, Harry M., ed. *The Definitive Dr. Jekyll and Mr. Hyde Companion*. Garland, 1983.

Genette, Gérard. *Palimpsests: Literature in the Second Degree*. University of Nebraska Press, 1997.

Gernsheim, Helmut. *Julia Margaret Cameron: Her Life and Photographic Work*. Aperture, 1975.

Gilbert, Sandra, and Susan Gubar, eds. *The Madwoman in the Attic: The Woman Writer and the Nineteenth-Century Literary Imagination*. Yale University Press, 2000. Originally published 1979.

Girveau, Bruno. *Once Upon a Time, Walt Disney: The Sources of Inspiration for the Disney Studios*. Prestel, 2006.

Glavin, John. *After Dickens: Reading, Adaptation, and Performance*. Cambridge University Press, 1999.

———, ed. *Dickens Adapted*. Routledge, 2012.

———, ed. *Dickens on Screen*. Cambridge University Press, 2003.

Godwin, William. *Collected Novels and Memoirs of William Godwin*, edited by Mark Philp et al. 8 vols. Pickering, 1992.

———. Unpublished letter to Mary Shelley (1823). Huntington Library HM11634.

Goethe, Johann Wolfgang von. *Conversations of Goethe with Eckermann and Soret*. 2 vols. Translated by John Oxenford. Smith, Elder & Co., 1850. https://archive.org/details/conversationsofgo1goetuoft.

———. *Faust*. Translated by Albert Stapfer. Illustrations by Eugène Delacroix. Motte, 1828. http://gallica.bnf.fr/ark:/12148/bpt6k134831w/f99.planchecontact.

Gold, Arthur, and Robert Fizdale. *The Divine Sarah: A Life of Sarah Bernhardt*. Vintage Books, 1992.

Golden, Catherine J., ed. *Book Illustrated: Text, Image, and Culture 1770–1930*. Oak Knoll Press, 2000.

Goldman, Paul. *John Everett Millais: Illustrator and Narrator*. Lund Humphries in Association with Birmingham Museums and Art Gallery, 2004.

———. *Victorian Illustration: The Pre-Raphaelites, the Idyllic School and the High Victorians*. Lund Humphries, 2004.

Goldstein, Robert Justin. *The Frightful Stage: Political Censorship of the Theater in Nineteenth-Century Europe*. Berghan Books, 2009.

———. "Political Theater Censorship in Nineteenth-Century France in Comparative European Perspective." *European History Quarterly* 40, no. 2 (2010): 240–65.

Goodman, Walter. *The Keeleys On Stage and At Home*. Bentley and Son, 1895.

Greenwald, Helen M. *The Oxford Handbook of Opera*. Oxford University Press, 2014.

Gribble, Jennifer. *The Lady of Shalott in the Victorian Novel*. London: Macmillan, 1983.

Griggs, Yvonne. *The Bloomsbury Introduction to Adaptation Studies: Adapting the Canon in Film, TV, Novels, and Popular Culture*. Bloomsbury, 2016.

Groom, Gloria. "Art, Illustration, and Enterprise in Late Eighteenth-Century English Art: A Painting by Philippe Jacques de Loutherbourg." *Art Institute of Chicago Museum Studies* 18, no. 2 (1992): 124–35 and 184–87.

Grossman, Julie. *Literature, Film, and Their Hideous Progeny: Adaptation and ElasTEXTity*. Palgrave Macmillan, 2015.

Guillory, John. "Genesis of the Media Concept." *Critical Inquiry* 36, no. 2 (2010): 321–62.

Hadley, Elaine. *Melodramatic Tactics: Theatricalized Dissent in the English Marketplace, 1800–1885*. Stanford University Press, 1995.

Haining, Peter, ed. *The Shilling Shockers: Stories of Terror from the Gothic Bluebooks*. St. Martin's, 1978.

Hambridge, Katherine, and Jonathan Hicks, eds. *The Melodramatic Moment: Music and Theatrical Culture, 1790–1820*. University of Chicago Press, 2018.

Hamilton, James. *A Strange Business: A Revolution in Art, Culture, and Commerce in 19th Century London*. Pegasus Books, 2015.

Hand, Richard J. "Populism and Ideology: Nineteenth-Century Fiction and Cinema." In *Interventions: Rethinking the Nineteenth Century*, edited by Andrew Smith and Anna Barton, 188–206. Manchester University Press, 2017.

Harvey, J. R. *Victorian Novelists and Their Illustrators*. New York University Press, 1971.

Hassler-Forest, Dan, and Pascal Nicklas, eds. *The Politics of Adaptation: Media Convergence and Ideology*. Palgrave Macmillan, 2015.

Hausken, Liv. "Textual Theory and Blind Spots in Media Studies." In *Narrative Across Media: The Languages of Storytelling*, edited by Marie-Laure Ryan, 391–403. University of Nebraska Press, 2004.

Hawkins, Ann, and Georgianna Ziegler. "Marketing Shakespeare: The Boydell Gallery, 1789–1805, & Beyond." The Folger Library Digital Collections. 2018. https://folgerpedia.folger.edu/Marketing_Shakespeare:_the_Boydell_Gallery,_1789%E2%80%931805,_%26_Beyond.

Hawkins, Ann R., and Maura Ives, eds. *Women Writers and the Artifacts of Celebrity in the Long Nineteenth Century*. Ashgate, 2012.

Heinrich, Anselm, Kate Newey, and Jeffrey Richards, eds. *Ruskin, the Theatre, and Victorian Visual Culture*. Palgrave Macmillan, 2009.

"Her Majesty's Theatre," *Times*, March 11, 1844: 5. The Times Digital Archive, 1785–2013. Gale Cengage. https://www.gale.com/c/the-times-digital-archive.

Hemmings, F. W. J. *Theatre and State in France, 1760–1905*. Cambridge University Press, 1994.

———. *The Theatre Industry in Nineteenth-Century France*. Cambridge University Press, 1993.

Hill, Jonathan E. "Cruikshank, Ainsworth, and Tableau Illustration." *Victorian Studies* 23, no. 4 (Summer 1980): 429–59.

Hitchcock, Susan. *Frankenstein: A Cultural History*. Norton, 2007.

Hoagwood, Terence, Kathryn Ledbetter, and Martin M. Jacobsen, eds. *L. E. L.'s "Verses" and* The Keepsake *for 1829*. Romantic Circles (1998). Romantic Circles. https://romantic-circles.org/editions/lel/index.html.

Hoeren, Thomas. "Charles Dickens and the International Copyright Law." *Journal of the Copyright Society of the USA* 63, no. 2 (Spring 2016): 341–52.

Hoesterey, Ingeborg. *Pastiche: Cultural Memory in Art, Film, Literature*. Indiana University Press, 2001.

Hoeveler, Diane Long. "*Frankenstein*, Feminism, and Literary Theory." In *The Cambridge Companion to Mary Shelley*, edited by E. Schor, 45–62. Cambridge University Press, 2004.

———. *Gothic Feminism: The Professionalization of Gender from Charlotte Smith through the Brontës*. Pennsylvania State University Press, 1998.

———. *Gothic Riffs: Secularizing the Uncanny in the European Imaginary, 1780–1820*. Ohio State University Press, 2010.

———. "Illustrating Thomas Holcroft's *A Tale of Mystery* as Physiognomical Tableaux Vivant." In *Re-Viewing Thomas Holcroft, 1745–1809*, edited by Miriam L. Wallace and A. A. Markley, 103–20. Ashgate, 2012.

———. "The Temple of Morality: Thomas Holcroft and the Swerve of Melodrama." *European Romantic Review* 14 (2003): 49–63.

Hogg, James, ed. *King Arthur through the Ages*. 2 vols. Garland Reference Library of the Humanities, 1990.

Hollington, Michael, ed. *The Reception of Charles Dickens in Europe*. 2 vols. Bloomsbury, 2013.

Houfe, Simon. *The Dictionary of 19th Century British Book Illustrators and Caricaturists*. The Antique Collectors' Club, 1978 (revised 1996).

House, Madeline, and Graham Storey, eds. *The Letters of Charles Dickens*. Clarendon, 1965.

Hugo, Victor. *The Dramas of Victor Hugo: Mary Tudor, Marion De Lorme, Esmeralda*. Vol. 3. Collier & Son, 1901.

———. *Notre-Dame de Paris*, edited and translated by J. Sturrock. Penguin, 2004.

Hume, Robert D. *Henry Fielding and the London Theatre, 1728–1737.* Clarendon, 1988.

Hunt, John Dixon, David Lomas, and Michael Corris, eds. *Art, Word and Image: Two Thousand Years of Visual/Textual Interaction.* Reaktion Books, 2010.

Hutcheon, Linda. *A Theory of Adaptation.* New York and London: Routledge, 2006.

———. *A Theory of Parody: The Teachings of Twentieth-Century Art Forms.* Chicago: University of Illinois Press, 2000. Originally published by Methuen, 1985.

Hutcheon, Linda, and Michael Hutcheon, "Adaptation and Opera." *The Oxford Handbook of Adaptation Studies,* edited by Thomas Leitch, 305–23. Oxford University Press, 2017.

Huyssen, Andreas. *After the Great Divide: Modernism, Mass Culture, Postmodernism.* Indiana University Press, 1987.

Inchbald, Elizabeth. "To the Artist." *Artist* (June 13, 1807): 14.

Inglis, Fred. *A Short History of Celebrity.* Princeton University Press, 2010.

Jackson, Peter. *A Pollock's Toy Theatre: The Britannia, Pollocks Characters and Scenes in the Forty Thieves.* Pollock's Toy Theatres, Limited, 1976.

James, Elizabeth, and Helen R. Smith. *Penny Dreadfuls and Boys' Adventures: The Barry Ono Collection of Victorian Popular Literature in the British Library.* The British Library, 1998.

Jameson, Frederic. *Postmodernism; or, The Cultural Logic of Late Capitalism.* Duke University Press, 1991.

Jellenik, Glenn. "On the Origins of Adaptation, as Such: The Birth of a Simple Abstraction." In *The Oxford Handbook of Adaptation Studies,* edited by Thomas Leitch, 36–52. Oxford University Press, 2017.

Jenkins, Henry. "Adaptation, Extension, Transmedia." *LFQ: Literature/Film Quarterly* 45, no. 2 (Spring 2017). http://www.salisbury.edu/lfq/_issues/first/adaptation_extension_transmedia.html.

———. *Convergence Culture: Where Old and New Media Collide.* New York University Press, 2006.

———. *Fans, Bloggers, and Gamers: Exploring Participatory Culture.* New York University Press, 2006.

———. *Participatory Culture in a Networked Era: A Conversation on Youth, Learning, Commerce, and Politics.* Polity Press, 2015.

———. *Reading in a Participatory Culture: Remixing Moby-Dick for the English Literature Classroom.* Teachers College Press, 2013.

———. *Spreadable Media: Creating Meaning and Value in a Networked Culture.* New York University Press, 2006.

———. *Textual Poachers: Television Fans and Participatory Culture.* 2nd ed. Routledge, 2013. Originally published 1992.

Jenkins, Ian. *Archeologists and Aesthetes: The Sculpture Galleries of the British Museum in the Nineteenth Century.* British Museum, 1992.

Jenkins, Rebecca. *Fanny Kemble: A Reluctant Celebrity.* Simon and Schuster, 2005.

Jobert, Barthélémy. *Delacroix.* Princeton University Press, 1997.

John, Juliet. *Dickens and Mass Culture.* Oxford University Press, 2010.

Johnson, Dorothy. *David to Delacroix: The Rise of Romantic Mythology.* University of North Carolina Press, 2011.

Johnson, Edgar. *Sir Walter Scott: The Great Unknown.* 2 vols. Macmillan, 1970.

Johnson, Lee. "Delacroix and *The Bride of Abydos.*" *Burlington Magazine* 114, no. 834 (September 1972): 579–85.

Jones, David J. *Gothic Machine: Textualities, Pre-Cinematic Media and Film in Popular Visual Culture, 1670–1910.* University of Wales Press, 2011.

Kaenel, Phillipe, ed. *Doré: Master of Imagination.* Musée d'Orsay/Flammarion/National Gallery of Canada, 2014.

Kahan, Jeffrey. *The Cult of Kean.* Ashgate, 2006.

Keats, John. *Complete Poems and Selected Letters of John Keats,* edited by Edward Hirsch and Tim Pollock. Random House, 2009.

Kelly, Ann Cline. *Jonathan Swift and Popular Culture.* Palgrave Macmillan, 2002.

Kérchy, Anna. *Alice in Transmedia Wonderland: Curiouser and Curiouser New Forms of a Children's Classic.* MacFarland, 2016.

Kerr, John A. *The Monster and Magician: or, The Fate of Frankenstein: A Melo-dramatic Romance, in Three Acts.* J. & H. Kerr, 1826. Reprinted in Steven Forry, *Hideous Progenies: Dramatizations of* Frankenstein *from Mary Shelley to the Present,* 205–26. University of Pennsylvania Press, 1990.

Keymer, Thomas, and Peter Sabor, eds. *The Pamela Controversy: Criticisms and Adaptations of Samuel Richardson's* Pamela. 6 vols. Pickering & Chatto, 2001.

Kinservik, Matthew J. *Disciplining Satire: The Censorship of Satiric Comedy on the Eighteenth-Century London Stage.* Bucknell University Press, 2002.

Kirkpatrick, Robert J. *From the Penny Dreadful to the Ha'penny Dreadfuller: A Bibliographical History of the British Boys' Periodical, 1762–1950.* The British Library/Oak Knoll Press, 2013.

Kitton, Frederic. *Charles Dickens and His Illustrators.* George Redway, 1899. http://www.gutenberg.org/files/40410/40410-h/40410-h.htm.

Klancher, Jon. *The Making of English Reading Audiences, 1790–1832.* University of Wisconsin Press, 1987.

Klonsky, Milton. *Blake's Dante: The Complete Illustration to the Divine Comedy.* Harmony Books, 1980.

Knowles, Ric. *Reading the Material Theatre.* Cambridge University Press, 2004.

Koger, Alicia Kae. "Calendar for 1836–1837." In *The Adelphi Calendar Project,* edited by Alfred L. Nelson, Gilbert B. Cross, Joseph Donohue. 1988–2016. https://www.umass.edu/AdelphiTheatreCalendar/.

Kohlke, Marie-Luise. "Adaptive/Appropriative Reuse in Neo-Victorian Fiction: Having One's Cake and Eating It Too." In *Interventions: Rethinking the Nineteenth Century,* edited by Andrew Smith and Anna Barton, 169–87. Manchester University Press, 2017.

Komporaly, Jozefina. *Radical Revival as Adaptation: Theatre, Politics, Society.* Palgrave Macmillan, 2017.

Kooistra, Lorraine. *The Artist as Critic: Bitextuality in Fin-de-Siècle Illustrated Books.* Ashgate, 1995.

———. *Christina Rossetti and Illustration: A Publishing History.* Ohio University Press, 2002.

———. *Poetry, Pictures, and Popular Publishing: The Illustrated Gift Book and Victorian Visual Culture, 1855–1875.* Ohio University Press, 2011.

Kraus, Chris, Simon Goldhill, Helene Foley, and Jaś Elsner, eds. *Visualizing the Tragic: Drama, Myth, and Ritual in Greek Art and Literature.* Oxford University Press, 2007.

Kreissman, Bernard. *Pamela-Shamela: A Study of the Criticisms, Burlesques, Parodies, and Adaptations of Richardson's* Pamela. University of Nebraska Press, 1960.

Kucich, John, and Diane Sadoff, eds. *Victorian Afterlife: Postmodern Culture Rewrites the Nineteenth Century.* University of Minnesota Press, 2000.

Kunzle, David. *Gustave Doré: Twelve Comic Strips.* University Press of Mississippi, 2015.

Lacy, Norris J., ed. *Text and Intertext in Medieval Arthurian Literature.* Garland, 1996.

Lagorio, Valerie M., and Mildred Leade Day, eds. *King Arthur Through the Ages.* Vol 2. Garland Reference Library of the Humanities, 1990.

Laird, Karen. *The Art of Adapting Victorian Literature, 1848–1920: Dramatizing* Jane Eyre, David Copperfield, *and* The Woman in White. Routledge, 2015.

Lambdin, Laura Cooner, and Robert Thomas Lambdin. *Camelot in the Nineteenth Century: Arthurian Characters in the Poems of Tennyson, Arnold, Morris, and Swinburne.* Greenwood Press, 2000.

Landow, George P., ed. *Ladies of Shalott: A Victorian Masterpiece and Its Contexts.* Brown University Press, 1985.

Layard, George Somes. *Tennyson and His Pre-Raphaelite Illustrators.* Elliot Stock, 1894.

Leader, Zachary. *Revision and Romantic Authorship.* Oxford University Press, 1996.

Lee, Jonathan Rey, "The Plastic Art of LEGO: An Essay into Material Culture." In *Design, Mediation, and the Posthuman,* edited by Dennis M. Weiss, Amy D. Propen, and Colbey Emmerson Reid, 95–112. Lexington Books, 2014.

Léger-St-Jean, Marie. *Price One Penny: A Database of Cheap Literature, 1837–1860.* [12 July 2018]. Faculty of English, Cambridge [15 October 2018] 2010–2018. http://priceonepenny.info.

Leitch, Thomas. "Adaptation, the Genre." *Adaptation* 1, no. 2 (2008): 106–20.

———. "The Adapter as Auteur: Hitchcock, Kubrick, Disney." In *Books in Motion: Adaptation, Intertextuality, Authorship,* edited by Mireia Aragay, 107–24. Rodopi, 2005.

———. *Film Adaptation and Its Discontents: From* Gone with the Wind *to* The Passion of the Christ. Johns Hopkins University Press, 2007.

———, ed. *The Oxford Handbook of Adaptation Studies.* Oxford University Press, 2017.

———. "Vampire Adaptation." *Journal of Adaptation in Film & Performance* 4, no. 1 (2011): 5–16.

Lennox-Boyd, Christopher. "The Prints Themselves: Production, Marketing, and their Survival." In *The Boydell Shakespeare Gallery,* edited by Walter Pape and Frederick Burwick, 45–53. Peter Pomp, 1996.

Lewis, Matthew. *The Monk.* Oxford World Classics, 2016. Originally published 1796.

Lezra, Esther M. "Monsters in Motion: Tracing the Silences in John Gabriel Stedman and William Blake." *Arthurium: A Caribbean Studies Journal* 4, no. 1 (June 2006): n.p.

Litvack, Leon. "Dickens's Dream and the Conception of Character." *Dickensian* 103 (2007): 5–36.

Liesenfeld, Vincent J. *The Licensing Act of 1737.* University of Wisconsin Press, 1984.

Lockhart, John Gibson. *Memoirs of the Life of Sir Walter Scott.* Baudry's European Library, 1837.

Looser, Devoney. *The Making of Jane Austen.* Johns Hopkins University Press, 2017.

Lupack, Alan. *The Oxford Guide to Arthurian Literature and Legend.* Oxford University Press, 2005.

Lynch, Deidre Shauna. *The Economy of Character: Novels, Market Culture, and the Business of Inner Meaning.* University of Chicago Press, 1998.

Lynch, Jack. *Becoming Shakespeare: The Unlikely Afterlife that Turned a Provincial Playwright into the Bard.* Walker & Company, 2007.

MacCabe, Colin, Kathleen Murray, and Rick Warner, eds. *True to the Spirit: Film Adaptation and the Question of Fidelity.* Oxford University Press, 2011.

MacCarthy, Fiona. *Byron: Life and Legend.* Farrar, Straus and Giroux, 2002.

Mack, Robert L. *The Genius of Parody: Imitation and Originality in Seventeenth- and Eighteenth-Century English Literature.* Palgrave Macmillan, 2007.

Mainardi, Patricia. *Another World: Nineteenth-Century Illustrated Print Culture.* Yale University Press, 2017.

Malan, Dan, ed. *Charles Dickens'* A Christmas Carol *with 45 Lost Gustave Doré Engravings (1861) and 150 Other Victorian Illustrations.* MCE Publishing, 1996.

———. *Gustave Doré: Adrift on Dreams of Splendor.* Malan Classical Enterprises, 1995.

Malley, Shawn. *From Archaeology to Spectacle in Victorian Britain: The Case of Assyria, 1845–1854.* Ashgate, 2012.

Mancoff, Debra N. *The Arthurian Revival in Victorian Art.* Garland Publishing, 1990.

———. *The Return of King Arthur: The Legend Through Victorian Eyes.* Harry N. Abrams, Inc. Publishers, 1995.

Mangham, Andrew, ed. *Wilkie Collins: Interdisciplinary Essays.* Cambridge Scholars Publishing, 2007.

Marcoux, J. Paul. *Guilbert de Pixerécourt: French Melodrama in the Early Nineteenth Century.* Peter Lang, 1992.

Marshall, Gail, ed. *Shakespeare in the Nineteenth Century.* Cambridge University Press, 2012.

Marshall, P. David. *Celebrity and Power: Fame in Contemporary Culture.* University of Minnesota Press, 1997.

Masson, David, ed. *The Collected Writings of Thomas De Quincey.* Vol 12. A. & C. Black, 1897.

Mayhew, Henry. "Letter XXXVIII: Monday, February 25, 1850." *Letters to the Morning Chronicle, 1849–1850.* https://www.victorianlondon.org/mayhew/mayhew38.htm.

McDayter, Ghislaine. *Byromania and The Birth of Celebrity Culture.* State University of New York Press, 2009.

McGavran, James Holt, ed. *Literature and the Child: Romantic Continuations, Postmodern Contestations.* University of Iowa Press, 1999.

McPharlin, Paul. *The Puppet Theatre in America: A History.* Harper & Brothers Publishers, 1949.

McPherson, Heather. *Art and Celebrity in the Age of Reynolds and Siddons.* Penn State University Press, 2017.

———. "Picturing Tragedy: *Mrs Siddons as the Tragic Muse* Revisited," *Eighteenth-Century Studies* 33, no. 3 (Spring 2000): 401–21.

Meer, Sarah. *Uncle Tom Mania: Slavery, Minstrelsy, and Transatlantic Culture in the 1850s.* University of Georgia Press, 2005.

Meikle, Kyle. *Adaptations in the Franchise Era, 2001–2016.* Bloomsbury, 2019.

Meisel, Martin. *Realizations: Narrative, Pictorial, and Theatrical Arts in Nineteenth-Century England.* Princeton University Press, 1983.

Mellby, Julie L. "Delacroix's *Faust*." Graphic Arts: Exhibitions, Acquisitions, and other highlights from the Graphic Arts Collection, Princeton University Library. November 26, 2009. https://www.princeton.edu/~graphicarts/2009/11/delacroixs_faust.html.

Melot, Michel. *The Art of Illustration*. Rizzoli International Publications, 1984.

Melville, Joy. *Ellen Terry*. Haus Books, 2006.

Messenger, Ann. "Novel into Play: Aphra Behn and Thomas Southerne." In *His and Hers: Essays in Restoration and Eighteenth-Century Literature*, 41–70. University Press of Kentucky, 1986.

Meyer, Andrea, and Bénédicte Savoy, eds. *The Museum Is Open: Towards a Transnational History of Museums 1750–1950*. De Gruyter, 2014.

Miller, Henry. *Politics Personified: Portraiture, Caricature, and Visual Culture in Britain, c. 1830–80*. Manchester University Press, 2015.

Milner, Henry M. *Frankenstein; or, The Man and the Monster! A Peculiar Romantic, Melo-dramatic Pantomimic Spectacle, in Two Acts*. John Duncombe, 1826. Reprinted in Steven Forry, *Hideous Progenies: Dramatizations of Frankenstein from Mary Shelley to the Present*, 187–204. University of Pennsylvania Press, 1990.

Milton, John. *The Complete Works of John Milton*, edited by Thomas Corns, Gordon Campbell, et al. 11 vols. Oxford University Press, 2008–2013.

Mole, Tom. *Byron's Romantic Celebrity: Industrial Culture and the Hermeneutic of Intimacy*. Palgrave Macmillan, 2007.

———, ed. *Romanticism and Celebrity Culture, 1750–1850*. Cambridge University Press, 2009.

———. *What the Victorians Made of Romanticism: Material Artifacts, Cultural Practices, and Reception History*. Princeton University Press, 2017.

Moll, Richard J. *Before Malory: Reading Arthur in Later Medieval England*. University of Toronto Press, 2003.

Moore, Thomas. *Life of Lord Byron, with His Letters and Journals*. 6 vols. London: John Murray, 1854.

Morgan, Jo-Ann. *Uncle Tom's Cabin as Visual Culture*. University of Missouri Press, 2007.

Morgan, Simon. "Crossing Boundaries: Harriet Beecher Stowe as Literary Celebrity and Anti-Slavery Campaigner." *Celebrity Studies* 8, no. 1 (2017): 162–66.

Moretti, Franco. *Distant Reading*. Verso, 2013.

Mullins, Paul R. *The Archaeology of Consumer Culture*. University Press of Florida, 2011.

Mulrooney, Jonathan. *Romanticism and Theatrical Experience: Kean, Hazlitt, and Keats in the Age of Theatrical News*. Cambridge University Press, 2018.

Murray, Simone. *The Adaptation Industry: The Cultural Economy of Contemporary Literary Adaptation*. Routledge, 2012.

Musser, Benjamin. *Diary of a Twelve-Year-Old*. Caxton Printers, 1932.

Nealon, Jeffrey T., and Caren Irr, eds. *Rethinking the Frankfurt School: Alternative Legacies of Cultural Critique*. State University of New York Press, 2002.

Neiman, Elizabeth A. *Minerva's Gothics: The Politics and Poetics of Romantic Exchange, 1780–1820*. University of Wales Press, 2019.

———. "A New Perspective on the Minerva Press's 'Derivative' Novels: Authorizing Borrowed Material." *European Romantic Review* 26, no. 5 (2015): 633–58.

Nelson, Alfred L., Gilbert B. Cross, and Joseph Donohue, eds. *The Adelphi Theatre Project 1806–1900*. 1988–2016. https://www.umass.edu/AdelphiTheatreCalendar/.

Nenadic, Stana. "Romanticism and the Urge to Consume in the First Half of the Nineteenth Century." In *Consumers and Luxury: Consumer Culture in Europe 1650–1850*, edited by Maxine Berg and Helen Clifford, 208–27. Manchester University Press, 1999.

Newell, Kate. *Expanding Adaptation Networks: From Illustration to Novelization*. Palgrave Macmillan, 2017.

Newey, Katherine. "Melodrama and Metatheatre: Theatricality in Nineteenth-Century Theatre." *Journal of Dramatic Theory and Criticism* (1997): 85–100.

Nichols, Harold. "The Acting of Thomas Potter Cooke." *Nineteenth-Century Theatre Research* 5, no. 2 (1977): 73–84.

Norton, Rictor, ed. *Gothic Readings: The First Wave, 1764–1840*. Leicester University Press. 2000.

Norwood, Janice. "The Britannia Theatre: Visual Culture and the Repertoire of a Popular Theatre." In *Ruskin, the Theatre, and Victorian Visual Culture*, edited by Anselm Heinrich, Kate Newey, and Jeffrey Richards, 135–53. Palgrave Macmillan, 2009.

Oakley, John H. *The Greek Vase: Art of the Storyteller*. The J. Paul Getty Museum, 2013.

O'Flinn, Paul. "Production and Reproduction: The Case of *Frankenstein*." *Literature and History* 9, no. 2 (1983): 194–213.

Olsen, Victoria C. "Idylls of Real Life." *Victorian Poetry* 33, no. 3/4 (1995): 371–89.

O'Malley, Andrew. *Children's Literature, Popular Culture, and* Robinson Crusoe. Palgrave Macmillan, 2012.

O'Quinn, Daniel. *Staging Governance: Theatrical Imperialism in London, 1770–1800*. Johns Hopkins University Press, 2005.

Ormond, Leonee, ed. *The Reception of Alfred Tennyson in Europe*. Bloomsbury, 2017.

Ortiz-Robles, Mario. "Dickens Performs Dickens." *ELH: English Literary History* (Summer 2011): 457–78.

Page, Eugene Richard. *George Colman, the Elder: Essayist, Dramatist and Theatrical Manager, 1732–1794*. Columbia University Press, 1935.

Paraschas, Sotirios. *Reappearing Characters in Nineteenth-Century French Literature: Authorship, Originality, and Intellectual Property*. Palgrave Macmillan, 2018.

Parfait, Claire. *The Publishing History of* Uncle Tom's Cabin, *1852–2002*. Ashgate, 2007.

Pascoe, Judith. *The Sarah Siddons Audio Files: Romanticism and the Lost Voice*. University of Michigan Press, 2013.

Patten, Robert L. *Charles Dickens and 'Boz': The Birth of the Industrial Age Author*. Cambridge University Press, 2012.

———, ed. *Dickens and Victorian Print Cultures*. Ashgate, 2012.

Paulson, Ronald. *Don Quixote in England: The Aesthetics of Laughter*. Johns Hopkins University Press, 1997.

Peake, Richard Brinsley. *Another Piece of Presumption*. J. Duncombe, 1823. Reprinted in Steven Forry, *Hideous Progenies: Dramatizations of* Frankenstein *from Mary Shelley to the Present*, 161–76. University of Pennsylvania Press, 1990.

———. *Presumption; or, The Fate of Frankenstein*. J. Duncombe, 1823. Reprinted in Steven Forry, *Hideous Progenies: Dramatizations of* Frankenstein *from Mary Shelley to the Present*, 135–60. University of Pennsylvania Press, 1990.

Pearce, Lynne. *Woman / Image / Text: Readings in Pre-Raphaelite Art and Literature*. University of Toronto Press, 1991.

Pedlar, Valerie. "Opening up the Secret Theatre of Home: Wilkie Collins's 'The Woman in White' on the Victorian Stage." *Wilkie Collins Journal* 11 (2012): http://wilkiecollinssociety.org/opening-up-the-secret-theatre-of-home-wilkie-collinss-the-woman-in-white-on-the-victorian-stage/.

Perry, Gill, Joseph Roach, and Shearer West. *The First Actresses: Nell Gwyn to Sarah Siddons*. University of Michigan Press, 2011.

Pitcher, E. W. "Byron's 'The Deformed Transformed' Transformed: A Short Fiction Adaptation in 1825." *Keats-Shelley Journal* 33 (1984): 24–30.

Pittock, Murray, ed. *The Reception of Sir Walter Scott in Europe*. Continuum, 2007. Reprinted by Bloomsbury Academic, 2014.

Planché, James Robinson. *Maid Marian; or, The Huntress of Arlingford: A Legendary Opera in Three Acts*. Lowndes, 1822.

———. *Recollections and Reflections: A Professional Autobiography*. 2 vols. Tinsley Brothers, 1872.

Postle, Martin. *Joshua Reynolds: The Creation of Celebrity*. Tate Publishing, 2005.

Potter, Franz J. *The History of Gothic Publishing, 1800–1835: Exhuming the Trade*. Palgrave Macmillan, 2005.

———, ed. *The Monster Made by Man: A Compendium of Gothic Adaptations*. Zittaw, 2004.

Powell, David. *William West and the Regency Toy Theatre*. Sir John Soane's Museum, 2004.

Pyle, Eric. *William Blake's Illustrations for Dante's Divine Comedy: A Study of the Engravings, Pencil Sketches and Watercolors*. McFarland, 2015.

Radcliffe, Ann. *The Mysteries of Udolpho*, edited by Bonamy Dobrée and Terry Castle. Oxford University Press, 2008.

Randall, Marilyn. *Pragmatic Plagiarism: Authorship, Profit, and Power*. University of Toronto Press, 2001.

Raw, Laurence, and Define Ersin Tutan, eds. *The Adaptation of History*. McFarland, 2013.

Ray, Gordon Norton. *The Illustrator and the Book in England from 1790–1914*. The Piermont Morgan Library in association with Dover Publications, Inc., 1976.

Reid, Calvin. "'Birdman' Drives Interest in Carver Collection." *Publishers Weekly* (February 19, 2015). http://www.publishersweekly.com/pw/by-topic/industry-news/bookselling/article/65629-birdman-drives-interest-in-raymond-carver-collection.html.

Reynolds, Ernest. *Early Victorian Drama (1830–1870)*. Benjamin Blom, 1965.

Rhodes, Kimberley. *Ophelia and Victorian Visual Culture: Representing Body Politics in the Nineteenth Century*. Ashgate, 2008.

Richardson, Samuel. *The Novels of Samuel Richardson, Complete and Unabridged*. 19 vols. Classic Books, 1999.

Ricketson, Sam. *The Berne Convention for the Protections of Literary and Artistic Works, 1886–1986*. The Eastern Press, 1987.

Rigney, Anne. *The Afterlives of Walter Scott: Memory on the Move.* Oxford University Press, 2012.

Ritchie, Fiona, and Peter Sabor, eds. *Shakespeare in the Eighteenth-Century.* Cambridge University Press, 2012.

Robbins, John. "It Lives!: *Frankenstein, Presumption,* and the Staging of Romantic Science." *European Romantic Review* 28, no. 2 (2017): 185–201.

"Robert Louis Stevenson Archive: Film Versions of Jekyll and Hyde." RLS Website. http://www.robert-louis-stevenson.org/richard-dury-archive/films-rls-jekyll-hyde.html.

Robert, Valentine. "Cinema and the Work of Doré." In *Doré: Master of Imagination,* edited by Philippe Kaenel, 287–95. Musée d'Orsay/Flammarion/National Gallery of Canada, 2014.

Robinson, Charles E. "The Devil as Doppelgänger in *The Deformed Transformed*: The Sources and Meaning of Byron's Unfinished Drama." In *The Plays of Lord Byron: Critical Essays,* edited by Robert Gleckner and Bernard Beatty, 321–45. Liverpool University Press, 1997.

Roe, Albert S. *Blake's Illustrations to the Divine Comedy.* Princeton University Press, 1953.

Rose, Brian A. Jekyll and Hyde *Adapted: Dramatizations of Cultural Anxiety.* Greenwood, 1996.

Rose, Margaret A. *Parody//Meta-Fiction: An Analysis of Parody as a Critical Mirror to the Writing and Reception of Fiction.* Croom Helm, 1979.

Rowland, Ann Wierda. *Romanticism and Childhood: The Infantilization of British Literary Culture.* Cambridge University Press, 2015.

Roy, Donald. *Plays by James Robinson Planché.* Cambridge University Press, 1986.

Ruzicka, Jeannie, ed. *Gustave Doré: Illustrations to* Don Quixote. St. Martin's Press, 1974.

Ryan, Marie-Laure, ed. *Narrative across Media: The Languages of Storytelling.* University of Nebraska Press, 2004.

Ryan, Marie-Laure, and Jan-Noël Thon, eds. *Storyworlds across Media: Toward a Media-Conscious Narratology.* University of Nebraska Press, 2014.

Sadoff, Diane F. *Victorian Vogue: British Novels on Screen.* University of Minnesota Press, 2010.

Saggini, Francesca. *The Gothic Novel and the Stage: Romantic Appropriations.* Routledge, 2015.

Saggini, Francesca, and Anna Enrichetta Soccio, eds. *Transmedia Creatures: Frankenstein's Afterlives.* Bucknell University Press, 2018.

Saglia, Diego. "The Gothic Stage: Visions of Instability, Performances of Anxiety." In *Romantic Gothic: An Edinburgh Companion,* edited by A. Wright and D. Townshend. Edinburgh University Press, 2016.

Saklofske, Jon. "A Fly in the Ointment: Exploring the Creative Relationship between William Blake and Thomas Gray." *Word & Image* 19, no. 3 (2012): 166–79.

Sanders, Julie. *Adaptation and Appropriation.* Routledge, 2006. Reprinted 2016.

Santaniello, A. E., ed. "Introduction." *The Boydell Shakespeare Prints.* Arno Press, 1979.

Saunders, Clare Broome. *Women Writers and Nineteenth-Century Medievalism.* Palgrave Macmillan, 2009.

Schlicke, Paul. *Dickens and Popular Entertainment.* Allen & Unwin, 1985.

Schmidt, Rachel Lynn. *Critical Images: The Canonization of* Don Quixote *through Illustrated Editions of the Eighteenth Century.* McGill-Queen's University Press, 1999.

Schober, Regina. "Adaptation as Connection—Transmediality Reconsidered." In *Adaptation Studies: New Challenges, New Directions,* edited by Jorgen Bruhn, Anne Gjelsvik, and Eirik Frisvold Hanssen, 89–112. Bloomsbury, 2013.

Scolari, Carlos Alberto, Paolo Bertetti, and Matthew Freeman. *Transmedia Arachaeology: Storytelling in the Borderlines of Science Fiction, Comics, and Pulp Magazines.* Palgrave Macmillan, 2014.

Scott, Grant F. "Language Strange: A Visual History of Keats's 'La Belle Dame sans Merci.'" *Studies in Romanticism* 38, no. 4 (Winter 1999): 503–35.

———. *The Sculpted Word: Keats, Ekphrasis, and the Visual Arts.* University Press of New England, 1994.

Scott, Walter. *The Doom of Devorgoil: A Melodrama.* Cadell and Company, 1830. https://babel.hathitrust.org/cgi/pt?id=hvd.32044086800539;view=1up;seq=11.

———. *The Waverly Novels.* 24 vols. John D. Morris, 1892.

Semenza, Gregory. "Towards a Historical Turn?: Adaptation Studies and the Challenges of History." In *The Routledge Companion to Adaptation,* edited by Dennis Cutchins, Katja Krebs, and Eckart Voigts, 58–66. Routledge, 2018.

Shakespeare, William. *The New Oxford Shakespeare: The Complete Works,* edited by Gary Taylor, et al. 2 vols. Oxford University Press, 2017.

Shapiro, H. A. *Poet and Painter in Classical Greece.* Routledge, 2005.

Shelley, Mary Wollstonecraft. *Frankenstein; or, The Modern Prometheus,* edited by Susan J. Wolfson Longman Cultural Editions Series. 2nd ed. Pearson Education, 2007. Originally published 1818.

———. *The Letters of Mary Wollstonecraft Shelley,* edited by Betty T. Bennett. 3 vols. Baltimore: Johns Hopkins University Press, 1980–88.

———. *The Selected Letters of Mary Wollstonecraft Shelley,* edited by Betty T. Bennett. Johns Hopkins University Press, 1995.

Shelley, Percy Bysshe. *Shelley's Poetry and Prose,* edited by Neil Fraistat and Donald H. Reiman. Norton, 2002.

Shershow, Scott Cutler. *Puppets and "Popular" Culture.* Cornell University Press, 1995.

Sickmann Han, Carrie. "Pickwick's Other Papers: Continually Reading Dickens." *Victorian Literature and Culture* 44 (2016): 19–41.

Sigler, Carolyn, ed. *Alternative Alices: Visions and Revisions of Lewis Carroll's Alice Books: An Anthology.* University Press of Kentucky, 1997.

Simpson, Roger. *Radio Camelot: Arthurian Legends on the BBC, 1922–2005.* D. S. Brewer, 2008.

Slethaug, Gordon E. *Adaptation Theory and Criticism: Postmodern Literature and Cinema in the USA.* Bloomsbury, 2014.

Smart, Mary Ann. *Waiting for Verdi: Italian Opera and Political Opinion, 1815–1848.* University of California Press, 2018.

Smeed, J. W. *Don Juan: Variations on a Theme.* Routledge, 1990.

Smith, Andrew, and Anna Barton. *Interventions: Rethinking the Nineteenth Century.* Manchester University Press, 2017.

Smith, Andrew, and William Hughes, eds. *The Victorian Gothic: An Edinburgh Companion.* Edinburgh University Press, 2012.

Smith, Julianne. "J. P. Burnett's *Bleak House: A Drama in Three Acts.*" *Streaky Bacon: A Guide to Victorian Adaptations.* 2016. http://www.streakybacon.net/j-p-burnetts-bleak-house-a-drama-in-three-acts-by-julianne-smith/.

Smith, O. *Recollections of O. Smith, Comedian: During a Period of Fifty Years in the Profession,* edited by William W. Appleton. *Performing Arts Resource* 5 (1979).

Soane, George. *Der Freischütz: A Romantic Opera in Three Acts.* 3rd ed. Simpkin and Marshall, 1825. https://babel.hathitrust.org/cgi/pt?id=uc1.31175005738722;view=2up;seq=4.

Soubigou, Gilles. "French Portraits of Byron, 1824–1880." *Byron Journal* 36, no. 1 (2008): 45–55.

———. "Gustave Doré: Interpreter of Tennyson's *Idylls of the King.*" *The Reception of Alfred Tennyson in Europe,* edited by Leonee Ormond, 63–84. Bloomsbury, 2017.

Speaight, George. *Juvenile Drama: The History of the English Toy Theatre.* Macdonald & Co. Publishers, 1946. Reprinted as *The History of the English Toy Theatre.* Pays, Inc. 1969.

Spencer, Jane. *Aphra Behn's Afterlife.* Oxford University Press, 2000.

St. Clair, William. *The Reading Nation in the Romantic Period.* Cambridge University Press, 2004.

Stam, Robert. "Beyond Fidelity: The Dialogics of Adaptation." In *Film Adaptation,* edited by James Naremore. Rutgers University Press, 2000.

———. *Literature through Film: Realism, Magic, and the Art of Adaptation.* Blackwell, 2005.

Stam, Robert, and A. Raengo, eds. *Literature and Film: A Guide to the Theory and Practice of Film Adaptation.* Blackwell, 2005.

Stavans, Ilan. *Quixote: The Novel and the World.* W. W. Norton, 2016.

Stein, Atara. *The Byronic Hero in Film, Fiction, and Television.* Southern Illinois University Press, 2004.

Stephens, John Russell. *The Profession of the Playwright: British Theatre 1800–1900.* Cambridge University Press, 1992.

Stevenson, Brenda E. "*12 Years a Slave*: Narrative, History, and Film." *Journal of African American History* 99, no. 1–2 (2014): 106–18.

Stevenson, Robert Louis. "A Penny Plain and Twopence Coloured." In *Memories and Portraits,* 198–211. Charles Scribner's Sons, 1907.

Stillinger, Jack. *Multiple Authorship and the Myth of Solitary Genius.* Oxford University Press, 1991.

Stone, Geo. Winchester, Jr., ed. *The Stage and the Page: London's 'Whole Show' in the Eighteenth-Century Theatre.* University of California Press, 1981.

Stoneman, Patsy. *Brontë Transformations: The Cultural Dissemination of* Jane Eyre *and* Wuthering Heights. 2nd ed. Edward Everett Root Publishers, 2018.

———. Jane Eyre *on Stage, 1848–1898: An Illustrated Edition of Eight Plays with Contextual Notes.* Ashgate, 2007.

Stowe, Harriet Beecher. *Uncle Tom's Cabin: Authoritative Text, Backgrounds and Contexts.* W. W. Norton, 2018.

Stuart, Roxana. *Stage Blood: Vampires of the Nineteenth-Century Stage.* Bowling Green State University Popular Press, 1994.

Swift, Jonathan. *Gulliver's Travels: Based on the 1726 Text,* edited by Albert J. Rivero. W. W. Norton, 2002.

Szwydky, Lissette Lopez. "Forms and Media: Adapting Tragedy." In *A Cultural History of Tragedy. Volume 5: The Age of Empire*, edited by Michael Gamer and Diego Saglia, 23–43. Bloomsbury, 2019.

———. "*Frankenstein*'s Spectacular Nineteenth-Century Stage History and Legacy." In D. Cutchins and D. Perry, eds. *Adapting Frankenstein: The Monster's Eternal Lives in Popular Culture*. Manchester: Manchester University Press, 2018.

———. "Rewriting the History of Black Resistance: The Haitian Revolution, Jamaican Maroons, and the 'History" of Three-Fingered Jack in English Popular Culture, 1799–1830." In *Circulations: Romanticism and the Black Atlantic*, edited by Paul Youngquist and Frances Botkin. Romantic Circles Praxis Series, 2011. https://romantic-circles.org/praxis/circulations/HTML/praxis.2011.szwydky.html.

———. "Victor Hugo's *Notre-Dame* on the Nineteenth-Century London Stage." *European Romantic Review* 21, no. 4 (2010): 469–87.

Tambling, Jeremy. "Scott's 'Heyday' in Opera." In *The Reception of Sir Walter Scott in Europe*, edited by Murray Pittock, 283–92. Bloomsbury, 2014.

Tennyson, Alfred. *The Works of Alfred Lord Tennyson*, edited by K. Hodder. Wordsworth Editions Limited, 2008.

"Theatres: English Opera House," *London Morning Post*, July 30, 1823: 3. *The British Newspaper Archive*. https://www.britishnewspaperarchive.co.uk/viewer/bl/0000174/18230730/014/0003.

Thomas, Julia. "Reflections on Illustration: The *Database of Mid-Victorian Wood-Engraved Illustration (DMVI)*." *Journal of Illustration Studies* (2007). http://jois.uia.no/articles.php?article=37.

Thomas, Kaitlin. "Everything's an Adaptation: You Won't Believe How Many Current TV Shows Began as Something Else." (August 28, 2014). http://www.tv.com/news/tv-show-adaptations-140909871911/.

Thomson, Douglass H., Jack G. Voller, and Frederick S. Frank, eds. *Gothic Writers: A Critical and Bibliographical Guide*. Greenwood Press, 2002.

Thomson, Peter. *The Cambridge Introduction to English Theatre, 1660–1900*. Cambridge University Press, 2006.

Thon, Jan-Noël. *Transmedial Narratology and Contemporary Media Culture*. University of Nebraska Press, 2016.

Thorburn, David, and Henry Jenkins, eds. *Rethinking Media Change: The Aesthetics of Transition*. MIT Press, 2004.

Throsby, Corin. "Byron, Commonplacing, and Early Fan Culture." In *Romanticism and Celebrity Culture, 1750–1850*, edited by Tom Mole, 227–44. Cambridge University Press, 2009.

Tromp, Marlene, Pamela K. Gilbert, and Aeron Haynie, eds. *Beyond Sensation: Mary Elizabeth Braddon in Context*. State University of New York Press, 2000.

Tuite, Clara. *Lord Byron and Scandalous Celebrity*. Cambridge University Press, 2015.

Tunbridge, Laura. "From Count to Chimney Sweep: Byron's 'Manfred' in London Theatres." *Music & Letters* 87, no. 2 (2006): 212–36.

Viscomi, Joseph. *Blake and the Idea of the Book*. Princeton University Press, 1993.

———. "Blake's Illuminated Word." In *Art, Word and Image: Two Thousand Years of Visual/Textual Interaction*, edited by John Dixon Hunt, David Lomas, and Michael Corris, 87–110. London Reaktion Books, 2010.

Vogler, Richard A. "Cruikshank and Dickens: A Reassessment of the Role of Artist and the Author." *Princeton University Library Chronicle* 35, no. 1–2 (1973–74): 61–91.

Waite, Arthur Edward. *The Quest for Bloods: A Study of the Victorian Penny Dreadful*. Printed for Private Circulation, 1997. Original publication c. 1920.

Waterfield, Giles. *The People's Galleries: Art Museums and Exhibitions in Britain, 1800–1914*. Yale University Press, 2015.

The Waverley Dramas: Kenilworth, Rob Roy, Guy Mannering, Ivanhoe &c. G. Routledge, 1823. Reissued in 1845.

Weber, Brenda R. *Women and Literary Celebrity in the Nineteenth Century*. Routledge, 2016.

Welcher, Jeanne K., and George E. Bush Jr., eds. *Gulliveriana*. 8 vols. Scholars' Facsimiles & Reprints, 1970.

Weltman, Sharon Aronofsky. "1847: Sweeney Todd and Abolition." *BRANCH: Britain, Representation and Nineteenth-Century History*, edited by Dino Franco Felluga. *Romanticism and Victorianism on the Net*. 2013. http://www.branchcollective.org/?ps_articles=sharon-aronofsky-weltman-1847-sweeney-todd-and-abolition.

———. "Theater, Exhibition, and Spectacle in the Nineteenth Century." In *A Companion to British Literature*. Vol 4: Victorian and Twentieth-Century Literature, 1837–2000, edited by Robert Demaria Jr., Heesok Chang, and Samantha Zacher, 68–88. Malden and Oxford: Wiley Blackwell, 2014.

West, Shearer. "The Photographic Portraiture of Henry Irving and Ellen Terry." In *Ruskin, the Theatre, and Victorian Visual Culture*, edited by Anselm Heinrich, Katherine Newey, and Jeffrey Richards, 187–215. Palgrave Macmillan, 2009.

"What Jane Saw." Liberal Arts Development Studio at The University of Texas at Austin. www.whatjanesaw.org.

Whitaker, Muriel. *The Legends of King Arthur in Art*. D. S. Brewer, 1990.

White, Colin. *The Enchanted World of Jessie M. King*. Canongate, 1989.

White, Henry Adelbert. *Sir Walter Scott's Novels on the Stage*. Yale University Press, 1927.

Whitehead, Christopher. *The Public Art Museum in Nineteenth-Century Britain*. Ashgate, 2005.

Williams, Carolyn. *Gilbert and Sullivan: Gender, Genre, Parody*. Columbia University Press, 2010.

Williams, Raymond. *Culture and Society, 1780–1950*. Columbia University Press, 1958. Reprint 1983.

Wilstach, Paul. *Richard Mansfield: The Man and the Actor*. Charles Scribner's Sons, 1909.

Winn, Peter Charles. "The 'Terrible' Fitzball: The Work of a Hack Dramatist, 1817–1873." PhD diss., Cornell University, 1979.

Winter, William. *Life and Art of Richard Mansfield*. Moffat, Yard and Company, 1910.

Winton, Calhoun. "Dramatic Censorship." In *The London Theatre World 1660–1800*, edited by Robert D. Hume, 286–308. Southern Illinois University Press, 1980.

Wirtén, Eva Hemmungs. *No Trespassing: Authorship, Intellectual Property Rights, and the Boundaries of Globalization*. University of Toronto Press, 2004.

Wise, Winifred. *Fanny Kemble: Actress, Author, Abolitionist*. G. P. Putnam's Sons, 1966.

Wittreich, Joseph Anthony. "A Note on Blake and Fuseli." *Blake: An Illustrated Quarterly* 3, no. 1 (1969): 3–4.

Wright, Beth S. "'Seeing with the Painter's Eye': Sir Walter Scott's Challenge to Nineteenth-Century Art." In *The Reception of Sir Walter Scott in Europe*, edited by Murray Pittock, 293–312. Continuum, 2007. Reprint Bloomsbury, 2014.

Wolf, Mark J. P. *Building Imaginary Worlds: The Theory and History of Subcreation.* Routledge, 2012.

Wollstonecraft, Mary. *Vindication of the Rights of Woman* and *The Wrongs of Woman; or, Maria,* edited by Anne K. Mellor and Noelle Chao. Pearson Longman, 2007.

Woo, Celestine. "Sarah Siddons's Performances as Hamlet: Breaching the Breeches Part." *European Romantic Review* 18, no. 5 (2007): 573–95.

Wootton, Sarah. *Consuming Keats: Nineteenth-Century Representations in Art and Literature.* Palgrave Macmillan, 2006.

Worrall, David. *Celebrity, Performance, Reception: British Georgian Theatre as Social Assemblage.* Cambridge University Press, 2013.

———. *Theatric Revolution: Drama, Censorship and Romantic Period Subculture, 1773–1832.* Oxford University Press, 2006.

Youngquist, Paul. *Madness and Blake's Myth.* Pennsylvania State University Press, 1990.

Zafran, Eric, Robert Ronsenblum, and Lisa Small. *Fantasy and Faith: The Art of Gustave Doré.* Yale University Press, 2007.

Zall, Paul M. "Wordsworth and the Copyright Act of 1842." *PMLA* 70, no. 1 (1955): 132–44.

Zemer, Lior. *The Idea of Authorship in Copyright.* Ashgate, 2007.

Zemka, Sue. "The Death of Nancy 'Sikes,' 1838–1912." *Representations* 110 (2010): 29–57.

INDEX

Illustrations are in **bold**.

Adaptation (2002), 46
adaptation: abridgements, 2, 23–24, 67, 178, 180, 218; allusions, 10, 14, 116–17, 123, 140, 182–83; approaches to study, 3–4, 9, 12–13, 17–18, 23–25, 29, 96, 123, 210–11, 221; appropriation, 3–6, 14, 25, 51, 119, 133–34, 146, 179–80, 190, 212, 218, 220; ballads, 5, 23, 99, 178, 180; caricatures, 5, 74, 87, 149, 150, 154; chapbooks, 6, 23–24, 178, 180–81, 183, 191, 205; derivative works, 1, 3, 10, 14, 19, 21, 73, 104, 152, 157–58, 158n42, 182, 210, 215; digital media, 3, 7, 66, 95, 111, 144, 177, 209, 214; extensions, 1–2, 4, 11, 17, 22, 116, 133, 137, 140–43, 147, 149, 155–58, 173, 176, 178–79, 202, 205, 207, 212, 221; hybridity, 61, 116, 126, 181, 188; mash-ups, 3–4, 52, 52n68, 142–43, 173, 180, 183–84, 214; metafiction, 45, 53, 61, 151, 179; off-shoots, 17, 160, 176; parodies, 1–2, 5, 11, 14, 20, 28n4, 29, 45, 47, 49, 53, 53n76, 54, 60, 61, 67–68, 132, 139, 147, 156, 178, 183, 218; pastiches, 20, 28n4, 29, 49, 53–54, 53n76, 60, 61; prequels, 3–4, 16, 142, 176; role of gender, 4, 21, 23–24, 100–101, 113–14, 161, 163, 165, 168–69, 172, 176, 181–83, 190–91, 206, 215; satire, 5, 69–70; sequels, 2, 5, 14, 16, 17, 139, 142, 146, 176, 178–79, 218; spin-offs, 14, 16, 17, 23, 160, 176, 209
Adelphi Theatre, 42, 48, 50–51, 76, 84, 85, 89, 91, 149
Adorno, Theodor, 16–17, 28–29, 37
Adventures of Baron Munchausen, The (culture-text), 129, 199, **199**
Ainsworth, William Harrison, 149, 155; *Jack Sheppard*, 149
Alary, Giulio, 71
Alexander, John White, 101, **103**
Aldridge, Ira, 73, 80
Alice's Adventures in Wonderland (Carroll), 121, 134, 192
Alighieri, Dante. *See* Dante
All Quiet on the Western Front (1930), 213
Allen, Grant, 200
Andrew, Dudley, 213
Apel, Johann August, 48
Arnold, Matthew, 165
art: art galleries, 74, 99, 104–5, 109–10, 136; ekphrasis, 10, 22, 98–99, 104, 133, 136, 149; fine art, 7, 72, 98–99, 105–6, 111, 113–14, 175–76, 180, 188, 206; high art, 4, 8–9,

10n25, 30, 39, 74, 108, 110–11, 117, 124, 189; literary art galleries, 21, 105–14, 132, 136; paintings, 2, 5–7, 12, 16, 19–21, 23–24, 61, 68, 70, 74–75, 97–101, 104–19, 123–26, 129, 133–36, 143–44, 148, 161–63, 165–66, 175–76, 188–89, 202, 206, 215

Austen, Jane, 49n63, 159, 172, 182, 209–10, 220; *Northanger Abbey*, 49n63, 182–83; *Pride and Prejudice*, 4

Austenland (Hale), 209–10

Bakhtin, Mikhail, 10
Balzac, Honoré de, 132
Barnett, Jane, 46–47
Barry, Michael, 209
Batman (culture-text), 46–49, 139, 206
Behn, Aphra, 2, 4–5; *Oroonoko: or, The Royal Slave*, 4–5
Behrendt, Stephen, 118n50, 119
Béraud, Antony, 6, **55, 56, 57, 58, 59,** 184; *Le Monstre et le Magicien*, 6, 48n58, **55, 56, 57, 58, 59,** 184, 217
Berlioz, Hector, 70, 73
Berminghan, Ann, 27
Bernhardt, Sarah, 73, 79, 80, **82**
Bertin, Louise, 73
Bible, 7, 116, 118, 119
Birdman or (The Unexpected Virtue of Ignorance) (2014), 46–49, 46n51, 47n54, 213
Black Eyed Susan, 198
Blake, William, 16, 22, 98, 104, 115–21, 118n50, 119n53, **120, 122,** 123–24, 126, 129, 134, 160–62; *The Circle of the Lustful*, **122**; *Satan Arousing the Rebel Angels*, **120**; *Songs of Innocence and of Experience*, 117; "The Tyger," 117
Boccaccio, Giovanni, 99; *The Decameron*, 99
Bolton, H. Philip, 7, 7n16, 83
Boucicault, Dion, 20, 43, 87, 94; *The Corsican Brothers; or, The Fatal Duel*, 43
Boydell, John, 106–13, 132, 134
Boydell Shakespeare Gallery, 106–9, 112, **112**
Braddon, Mary Elizabeth, 5, 169, 190; *Lady Audley's Secret*, 5
Brewer, David, 156
Brickdale, Eleanor Fortescue, 169
Brontë, Charlotte, 5, 168, 172, 189–90, 220; *Jane Eyre*, 4, 5, 139, 190, 214; *Villette*, 168

Brontë, Emily, 172, 189, 220; *Wuthering Heights*, 4
Brooks, Mel, 50, 52, 53n71
Brooks, Peter, 92
Brougham, John, 94
Browne, Hablot Knight, 22, 148, 150
Bruhn, Jørgen, 123
Brylowe, Thora, 105, 105n12
Bulwer-Lytton, Edward, 23
Burwick, Frederick, 39, 70, 109
Buss, Robert William, 143–44, **143,** 148
Byron, Lord George Gordon, 20, 22, 34, 39, 67–74, 75n34, 94, 100, 116, 125–26, **125, 127,** 129, 154, 160, 183–84, 188, 218; *The Bride of Abydos*, 69, 126; *Cain*, 69; *Childe Harold's Pilgrimage*, 68–70; *The Corsair*, 39, 69, **127**; *The Deformed Transformed*, 184; *Don Juan*, 69–70, 116; *Fragment of a Novel*, 75n34; *The Giaour*, 69, 126; *Manfred*, 69–70; *Marino Faliero, Doge of Venice*, 71, 125; *Mazeppa*, 69, 75n34; *Sardanapalus*, 70–71, 110, 125, **125**; *The Two Foscari*, 71

Calè, Luisa, 105
Camelot (culture-text), 22–23, 142, 159–73; *A Connecticut Yankee in King Arthur's Court* (Twain), 166; *The Defence of Guenevere and Other Poems* (Morris), 165; *The Defense of Queen Guinevere* (King), **171**; *History of the Kings of England* (Monmoth), 161; *Idylls of the King* (Tennyson), 23, 129, 161–69; *King Arthur: Legend of the Sword* (2017), 170; "The Last Tournament" (Tennyson), 165; "Launcelot and Elaine" (Tennyson), 161; *Le Morte d'Arthur* (Malory), 23, 161; "The Maying of Guenevere" (Morris), 165; *The Parting of Launcelot and Guinevere* (Cameron), **167**; *Vivien and Merlin* (Cameron), 165, **166, 167**; *Vivien and Merlin Repose* (Doré), 163, **164**
Cameron, Julia Margaret, 23, 163, 165, **166, 167,** 169–70
canon and canonization, 10, 16, 21, 25, 39, 83, 94–95, 104–5, 114, 126, 132, 144, 155–56, 159–60, 162, 165, 172–73, 175, 180, 188, 192, 207, 210–13
capitalism, 1, 4, 6, 28, 61, 151, 160, 180, 200
Cardwell, Sarah, 143, 220–21
Carroll, Lewis, 136, 192, 206

Index

Carver, Raymond, 46, 46n51, 213; "What We Talk About When We Talk About Love," 46, 46n51, 213

celebrity, 7, 9, 19–21, 47n56, 63–64, 66–70, 72–77, 79, 83, 85, 87–88, 124, 136, 144, 147, 150, 152–55, 205, 211, 216, 218. *See also* cultural icons

censorship, 19, 30–38, 83, 92–93, 95

Cervantes, Miguel de, 2, 22, 90, 129, **130**; *Don Quijote de la Mancha*, 2, 90, 129, **130**, 133

children's media, 9, 24, 178, 192, 200, 206

Christmas Carol, A (culture-text), 17–18, 121, 129, 129n74, 140, 142–44, **145**; *A Christmas Carol* (Barnett), **145**; *A Christmas Carol* (Dickens), 4, 17–18, 121, 129, 129n74, 140–44, 154

Clifton, Stephen, 87

Cole, William, 194

Coleridge, Samuel Taylor, 109, 129, **131**, 189; *The Rime of the Ancient Mariner*, 129, **131**

Colin, Alexandre-Marie, 70, **71**; *Byron as Don Juan, with Haidee*, 70, **71**, 83

Collins, Wilkie, 5–6, 158, 190; *The Moonstone*, 5–6; *The Woman in White*, 5–6, 214

Colman, George (the Elder), 2n4, 82

Colman, George (the Younger), 32–33, 65, 82–83; *The Iron Chest*, 32–33, 65, 83

comic books, 17, 41, 66, 111, 178–79, 184, 206–7, 218

commercialism, 1–2, 14, 21, 27–30, 39, 60–61, 64–68, 73, 88, 91–96, 97, 100, 105, 108, 110–15, 124, 129, 133, 142, 146–51, 155–57, 172–74, 175–78, 192, 194, 200, 204–7, 210–14, 216, 219–20; advertising, 19–20, 43, 45, 83, 88, 107, 111, 144, 155, 184, 194, 199; commercial products, 6, 11, 16, 142, 173, 176, 206; income and royalties, 24, 67, 84, 95, 113, 151, 154–57, 158n42; marketing, 5, 43, 45, 50, 63, 67, 77, 107, 111, 153, 155–56, 155n32, 198–200; merchandise and merchandizing, 14, 19, 23, 28, 175–79, 192, 205–6

Cooke, Thomas Potter, 20, 41, 48, **55**, 65, 73, 75, 76, 84, 89, 198

Cooper, James Fenimore, 7, 39, 84; *The Pilot*, 7, 39, 84, 89; *The Red Rover*, 7, 39, 198

copyright laws, 6, 11, 19, 21, 54, 67, 73, 95, 151–52, 154–59, 157n39, 173; Berne Convention for the Protection of Literary and Artistic Works, 11, 73, 157, 157n39, 159; Copyright Act of 1842, 152

Corrigan, Timothy, 9, 30, 39, 214

Corsair, The (culture-text), 39, 69, 71, **127**

Corsican Brothers; or, The Fatal Duel, The (culture-text), 43, **195**

costumes and costuming, 5, 20, 38, 45–47, 63, 74–75, 80, 89, 91, 92–93, 110, 150, 172, 177, 193

Covent Garden, 31, 43, **44**, 82, 87, 91

Cowen, Fredric Hymen, 71; *The Corsair*, 71

Cox, Jeffrey, 38

Cox, Philip, 34

critics and criticism, 2, 9–11, 22, 29, 54, 91–92, 94, 98, 100, 104, 105, 109, 115–18, 124, 126, 129, 146, 162–63, 168

Cruikshank, George, 129, 147–50, 154

cultural icons, 14, 75, 86, 95, 154–55, 168, 194, 210, 212, 216. *See also* celebrity

cultural production, 3, 13–14, 16, 28, 34, 38, 60, 63, 67, 74, 85, 96, 97–98, 104, 110, 113–14, 135, 139, 142, 147, 157, 177, 188, 194, 200, 206–7, 215

culture: commercial, 4, 14, 19–20, 25, 30, 142; consumer culture and consumerism, 1, 4, 17, 27–28, 61, 175, 200; convergence, 14–17, 24, 64, 104, 110, 114, 123, 159, 176–78; high, 11, 31, 97, 104–5, 109, 111–12, 114, 180, 206–7, 215; industry, 29, 37, 60–61, 156, 191, 210, 214; mass, 4, 7, 8–9, 37, 39, 69, 74, 92, 97–98, 104, 114, 124, 144, 175–76, 178, 180–82, 188, 206–7, 216, 220; participatory, 23–24, 95, 105, 175–78, 197, 200–206; popular, 1, 4, 8, 10, 17, 20, 29–31, 38, 60–61, 72, 93, 105, 109, 113–14, 140, 175–76, 180, 183, 191, 193, 210, 215, 220; print, 4, 54, 105–6, 111, 114, 123–24, 135, 148, 193, 207; visual, 22, 74, 108, 116, 133–34, 136, 147, 149

culture-texts, 14, 17–20, 22–23, 25, 29, 47–48, 53–54, 60, 63–64, 101, 114, 118–21, 123, 129, 132–35, 139–44, 155, 158–59, 165–66, 173–74, 175–76, 187, 192, 194, 206–7, 210–12, 217–20. *See also specific culture-texts*

Curtis, Gerard, 154, 155n32

Cutcheon, Dennis, 18

Daly, Charles, 115

Dante, 22, 118, 121, **122**, 123, 125, 132, 134, 162, 172; *The Divine Comedy*, 16, 118, 121, **122**, 123, 129; *The Inferno*, 121, **122**, 123

David Copperfield (culture-text), 86, 214

Davis, Paul, 17–18, 140

Davis, Tracy, 37
De Quincey, Thomas, 48; "The Fatal Marksman," 48
Defoe, Daniel, 2, 5, 178; *Robinson Crusoe*, 5, 24, 93n74, 204
Delacroix, Eugène, 22, 70, 104, 124–26, **125**, 126n70, **127, 128**, 129, 132, 134; *The Execution of the Doge Marino Faliero*, 125; *Faust in the Prison with Marguerite*, **128**; *La Mort de Sardanapalus*, 125, **125**
Denisoff, Dennis, 200
Dentith, Simon, 60
Dibdin, Thomas John, 39, 90n66, 94
Dibdin-Pitt, George, 21, 87, 94, 187; *The Pirate; or, The Wild Woman of Zetland*, 39
Dickens, Charles, 6, 7, 7n16, 9, 13, 20–22, 67, 73, 76, 79n41, 85, 86–87, 94–95, 98, 129n74, 136, 140, 142–44, 146–56, 158–59, 162, 168, 189, 197, 206, 210–12, 218, 220; *All the Year Round*, 86; *Barnaby Rudge*, 153; *Bleak House*, 7n16, 142, 154; *David Copperfield*, 214; *Great Expectations*, 143, 150; *Little Dorrit*, 168; *Martin Chuzzlewit*, 152–53; *Master Humphrey's Clock*, 153; *Nicholas Nickleby*, 87, 150–51, 154, 155, 210–12; *The Old Curiosity Shop*, 143, 153; *Oliver Twist*, 24, 85, 142, 144, 149–50, 193–94, 197; *Our Mutual Friend*, 150; *The Posthumous Papers of the Pickwick Club*, 144, 146, 148–50, 153; *Sketches by Boz Illustrative of Every-day Life and Every-day People*, 147–48, 154
Dickens' Dream (Buss), 143–44, **143**
Dickensian, 142–44, 173
Dicksee, Frank, 101, **101**
Dimond, William, 39; *The Pirate*, 39
Disher, Maurice, 93, 93n74
Divine Comedy, The (culture-text), 18, 118, **122**, 123, 129; *The Divine Comedy* (Dante), 16, 118, 121, **122**, 123, 129
Don Juan (culture-text): *Byron as Don Juan, with Haidee* (Colin), 70, **71**, 83; *Don Juan* (Byron), 69–70, 116
Don Quixote (culture-text), 18, 129, **130**, 133; *Don Quijote de la Mancha* (Cervantes), 2, 90, 129, **130**, 133; *Don Quijote in England* (Fielding), 2; *Don Quixotte!* (Fitzball), 76
Doré, Gustave, 22, 104, 121, **122**, 123–24, 129, 129n74, **130, 131**, 132–33, 163, **164**, 165, 189; *Les Travaux d'Hercule*, 132; *Paolo and Francesca*, **122**

Dracula (culture-text): *Dracula* (1930), 178, 213; *Dracula* (Stoker), 4, 52n68, 141, 158, 179–80; *Nosferatu* (1922), 158
Drury Lane, 31, 32, 48, 65, 75, 90, 125, 126
Ducray-Duminil, François Guillaume, 93n73, 188
Duff, David, 189
Dugué, Ferdinand, **59**
Dumas, Alexandre, 43, 132, 216n16
Dunbar, Pamela, 118, 118n50
Dupont, Pierre, 132
Duvernoy, Alphonse, 71
"Dwarf; or, The Deformed Transformed, The," 183–84, **185**

Eagan, Pierce, 149
Eco, Umberto, 141
education, 3, 12n33, 92–94, 99, 105, 110, 124, 172, 192, 204, 210, 220
Eliot, George, 168, 220
Elliott, Kamilla, 11–12, 98, 134
Endless Entertainment, 183–84, **185, 186,** 187
English Opera House, 32, 50, 64, 77, 79n41, 153, 217
engravers and engravings, 6, 21, 98, 105–9, 111–16, **112**, 124–29, 133, 136, 148, 155, 165, 194

fan fiction, 9, 15–16, 95, 177, 190, 190n28, 203, 206–7
fans and fandoms, 69, 141–42, 144, 173, 175–77, 182–84, 201, 207
Fantasmagoriana, 205
Farr, Liz, 200, 204
Fawcett, John, 32, 76; *Obi; or Three-Finger'd Jack*, 32, 48n60, 76, 219
Fielding, Henry, 1–2, 34–35, 82; *An Apology for the Life of Mrs. Shamela Andrews*, 1, 34; *Don Quijote in England*, 2; *The History of the Adventures of Joseph Andrews*, 1–2; *Pamela in Her Exalted State*, 2; *Tom Jones*, 82
film, 4, 8, 8n22, 11–13, 15, 17–18, 20, 22, 28, 30–31, 38–39, 41, 46, 49–50, 52–54, 52n68, 52n70, 60, 66, 76, 80, 98, 111, 114, 129, 133–34, 149, 155, 159, 165, 172–73, 178, 206–7, 210, 213–15, 217–18, 221; Academy Awards, 47n54, 213; Motion Picture Production Code (Hays Code), 30–31, 30n13. *See also individual film titles*

Fitzball, Edward, 21, 40, 42n44, 76, 84–94, 188, 201; *Don Quixotte!*, 76; *The Flying Dutchman; or, The Phantom Ship*, 89; *Giraldi; or, The Ruffian of Prague*, 90

Fitzsimons, Raymund, 154

folk tales, 32, 39, 42, 48, 76, 93, 99, 204, 212

Forry, Steven, 32

Fosca, François, 126

Frankenstein (culture-text), 18–19, 41, 43, 47–54, 48n58, 52n68, **55, 56, 57, 58, 59,** 60–61, 64–65, 75–76, 79, 84, 121, 141, 165, 179–80, 184, 188, 205, 217–18; *Abbott and Costello Meet Frankenstein* (1948), 49–50; *Another Piece of Presumption* (Peake), 50–51; *Frankenstein* (1931), 79, 178, 213; *Frankenstein; or, The Demon of Switzerland* (Milner), 52, 217, 217n19; *Frankenstein; or, The Man and The Monster* (Milner), 48, 52, 76, 184; *Frankenstein; or, The Model Man* (Henry), 47–49, 54, **59,** 76; *Frankenstein; or, The Modern Prometheus* (M. Shelley), 5–6, 41, 54, 61, 64–65, 76, 79, 121, 141, 165, 179, 184, 188, 205, 216–18; *Frankenstein; or, The Monster and the Magician* (Kerr), 48n58; *Frankenstein; or, The Vampire's Victim* (Henry), 52, 52n67; *House of Frankenstein* (1944), 52n68; *The Last Laugh* (Dickey and Goddard), 52; *The Monster and the Magician; or, The Fate of Frankenstein* (Kerr), 6, 43; *Le Monstre et le Magicien* (Merle and Béraud), 6, 48n58, **55, 56, 57, 58, 59,** 184, 217; "The Monster Made by Man; or, The Punishment of Presumption," 184, **186**; *Presumption; or, The Fate of Frankenstein* (Peake), 32, 41, 43, **44,** 45, 48, 50, 54, **55,** 64–65, 79, 184, 216–17; *Son of Frankenstein* (1939), 79; *Victor Frankenstein* (2015), 54; *Young Frankenstein* (1974), 49–50, 52–54, 52n70, 79

Freeman, Matthew, 17, 27

French Revolution, 92, 108, 203

Fuseli, Henry, 109–13, **112,** 132, 189; *The Enchanted Island before the Cell of Prospero*, **112**

Gamer, Michael, 83

games, 3, 15, 179, 206–7, 209; role-playing, 15, 177, 201, 207; video, 9, 66, 159, 176, 218, 221

Genette, Gerard, 10, 53n76

Gernsheim, Helmut, 165

Godwin, William, 32–33, 35, 64–65, 83, 216–17; *Caleb Williams; or, Things as They Are*, 65; *Political Justice*, 33, 65; *Things as They Are; or, The Adventures of Caleb Williams*, 32–33, 83

Goethe, Johann Wolfgang von, 22, 125–26, 126n70, **128,** 184; *Faust*, 126, **128,** 184, 188; *The Sorrows of Young Werther*, 139

Goldstein, Justin, 36

gothic styles, 23–24, 65, 76, 83, 89, 141, 175–76, 178–84, 189–91, 197, 205–7, 213, 218

Goya, Francisco de, 189

graphic novels, 3, 9, 66, 132, 149, 207, 209

Griggs, Yvonne, 220–21

Groom, Gloria, 113

Grosette, H. W., 188

Grossman, Julie, 18, 141, 218

Hadley, Elaine, 189

Hale, Shannon, 209

Halliday, Andrew, 21, 42–43, **44,** 86, 87, 94, 149–50, 152; *David Copperfield*, 86

Harrison, Florence, 169–70

Haymarket Theatre, 31, 34, 82–83, 188

Hazlewood, Colin Henry, 94, 198; *Alone in the Pirate's Lair*, 198

Hazlitt, William, 109

Hemans, Felicia, 113

history: cultural, 10n25, 12–13, 27, 47, 53, 72, 79–80, 87, 95, 123, 129, 165, 204–19; literary, 3–4, 7, 9, 22, 39, 61, 64, 72, 87, 99, 111, 115, 126, 134, 136, 140–41, 144, 148, 155, 177, 206, 211–12, 216, 219

Hoesterey, Ingeborg, 53

Hoeveler, Diane Long, 23, 180–81; *Gothic Riffs*, 23

Holcroft, Thomas, 188; *A Tale of Mystery*, 188

Horkheimer, Max, 16–17, 28–29

Hugo, Victor, 5–7, 9, 20–21, 42–43, 49n63, 72, 73, 76, 90, 91, 132, 158–59, 189–90, 218–19; *Hernani*, 72

Hume, Robert, 33

Hunchback of Notre-Dame (culture-text): *Esmerelda; or, The Deformed of Notre Dame* (Fitzball), 91; *La Esmeralda* (Hugo), 5–6, 40, 73; *Notre-Dame; or, The Gypsy Girl of Paris* (Halliday), 42–43, **44**; *Notre-Dame de Paris* (Hugo), 6–7, 42–43, 49n63, 73, 76, 90, 189–90, 218–19; *Quasimodo; or, They Gipsey Girl of Notre Dame* (Fitzball), 40, 91

Hunt, Leigh, 41, 64
Hunt, William Holman, 101, **102**, 162
Hutcheon, Linda, 29, 53n76, 60, 72, 187, 216n16

illustrated books, 5, 8, 17, 22, 61, 105–7, 111, 113–15, 124n66, 129, 132–33, 135–36, 147–49, 163, 170, 192, 216, 218
illustrations, 10, 14, 22–23, 28, 75, 97–98, 101, 104, 109, 111–21, 118n50, 119n53, 123–26, 129, 134–36, 144, 148–50, 153–55, 162, 175, 187–88, 210, 212
illustrators, 6, 21, 113, 115, 118, 137, 147, 152, 169
Inchbald, Elizabeth, 35
industrialization, 1, 4, 19, 28, 45, 97, 110, 142, 146–47, 156, 172, 175, 180, 193–94, 200
Inglis, Fred, 74
intertextuality, 10, 29, 45–46, 60–61, 72, 98–99, 116, 124, 133, 153, 170, 181–83, 202, 215
Invisible Man, The (1933), 178, 213
Irving, Henry, 73, 79, 80
Irving, Washington, 76; "Rip Van Winkle," 76
Isabella and the Pot of Basil (culture-text): *Isabella and the Pot of Basil* (Alexander), **103**; *Isabella & the Pot of Basil* (Hunt), **102**; *Isabella; or, The Pot of Basil* (Keats), 99

James, Henry, 134
Jameson, Frederic, 54
Jenkins, Henry, 15–17, 24, 27, 176–77
Jerrold, Douglas, 198
John, Juliet, 13, 144
Jones, David, 5, 24, 180–81
Jonze, Spike, 46

Kean, Charles, 110
Kean, Edmund, 80
Keaton, Michael, 46–47, 47n54, 49, 49n62
Keats, John, 98–101, 134, 189; *The Eve of St. Agnes*, 99; *Isabella; or, The Pot of Basil*, 99; "La Belle Dame sans Merci," 99, 100; "Ode on a Grecian Urn," 99; "On First Looking into Chapman's Homer," 99; "On Seeing the Elgin Marbles," 99
Keeley, Robert, 79, 79n41, 153
Kemble, Fanny, 73, 80

Kerr, John Atkinson, 6, 43, 48n58; *Frankenstein; or, The Monster and the Magician*, 48n58; *The Monster and the Magician; or, The Fate of Frankenstein*, 6, 43
King, Jessie M., 169–70, **171**
Kinservik, Matthew, 36
Kohlke, Marie-Louise, 172–73
Kooistra, Lorraine, 124n66, 135–36

"La Belle Dame sans Merci" (culture-text), 101; *La Belle Dame sans Merci* (Dicksee), **101**; "La Belle Dame sans Merci" (Keats), 99, 100; *La Belle Dame sans Merci* (Waterhouse), **100**
Laird, Karen, 214
Lamb, Caroline, 68
Lamb, Mary, 109
Lamdin, Laura Conner, 161
Lamdin, Robert Thomas, 161
Landon, Leticia Elizabeth, 113
Layard, Austen Henry, 110
Layard, George Somes, 162
League of Extraordinary Gentlemen, The (Moore and O'Neill), 52n68, 179
Leech, John, 150
legends, 7, 89, 93, 99, 129, 134, 142, 151, 159–62, 165–66, 169–70, 172, 201
Leitch, Thomas, 10, 11, 194, 215, 216n16
Lewis, Matthew, 5, 32, 35, **77**, 90, 184, 188, 189; *The Monk*, 32, **77**, 90, 188; *One O'Clock: or, The Knight and the Wood Demon*, 184
Lezra, Esther, 118
Liszt, Franz, 71
literacy, 4, 34, 36, 93–94, 104, 105, 111, 114–15, 163, 176–77, 188, 194, 202, 210
literary studies, 3, 9, 10n25, 11–12, 29, 211, 213, 218
Lloyd, Frederick, 42
Loder, Edward, 188
Logan, John, 179
Looser, Devoney, 210
Lyceum Theatre. *See* English Opera House
Lynch, Diedre, 157, 177, 216n17

Macklin, Thomas, 109–13, 132
Macready, William, 70, 80
magic lantern shows, 23, 176, 181, 189

Maid Marian (culture-text), 87–88; *Maid Marian* (Peacock), 87; *Maid Marian; or, The Huntress of Arlingford* (Planché), 87–88
Mainardi, Patricia, 148
Malley, Shawn, 110
Malory, Thomas, 23, 161–62, 168
Mancoff, Debra, 161–62, 166
Manfred (culture-text), 69–70
Mansfield, Richard, 7, 20, 73, 76–77, **78**, 79, 80, 158
Mayhew, Henry, 195
McPherson, Heather, 74
McTeer, Janet, 80
Meisel, Martin, 10–11, 97–98, 105, 148
Merle, Jean-Toussaint, 6, **55, 56, 57, 58, 59,** 184; *Le Monstre et le Magicien*, 6, 48n58, **55, 56, 57, 58, 59,** 184, 217
Milbanke, Annabella, 68
Millais, John Everett, 162, 162n52
Milner, Henry, 48, 51–52, 76, 184, 217n19; *Frankenstein; or, The Demon of Switzerland*, 52, 217, 217n19; *Frankenstein; or, The Man and The Monster*, 48, 52, 76, 184
Milton, John, 22, 99, 105, 118–20, 118n50, 119n53, 123, 132, 134, 162; *Paradise Lost*, 16, 99, 119–21, 129
Minerva Press, 24, 181–83, 190–91
Mole, Tom, 73, 116, 216n17
Moncrieff, William Thomas, 87, 150
Monk, The (culture-text): *The Monk* (Lewis), 32, **77,** 90, 188; *Raymond and Agnes; or The Castle of Lindenberg*, 32, **77,** 90, 188
Moretti, Franco, 156
Morris, William, 23, 160, 165, 168–70, **171**
Moxon, Edward, 162–63
Murnau, F. W., 158
Murray, Simone, 66
Murray, William Henry, 94
museums, 38, 99, 104–5, 110, 136, 193, 210, 215
Musser, Benjamin, 203–4
mythology, 7, 90, 93, 99, 116, 124, 141, 159, 179

Neiman, Elizabeth, 182, 191
Nenadic, Stana, 28
networks: 68, 115, 123, 140, 179; of adaptation, 64, 66–68, 72, 87, 93, 104–5, 114, 123, 133–34, 140, 149, 155, 158, 160, 174, 202, 217; of cultural production, 66, 69, 72, 95–96, 123; fan, 183; of intertextual exchange, 182; of literary celebrity, 74, 85; model of the adaptation industry, 66, 96, 133; of professionals, 64–66, 84–86, 96; social, 65–66, 84, 177
New Woman movement, 101, 169
Newell, Kate, 98, 104, 114–15, 133–34; *Expanding Adaptation Networks*, 114
Newey, Katherine, 47
Nicholas Nickleby (culture-text), 85, 87, 150–51, 154, 155, 210–12; *Nicholas Nickleby* (Dickens), 87, 150–51, 154, 155, 210–12; *Nickclas Nickleby; or, Doings at Do-the-Boys Hall* (Stirling), 85
Nodier, Charles, 43, 75; *Le Vampire*, 75
novels, 4, 8n22, 14–16, 24, 28–30, 34–35, 37, 40–42, 49n63, 60–61, 63, 66, 72, 83–90, 93–94, 111, 113, 115, 133, 139, 149, 154, 156–57, 168, 173, 175–77, 180, 183–84, 191, 209, 214, 218

O'Malley, Andrew, 191, 204
Oliver Twist (culture-text), 24, 85, 142, 144, 149–50, 193–94, 197, **197**
operas, 23, 68, 70–72, 72n24, 83–84, 89–91, 126, 165, 188
Opie, Amelia, 90, 90n66; "The Ruffian Boy," 90, 90n66
Oroonoko (culture-text), 4–5; *Oroonoko: A Tragedy*, 5; *Oroonoko: or, The Royal Slave*, 4–5

Pamela (culture-text), 1–2, 34; *An Apology for the Life of Mrs. Shamela Andrews*, 1, 34; *Pamela in Her Exalted State*, 2
Paradise Lost (culture-text), 18, 119, 129; *Paradise Lost* (Milton), 16, 99, 119–21, 129
patronage system, 20, 65–67, 96, 110–11, 124; Royal Academy of Arts, 110–11
Peacock, Thomas Love, 87–88; *Maid Marian*, 87
Peake, Richard Brinsley, 21, 41, 43–44, **44,** 48, 50–52, **55,** 64, 79, 184; *Another Piece of Presumption*, 50–51; *Presumption; or, The Fate of Frankenstein*, 32, 41, 43, **44,** 45, 48, 50, 54, **55,** 64–65, 79, 184, 216–17
Pearse, Lynne, 168
Penny Dreadful, 141, 173, 179, 214
penny dreadfuls, 180–81, 187, 192, 207
Perry, Dennis, 18

photographs and photography, 23, 39, 77, 133, 155, 163, 165
Pickersgill, Joshua, 183
Pickwick Papers (culture-text), 22, 85, 144, 146, 148–50, 153; *The Peregrinations of Pickwick; or, Boz-i-a-na The Pickwick Papers* (Rede), 85; *The Posthumous Papers of the Pickwick Club* (Dickens), 144, 146, 148–50, 153
pirate culture-texts: *Alone in the Pirate's Lair* (Hazlewood), 198; *The Pirate* (Dimond), 39; *The Pirate* (Planché), 39; *The Pirate* (Scott), 39; *The Pirate* (Terry), 83; *The Pirate; or, The Wild Woman of Zetland* (Dibdin-Pitt), 39
Pixerécourt, René-Charles Guilbert de, 93, 93n73, 188; *Coelina ou l'Enfant du Mystère*, 188
Planché, James Robinson, 21, 39, 43, 75, 87–88, 92–93; *Maid Marian; or, The Huntress of Arlingford*, 87–88; *The Pirate*, 39; *The Vampire, or The Bride of the Isles*, 43, 75
Poe, Edgar Allan, 129, 189; *The Raven*, 129
poetry, 34, 67, 69–70, 72, 87, 90, 98–99, 101, 105, 109, 117, 119, 125, 135, 156, 159–60, 163, 166, 169, 176, 189. See also individual authors
Polidori, John, 43, 75, 75n34; *The Vampyre*, 43, 75, 75n34
politics, 4, 6, 9, 14, 19–20, 33–34, 38–39, 41, 61, 68, 72–73, 75, 92, 96, 97, 108–11, 118, 126, 133, 140, 160, 166, 168–69, 173, 177, 181, 188–89, 204, 212
Potter, Franz J., 181, 184
Powell, Manushag, 39
Pre-Raphaelite Brotherhood, 21, 99–101, 114, 124n66, 134–35, 160, 162, 162n52
Prest, Thomas, 187
Pride and Prejudice (culture-text), 4, 209; *Pride and Prejudice* (Austen), 4
publishers and publishing, 6, 20–24, 35, 61, 64–67, 69, 84–85, 87–88, 95, 105–6, 114–15, 129, 132, 136, 152, 156, 163, 181, 183, 190, 194, 198–99, 202, 220
Pyle, Eric, 117

Rabelais, François, 129, 132
Radcliffe, Ann, 5, 35, 181, 188, 189
radio, 17, 111, 165, 218
realism, 75, 153, 165, 189–90

Rebeck, Theresa, 80; *Bernhardt/Hamlet*, 80
Rede, William, 85; *The Peregrinations of Pickwick; or, Boz-i-a-na The Pickwick Papers*, 85
Redington, John, **195**, 197, 199, **199**
Reynolds, Joshua, 74–75; *Mrs. Siddons as the Tragic Muse*, 75
Richardson, Samuel, 1–2, 178; *Clarissa; or, The History of a Young Lady*, 2, 2n4
Roe, Albert, 123
Rose, Brian, 17–18, 60, 140
Rossetti, Christina, 136, 192
Rossetti, Dante Gabriel, 100, 162
"Ruffian Boy, The" (culture-text), 90, 90n66
Ruskin, John, 135–36, 160
Rymer, James Malcolm, 187

Sadoff, Diane, 172
Saggini, Francesca, 217
Saglia, Diego, 188
Sanders, Julie, 119, 119n52, 211
Santaniello, A. E., 106
Saunders, Clare, 169
Schober, Regina, 123
Schumann, Robert, 70; *Manfred: Dramatic Poem with Music in Three Parts*, 70
Scott, Grant F., 99
Scott, Walter, 5, 9, 20, 24, 39, 67, 83–84, 88, 90, 94, 160, 182, 194, 218, *Bride of Lammermoor*, 83; *The Doom of Devorgoil*, 83; *The Fortunes of Nigel*, 90; *Guy Mannering*, 83; *Heart of Mid-Lothian*, 83; *Lady of the Lake*, 83; *Marmion*, 90; *Peveril of the Peak*, 90; *The Pirate*, 39; *Waverly*, 84, 90
Semenza, Gregory, 210
serializations, 22, 84–85, 111, 146–47, 176, 180, 198
Seymour, Robert, 148
Shakespeare, William, 12, 24, 79–80, 87, 92, 105, 106–9, 111–12, **112**, 114, 125, 132, 151, 159, 194, 212; *Hamlet*, 80; *Hamlet* (1900), 80; *The Tempest*, 111–12, **112**
Shelley, Mary Wollstonecraft, 5–6, 16, 20, 41, 47, 52, 64–65, 113, 179, 183–84, 188, 205, 213, 217–18; *Frankenstein; or, The Modern Prometheus*, 5–6, 41, 54, 61, 64–65, 76, 79, 121, 141, 165, 179, 184, 188, 205, 216–18; "The Transformation," 184
Shelley, Percy Bysshe, 34, 64–65, 121, 121n56, 182, 205; *Zastrozzi*, 205

Index

Sheridan, Richard Brinsley, 32, 65
Sickman Han, Carrie, 146
Siddal, Elizabeth, 100
Siddons, Sarah, 75, 80
Sigler, Carolyn, 192
Simon, Peter, **112**
"Sister Arts" tradition, 10, 21, 105, 105n12
Slethaug, Gordon, 210
Smart, Mary Ann, 72
Smith, O. (Richard John), 20, 48–49, 48n60, 65, 76, **77**
Soane, George, 48, 126
Soccio, Anna, 217
social class, 4, 8, 10, 21, 24, 31, 39, 45, 94, 98–99, 113, 144, 168, 176–78, 180–81, 188–91, 215
Southerne, Thomas, 5; *Oroonoko: A Tragedy*, 5
Southey, Robert, 90, 201; "The Inchcape Rock," 201; *Thalaba the Destroyer*, 90
souvenirs, 2, 6, 21, 23, 54, 75, 76–77, **78**, 79, 106–7, 178, 193, 204–5
Speaight, George, 193
spectacle and special effects, 19–20, 24, 34, 39–43, 45, 51, 60, 63, 89, 105, 110, 147, 181
Spencer, Herbert, 200
St. Clair, William, 217
Stam, Robert, 2
Stedman, John Gabriel, 117–18; *The Narrative of a Five Years Expedition against the Revolted Negroes of Surinam*, 117–18
Stephens, John Russell, 94
Stevenson, Robert Louis, 7, 76–77, 134, 158, 190, 200–203, 206; *Memories and Portraits*, 200–201; *The Strange Case of Dr. Jekyll and Mr. Hyde*, 7, 18, 76–77, 134, 158, 179, 188
Stirling, Edward, 85, 87, 94, 150, 153; *Nickolas Nickleby; or, Doings at Do-the-Boys Hall*, 85
Stoker, Bram, 52n68, 158, 179, 213; *Dracula*, 4, 52n68, 141, 158, 179–80
Stone, Marcus, 150
storyworlds, 15, 139–44, 151, 153–56, 159–60, 162, 165–66, 168, 170, 172–74, 176, 178–79, 181–82, 192, 206, 219
Stowe, Harriet Beecher, 7, 9, 73, 90, 94, 155–56; *Uncle Tom's Cabin*, 7, 24, 73, 90, 155–56
Strange Case of Dr. Jekyll and Mr. Hyde, The (culture-text), 18, **78**, 79–80, 140, 158, 179–80, 188; *The Strange Case of Dr. Jekyll and Mr. Hyde* (Stevenson), 7, 18, 76–77, 134, 158, 179, 188
Sullivan, Thomas Russell, 76–77, 79, 94, 158
superheroes, 46–47, 159, 176, 178–79, 206–7
Sweeney Todd (culture-text), 187; *The String of Pearls*, 187; *String of Pearls; or, The Fiend of Fleet Street* (Dibdin-Pitt), 187–88
Swift, Jonathan, 2, 5, 178; *Gulliver's Travels*, 5, 139

Tchiakovsky, Pyotr Ilyich, 70; *Manfred Symphony in B Minor*, Op. 58, 70
technology, 1, 4, 8, 15–16, 19–20, 23–24, 39, 45, 60–61, 74, 97, 105, 110, 113, 115–16, 135, 137, 140, 165, 180–81, 189, 193, 207, 221
television, 11–12, 15, 17, 22, 41, 66, 111, 114, 133, 139, 142–44, 155, 165, 172–73, 179, 206, 210, 214, 218, 220. *See also individual television shows*
Tennyson, Alfred Lord, 22–23, 116, 129, 160–63, 165, 168–69; "The Lady of Shalott," 161
Terry, Daniel, 83–84, 88–89, 126, 218; *Ivanhoe*, 83, 139; *The Pirate*, 83; *Rob Roy*, 83
Terry, Ellen, 73, 79, 80, **81**
theater, 2, 4–6, 17, 19–24, 28–31, 34–36, 38–42, 46–47, 50–53, 61, 67, 69–70, 75, 79, 82–83, 86, 89, 95, 97, 110, 126, 134, 147–53, 155–56, 181, 183–84, 187–88, 190, 193, 204–5, 209–10, 212, 216–18, 221; burlesques, 7, 31, 52, 69, 89; Examiner of Plays, 31–33, 35–37, 83; farces, 31, 50–51, 85, 88; harlequinades, 47, 49, 197; legitimacy, 9, 10n25, 31, 33, 37, 41, 69, 88, 188; Licensing Act of 1737, 33–34, 36; melodramas, 30–32, 37, 40, 47, 61, 75, 83, 88–89, 91–93, 93n73, 93n74, 180, 188–90, 197, 200, 218; minor theaters, 31–32, 37, 94, 188; nautical works, 7, 39, 75, 84, 198; pantomimes, 5, 76, 88, 178, 192, 197; patent system, 31, 37–38; Reform Act of 1832, 37; theatrical hacks, 21, 87, 94–95, 112–13, 150–51; Theatres Act of 1968, 31, 33; Theatres Licensing Act of 1737, 31; Theatres Regulation Act of 1843, 37
Thomas, Julia, 170
tourism, 9, 108, 110, 209–10
toys, 5, 6, 9, 15, 17, 23; action figures, 176–77, 179, 192, 200, 205, 206; toy theaters, 23–24, 175–76, 178, 192–206, **195**, 219
transmedia storytelling, 1–4, 7, 9–11, 13–17, 19–20, 24, 27–29, 39, 45–46, 61, 63,

66, 69, 101, 104–5, 110, 114, 116–17, 123, 134–35, 140–42, 146, 148–49, 159, 166, 168, 173–74, 175–77, 200, 204–7, 210, 212, 215–16, 221

Tristan and Isolde (culture-text): "Tristram and Iseult" (Arnold), 165; *Tristram of Lyonesse* (Swinburne), 165; *Tristan and Isolde* (Wagner), 165

Twain, Mark, 165–66

Uncle Tom's Cabin (culture-text): *Slave Life* (Taylor and Lemon), 76; *Uncle Tom's Cabin* (Stowe), 7, 24, 73, 90, 155–56

Universal Studios, 178–79, 213

Vampire, The (culture-text), *Le Vampire* (Nodier), 75; *The Vampire, or The Bride of the Isles* (Planché), 43, 75; *The Vampyre* (Polidori), 43, 75, 75n34

Verdi, Giuseppe, 71–72; *Ernani*, 72; *I due Foscari*, 71; *Il trovatore*, 72

Victorian period, 4, 7, 11–12, 22–23, 30, 34, 47–48, 52, 79–80, 87, 94, 99, 101, 109, 113, 116, 124n66, 132–34, 142–44, 156–66, 168–70, 172–73, 179, 181, 189–91, 204, 206, 209, 214, 217

"View of the Interior of the Shakespeare Gallery" (Wheatley), **107**

Viscomi, Joseph, 117

Wagner, Richard, 89, 165; *Der fliegende Holländer*, 89

Waterhouse, John William, **100**, 101, 161

web series, 3, 214, 218

Weber, Carl Maria von, 48; *Der Freischütz*, 48

Wells, H. G., 213

Weltman, Sharon Aronofsky, 187

West, William, 76, 193–96

Whale, James, 79

Wheatley, Francis, 106, **107**, 108

Wilde, Oscar, 179, 181, 206; *The Picture of Dorian Gray*, 141, 179–81

Wilkinson, Sarah, 190

Williams, Raymond, 96

Wootton, Sarah, 99–100

Wordsworth, William, 28, 152

world-building, 22–23, 142, 146, 150, 155n32, 173, 176, 178, 205

Zemka, Sue, 85

www.ingramcontent.com/pod-product-compliance
Lightning Source LLC
Chambersburg PA
CBHW020644230426
43665CB00008B/303